STANDING ON THE PROMISES

Mark W. Musse

STANDING ON
THE PROMISES

the promise keepers and the revival of manhood

Edited by **Dane S. Claussen**

The Pilgrim Press
Cleveland, Ohio

The Pilgrim Press, Cleveland, Ohio 44115
© 1999 by Dane S. Claussen

Printed in the United States of America on acid-free paper

04 03 02 01 00 99   5 4 3 2 1

Library of Congress Cataloging-in-Publication Data

Standing on the promises : the Promise Keepers and the revival of manhood / edited by Dane S. Claussen.
    p. cm.
  ISBN 0-8298-1307-1
  1. Promise Keepers (Organization). I. Claussen, Dane S., 1963– .
BV960.S73 1999
269'.23—dc21   99-047184

To Suttichai "Tom" Chuvessiriporn

contents

Preface   ix

Contributors   xiii

1. *Standing on the Promises* and the Broader Conversation   1
   Merle Longwood

PART 1: AN EVANGELICAL MEN'S MOVEMENT ON THE WORLD STAGE?

2. What the Media Missed about the Promise Keepers   17
   Dane S. Claussen

3. A Reaction to Declining Market and Religious Influence   34
   Judith L. Newton

4. Race and Religion at the Million Man March and the Promise Keepers'
   Stand in the Gap   44
   Steven L. Jones and William H. Lockhart

5. Biblical Interpretations That Influence Promise Keepers   56
   Marianne Ferguson

6. The Need to Develop Male Friendship   61
   George E. Sears

PART 2: PATRIARCHY, HOMOPHOBIA, AND RIGHT-WING POLITICS

7. How Promise Keepers See Themselves as Men Behaving Goodly   75
   John D. Keeler, Ben Fraser, and William J. Brown

8. Christianity, Feminism, and the Manhood Crisis   89
   John Stoltenberg

9. Patriarchy's Second Coming as Masculine Renewal   111
   Michael S. Kimmel

10. Godly Masculinities Require Gender and Power   121
    John P. Bartkowski

PART 3: WOMEN AS (MORE THAN) SUITABLE HELPERS?

11. Promise Keepers Welcomed Home by Wives   133
    Clella Iles Jaffe

12. Wives, Daughters, Mothers, and Sisters as Kept Women   143
    Lauren F. Winner

13. A Womanist/Feminist Lives with a Promise Keeper and Likes It   154
    Valerie Bridgeman Davis

14. Dale Came Home a Different Husband and Father   161
    Jeanne Parrott

15. Promise Keepers Has Not Changed Our Family   165
    Anonymous

16. Fulfilling God's Role for the Woman Is the Most Rewarding Feeling   167
    Marilyn Kenaga

Notes   169

preface

I have been asked several times by those who know me why I became interested in Promise Keepers (PK) and why I edited this book on PK. After all, I have never belonged to any men's movement group or any organization with an explicitly feminist agenda, and I certainly do not practice any brand of evangelical, charismatic, Pentecostal, or fundamentalist Christianity (in fact, quite the contrary). My interest in PK stemmed from questions about how the media would cover PK and why; PK's similarities to and differences from other men's movement organizations; PK's unusual emphases on race relations (covered quite a bit by media) and male friendship (hardly covered at all by media, although real male friendships in the United States are rare and yet would make better both men's lives and the entire culture and society); its posture on homosexuality (which PK has laudably deemphasized, even as PK unfortunately still condemns it); and generally how men (and women) in the United States would respond to PK.

In the final analysis, I recognize that most men in the United States are not hearing consistent messages about how to be a good husband, a good father, a good friend, or a good citizen from any authority, and thus PK is doing some good in these areas. Second, I believe that in the overwhelming majority of cases, a PK man who carries home with him extreme interpretations of PK teachings (from event speakers, books, or other publications) will have to implicitly negotiate his attempted implementation of those teachings in his own home. Thus, I do not think that all aspects of PK should be opposed by those who object to only some of its teachings any more than one should oppose a political party because one does not agree with every plank of its platform. In short, PK can be and probably should be supported by anyone who believes it is doing significantly more good than harm in both the short and the long term. To the inevitable question of what my own "agenda" is in studying PK, I would say that, as a result of this book and other research and journalism on PK, I hope that PK men and others who have been intoxicated by PK's success and potential will be more realistic and skeptical about it. And I hope that at least the most extreme of PK's opponents will understand enough about PK that they can offer credible, rather than reactionary and shrill, criticism.

Some scholars interested in Promise Keepers have been told that studying and writing about PK would give PK too much credit and credibility. But PK seems to have grown dramatically during its first few years while being almost completely ignored by scholars, and even while—if one listens to most PK men—receiving supposedly negative media coverage. In other words, PK's existence is almost entirely dependent upon its own merits as judged by participants and potential participants. I hope this book—even the parts of it with which I disagree—is a significant contribution to both academic research and public understanding of PK. But I am modest enough about my own efforts, knowledgeable enough of the deep-seated anti-intellectualism in U.S. culture,[1] and aware enough of so many scholars' inability and/or unwillingness to communicate clearly to a broad audience that I would not assume that scholars, particularly those in the humanities and social sciences, have such direct or immediate influence that we ultimately endorse an organization by only studying it; this would mean, among other results, that no one should write about Adolf Hitler. (Some people in the United States are so anti-intellectual that for them, scholarly attention to a subject may be an automatic negative; moreover, much scholarly research appears to nonscholars as critical—and thus negative—to begin with.) Second, scholars cannot simply ignore a subject that is important and interesting because they do not like it, which is not to say, of course, that more than a fraction of scholars can and should study PK. In conclusion, then, regardless of my feelings or conclusions about Promise Keepers, it is something that neither I nor many other scholars could ignore.

A book such as this is the product of many individuals' interests and efforts, from concept to completion. Professor Carol J. Pardun, now at the School of Journalism and Mass Communication, University of North Carolina–Chapel Hill, first encouraged me to research Promise Keepers' media coverage when both of us were at the A. Q. Miller School of Journalism and Mass Communications, Kansas State University, and she continues to believe in both the importance and the quality of my work. My master's thesis, which she directed, ultimately led to this book. Timothy Staveteig, the editor of Pilgrim Press, was particularly eager to publish this book and confident of my ability to edit it; I hope he is pleased. Lauren F. Winner, author of chapter 12, and George L. Daniels, now a doctoral student in the Henry W. Grady College of Journalism and Mass Communication, University of Georgia, have been especially enthusiastic about this book from the idea stage through the final proofreading, and I also hope they are satisfied with the result. I thank all of the contributors to this book, especially Professor Merle Longwood of Siena College, who was kind enough to write the first chapter for this book at Timothy Staveteig's request. Professor Andy P. Kavoori of the Grady College, UGA, read an early draft of this preface and chapter 2 and provided helpful advice. Professor Glen T. Cameron, now at the School of Journalism, University of Missouri–Columbia, facilitated my work on this book and another one during spring quarter 1998 at the Grady College, UGA. Professor Elizabeth "Elli" Lester Roushanzamir of the Grady College, UGA, tried hard to prevent the two books from interfering too much with my doctoral program's schedule, and she largely succeeded. Numerous scholars have helpfully commented on my master's thesis and conference papers about Promise Keepers, mythopoets, or the Men and Religion Forward Movement of 1911–12.

I owe an inestimable debt to Elizabeth A. R. Boleman-Herring, publishing editor at The Literate Chigger, Ink, Pendleton, South Carolina, who was a thorough, quick, and witty (in the margins, that is) line editor, as well as a true friend; of course, all remaining faults in the text are my responsibility alone. And finally, thanks and apologies to my relatives (particularly my parents) and friends (such as Phil Comer, Paul Featheringill, Professor Christopher Lane of Emory University, and especially Suttichai "Tom" Chuvessiriporn). I often neglected them, yet they cheerfully withstood some of my most stressful moments in 1998.

contributors

ANONYMOUS is a wife, mother, and grandmother who works in a lay biblical counseling ministry. She is a former Suitable Helpers staff member.

JOHN P. BARTKOWSKI, Ph.D., is assistant professor of sociology at Mississippi State University.

WILLIAM J. BROWN, Ph.D., is dean of the College of Communication and the Arts at Regent University, Virginia Beach, Virginia.

DANE S. CLAUSSEN, Ph.D., is assistant professor of communication and mass media at Southwest Missouri State University, Springfield.

VALERIE BRIDGEMAN DAVIS, Ph.D., is assistant professor of religion at Huston-Tillotson College, in Austin, Texas.

MARIANNE FERGUSON, Ph.D., is associate professor in the Department of Philosophy and Religious Studies at Buffalo State College.

BEN FRASER, Ph.D., is associate professor in the College of Communication and the Arts at Regent University, Virginia Beach, Virginia.

CLELLA ILES JAFFE, Ph.D., is associate professor of communication arts at George Fox University, Newberg, Oregon.

STEVEN L. JONES, Th.M., is a doctoral student in sociology at the University of Virginia.

MARILYN KENAGA is a wife and mother who is a former member of the board and staff of Suitable Helpers. She now is active in other church and community activities.

JOHN D. KEELER, Ph.D., is professor in the College of Communication and the Arts at Regent University, Virginia Beach, Virginia.

MICHAEL S. KIMMEL, Ph.D., is associate professor of sociology at the State University of New York at Stony Brook.

WILLIAM H. LOCKHART, M.Div., is a doctoral candidate and instructor in sociology at the University of Virginia.

MERLE LONGWOOD, Ph.D., is professor of religious studies at Siena College, former cochair of Men's Studies in Religion in the American Academy of Religion, and coeditor of *Redeeming Men: Religion and Masculinities* (Westminster John Knox, 1996).

JUDITH L. NEWTON, Ph.D., is professor and director of women's studies at the University of California at Davis.

JEANNE PARROTT is a wife, mother, and grandmother who serves on the board and staff of Suitable Helpers. She also works for the National Day of Prayer organization in Colorado Springs, Colorado.

GEORGE E. SEARS, D.Min., is pastor of the Comox Community Baptist Church in Comox, British Columbia.

JOHN STOLTENBERG, M.Div., M.F.A., is an author, journalist, frequent public speaker and workshop leader, cofounder of Men Against Pornography, and former managing editor of *Essence*, *Working Woman*, and *Lear's* magazines.

LAUREN F. WINNER is the Richard Hofstadter Fellow in the Department of History, Columbia University.

1

Standing on the Promises
and the Broader Conversation

Merle Longwood

I was pleased to be asked to contribute the introductory chapter to this collection of essays on the Promise Keepers. I do not identify myself as a "Promise Keeper," nor, as a Lutheran, am I a member of a church that is part of the evangelical family of churches—except in the very broadest sense of the term—from which the Promise Keepers (PK) draws most of its leaders and active participants. Having said this, I want to acknowledge that it is not easy to categorize PK participants.

The Religious Diversity of Promise Keepers

Among this book's contributors, John Stoltenberg has most clearly recognized the diversity of religious perspectives of those who identify with this movement. He describes the Promise Keepers as "a personalist revival movement" that is involved in "the delicate task of building a big-tent coalition among charismatics, Pentecostals, and evangelicals (Southern Baptists, Southern Methodists, and such) plus a sizable contingent of Roman Catholics." If one were to pursue more systematic empirical research into the backgrounds of those who have participated in PK activities, one would discover an even broader diversity of religious perspectives within this "big-tent coalition" than Stoltenberg describes; many events have attracted significant numbers of mainstream ecumenical Protestants in addition to those from churches mentioned by Stoltenberg. Moreover, some of Stoltenberg's terms describing the "big-tent coalition" require clarification. For example, "evangelicals" is one such term, and it refers to a broader range of religious traditions than the Southern Baptists and Southern Methodists listed by Stoltenberg.

Donald W. Dayton and Robert K. Johnston, drawing upon their years of working together as cochairs of the Evangelical Theology Group of the American Academy of Religion, cast their net broadly as they solicited essays for their collection, so as to include Lutheranism, for example, as one expression of American evangelicalism. Lutheran theologian Mark Ellingson's essay, however, demonstrates how Lutheranism in this country and abroad, despite retaining "evangelical" as a self-identifying description, is not in the evangelical coalition. But he acknowledges that some Lutherans "who are compatible with neopietist convictions—sharing the pietist emphasis on sanctification and critical perspectives toward Roman Catholicism, as well as the orthodox concern with theories of biblical inspiration and polemics—are at home in the evangelical coalition."[1]

In fact, what is meant by "evangelical" is a continuing debate among scholars, and Dayton and Johnston disagree about whether the category of "evangelical" is a useful one.[2] I use the term in this chapter although I am aware of its ambiguities. I propose that we accept Gabriel Fackre's as a working definition of "evangelical Christianity," when he suggests that the term refers to "those who espouse and experience justification and scriptural authority in an intensified way: personal conversion and a rigorous moral life, on the one hand, and concentrated attention on the Bible as a guide to conviction and behaviour on the other, with a special zeal for dissemination of Christian faith so conceived."[3]

The most important element in this definition probably is the emphasis on personal conversion.[4] Note that it does not equate evangelicalism with fundamentalism, and Martin Marty, one of the most knowledgeable scholars of Protestantism in the United States, believes that evangelicalism usually has more in common with and has more affinities to mainline Protestantism than to fundamentalism.[5] Johnston makes the further observation that "evangelicals largely resent the label fundamentalist, and vice versa."[6]

To understand more fully the diversity of perspectives within the PK movement, it would also be helpful to define more precisely other terms used here by Stoltenberg and other authors, including the terms "fundamentalists," "charismatics," and "Pentecostals," especially because these terms seem to be used interchangeably in some of these essays.

Having said that I am not a Promise Keeper, I also want to acknowledge that I am not a total outsider to this movement. I have attended PK stadium conferences and what may have been the Promise Keepers' zenith event, the Stand in the Gap: A Sacred Assembly of Men held on the Mall in Washington, D.C., in October 1997. Some have claimed this was the largest gathering of people ever assembled at that location, when several hundred thousand men[7] gathered for a day of personal repentance and prayer for the nation. And I have had many opportunities to meet and talk with men who are active, ongoing PK participants, both those who have attended large stadium events and those who have become involved in small "accountability" groups that have committed themselves to carry out the movement's work in their own communities. I have two brothers-in-law and three nephews-in-law (two of whom are clergy in evangelically oriented congregations)—all in the western part of the United States—who have been actively involved in Promise Keepers.

Finally, I have had conversations about PK with several clergy in my denomination. Most of these pastors discuss it in glowing terms. They have experienced its impact by attending stadium events and/or by observing the lives of PK men in their congregations. Typically they describe the rallies as "wonderful" or "Spirit-filled" events. On the other hand, other pastors are at least mildly critical, expressing their concern that PK's underlying theology shifts the focus from God's work to our will, which, they believe—from a Lutheran perspective—is a shaky foundation for real personal and social change. Taking a cue from their spiritual mentor, Martin Luther, some clergy express the fear that the emotionalism they perceive as widespread in PK can too easily become manipulative. Putting all of this aside, I develop my reflections in this chapter primarily as a longtime scholar-teacher in men's studies in religion who has been observing (rather than participating in) this particular men's spiritual movement for several years. As I have read broadly in the secondary literature on PK, my impression is that most attempts to analyze it have come from the popular press, whose writers have tended to view PK as if it emerged ex nihilo. Very few have compared this burst of male religious enthusiasm with any previous movements nor have they provided serious analysis of what has been happening in the wider culture to give rise to this popular movement among religiously conservative men.

Few efforts to advance the religiosity of U.S. men in the twentieth century have attracted the attention given to PK, which grew exponentially during the early part of the 1990s. In eight years of conferences, the Promise Keepers organization says it reached more than 3.2 million men through stadium and arena events.[8] The peak years seem to have been 1996, when 1.1 million men attended twenty-two stadium rallies, and 1997, when more than 600,000 men attended the national Stand in the Gap, in addition to 638,297 who attended eighteen regional stadium conferences.[9] And for several years a large number of clergy attended PK conferences arranged especially for them in locations throughout the country. The numbers of participants attending the stadium conferences have decreased since then. Promise Keepers reports that about 450,000 men attended its nineteen conferences in 1998, and it has scaled down expectations even more as it planned only fourteen conferences in 1999.[10]

This collection of essays is a welcomed contribution to an ongoing discussion taking place in religious and secular circles concerning the significance of the rise—and as it now appears the gradual waning—of the Promise Keepers as a cultural and religious phenomenon of the late twentieth century. Although much has been written about this men's evangelical movement from many angles, the stances of writers responding to it often have been highly polemical. This volume's contributors include both women and men, with a wide range of perspectives—those who oppose the movement (although few of them are sharply polemical), those who are closely connected to the movement, and those who simply question it. Their range of disciplinary expertise is broad, with five contributors in the field of communications (Claussen, Keeler, Fraser, Brown, and Jaffe), four in sociology (Bartkowski, Kimmel, Jones, and Lockhart), four in religious studies (Sears, Ferguson, Winner, and Bridgeman Davis), two writing from the perspective of women's studies or gender studies (Newton and Stoltenberg), and three who are identified by their relationship with PK men (Parrott, Anonymous, and Kenaga); this last category would include Bridgeman Davis, too, who is a spouse of a Promise Keeper, but whom I have placed in the category of religious studies because she is, in addition to being a "happily married womanist" who "sleeps with" a Promise Keeper, a scholar of feminisms and religious studies.

These essays approach PK from a wide diversity of viewpoints, and I will not attempt to explore exhaustively the richness of the content and implications of all the material these authors have put before us. Rather, I will lift up a few themes and issues that could be used to draw the authors into dialogue with one another and with others who have reflected on this movement. I also suggest areas in which further research could prove fruitful.

An Evangelical Men's Movement on the World Stage?

Apart from the two contexts of evangelical Christianity and the men's movements in the twentieth century, PK cannot be sufficiently understood, and its significance cannot be fully appreciated. Placing PK within these larger contexts opens up a fuller understanding of it as an effort to reshape the masculine ideal by admitting the spiritual as manly. PK is the latest expression of a larger and growing dissatisfaction with traditional definitions of male spirituality and identity in U.S. culture.[11] These stirrings of dissatisfaction had their beginnings in the nineteenth century and have reverberated in various forms throughout the current century, including the recent mythopoetic movement associated with Robert Bly,[12] Michael Meade,[13] and others. Although it may be true that PK is becoming passé, for reasons that Dane Claussen hypothesizes in relation to the declining attendance at its stadium events, the issues that prompted its rise are enduring and worthy of careful attention.

Claussen, and to a lesser extent Michael Kimmel, has made a significant effort to place PK within a broad historical framework, demonstrating that PK is not totally new in the history of American evangelicalism. Claussen begins his account in 1991 with the first regional gathering at the University of Colorado that attracted 4,200 men. I would move the origin back one year to 1990 when then University of Colorado football coach Bill McCartney developed a local fellowship of seventy-two men focusing on prayer, fasting, and mutual encouragement. Including this earlier group experience helps us understand more fully the small local fellowships that PK has attempted to make the foundation of PK, even though these cell groups receive little attention from most movement interpreters, who focus almost exclusively on the large rallies. For example, in this collection, George Sears's chapter, emphasizing the ways in which PK could be helpful for encouraging the development of male friendship, would have been more convincing if it focused more on the experiences of men in these local groups, and less on the stadium conferences, as the model for men relating to other men.

In tracing the development of Muscular Christianity, a set of initiatives intended to fight cultural degeneration, with particular reference to its most famous exemplar, Billy Sunday, both Claussen and Kimmel refer to the remarkable similarities between movements in the first two decades of this century and the PK rallies of the 1990s. The earlier movements were also often for men only, the leaders encouraged men to live their lives according to certain promises, and they held up Jesus as the model of masculinity. Claussen goes beyond Kimmel's historical comparison when he sharply differentiates the Men and Religion Forward Movement of 1911–12 from Muscular Christianity and proposes a number of reasons for the distinction, making the case, finally, that PK shares far more with the Billy Sunday version of Muscular Christianity than with the attempts to masculinize Christianity of the Men and Religion Forward Movement. Other scholars clearly view this differently, and further investigation by historians would be useful in this area. It would be helpful to examine connections between these movements and the way in which in the mid-1800s Protestant elders provided a home away from home for their juniors in the Young Men's Christian Association, as well as the founding of the Boy Scouts in the early 1900s in reaction to men's fears that their sons would become sissies as they turned citified.

The other context within which to place PK is the men's movements of the late-twentieth-century United States. Here Claussen draws upon solid, scholarly interpretations to describe the component movements that in the aggregate are usually called by scholars, as well as by the mass media, "the men's movement." Kimmel briefly compares PK to mythopoetism and its leaders Robert Bly and Sam Keen, but he really does not develop this comparison to any extent. Judith Newton alludes to "previous men's movements" without specifying to which ones she is referring on the 1990s' "explosion of discourse on masculinities," and John Stoltenberg contrasts PK with secular men's movements without saying to which movements he is referring. This book would have been strengthened if someone, perhaps Claussen in chapter 2, had brought in the work of the philosopher Kenneth Clatterbaugh, who has developed the most sustained work of which I am aware on the categorization of men's movements and perspectives on men and masculinity.[14] Clatterbaugh recognizes that these perspectives are sociopolitical, each offering an agenda for society as a whole, and that they are continually changing.

Yet the wider cultural context also needs to be taken into consideration for a full understanding of Promise Keepers. Two of the chapters are particularly effective in this area. They provide important clues about how this movement and others have emerged in part as reactions to marked changes in gender roles both in religious culture and in U.S. culture as a whole so that we can appreciate how each movement presumes an image of "the ideal male"—the muscular Christian man, the religious man, the responsible black man, or the Promise Keeper.

More than any other author in this collection, Newton explains PK's emergence within the context of more broadly based developments in evangelical, fundamentalist, and Pentecostal-charismatic Christianity. Moreover, she relates these developments in conservative Christianity to many worldwide changes brought about by transnational corporations, responses to the end of the Cold War, the decline of Marxist-Leninist influences and of nationalist movements, and other effects brought about by transnational capitalism. It would have been helpful if Newton had given more careful attention to the distinctions between, as well as the overlappings among, the movements of evangelicalism, fundamentalism, and Pentecostalism. She is aware of the differences and connections, and she suggests that PK combines elements of all three, but when she elaborates upon her interpretation of this movement's expansion, she gravitates toward Pentecostalisms, and I do not believe this is the most accurate way to describe the movement.

To illustrate the complexities of the relationships between PK and various strands within the evangelical and other Christian communities, we can look at a spectrum of critical responses to the movement ranging from Right to center to Left within what I am broadly calling evangelicalism.

This is best illustrated with two quite different but representative critiques from the Right found in U.S. evangelical Christian circles. Gil Rugh, pastor of Indian Hills Community Church in Lincoln, Nebraska, wrote a booklet in which he sharply criticized PK for claiming to represent Jesus Christ, though in fact it does not do so.[15] Rugh believes that this new movement does not preach a pure gospel or address human spiritual growth from an accurate interpretation of God's Word. He is deeply critical of the movement's expression of ecumenism, which he believes sets aside crucial *like Christian Coalition, Moral Majority,*

theological issues in order to promote a unity that is not really a biblical unity. He is convinced that PK's plan for producing godliness is not in accord with God's plan. Finally, he is particularly concerned that some PK leaders— probably especially Bill McCartney, though he does not name names—are men associated with the Vineyard movement, which he believes is characterized by unsound theology, such as the belief that new revelations of God continue to come to particular men in this new age.[16]

A quite different response, well informed by feminist biblical scholarship, was developed by Laurie Coene Dashnau.[17] Dashnau sharply criticized the teachings of PK leaders for their sloppy exegesis, lack of careful examination of scripture verses' contexts, and in general lack of consistency with biblical teaching. It is interesting to compare her perspective with that of Marianne Ferguson in this volume, who is also concerned about how PK uses the Bible. But Ferguson is convinced that what is needed is for those in the movement to adopt the historical-critical method of interpreting Scripture to which she says "most 'mainline' Protestant denominations subscribe." This is somewhat different from Dashnau, who attempts to articulate her position within a framework that evangelical Christians could find acceptable. That is, Ferguson seems to be suggesting that a better understanding of the Bible than that found in the evangelical Christian communities would be in frameworks of interpretation more likely to be found within mainline denominations. It is probably true that neither Dashnau nor Ferguson would find her views easily accepted within PK circles, but Dashnau would have a better chance of receiving a hearing because she is able to address them in a language that they share in common rather than proposing an entirely different framework of interpretation.

To represent a position in evangelical Christianity's center, I have chosen the writings of L. Dean Allen, who has delivered papers and published several articles on the Promise Keepers, often reporting on movement events as they have occurred.[18] He is cautiously supportive of the movement and is especially hopeful about its potential for interracial healing. However, as a Baptist with roots in the South, he is particularly concerned about the need to maintain a separation between church and state, and he fears the potential for partisan political affiliation within the movement. He was especially concerned about crossing inappropriate boundaries when PK decided to hold its national "day of worship and prayer" on the Mall in Washington, D.C., in October 1997.[19]

Several *Sojourners* articles represent voices of the Left within the evangelical Christian community.[20] Taken together, these articles express mild support for PK, but they raise a number of questions about the lack of a clear articulation of social justice in relation to the structures of society, particularly in the area of interracial relations.

Whether one uses the category of Pentecostalism or other terms that I would prefer to describe this movement, Newton has performed a valuable service by informing readers that the Promise Keepers movement has already spread to Canada and New Zealand. She could also have added Germany, South Africa, and the United Kingdom as countries that have PK organizations granted official status by PK's national board. In fact, representatives from forty countries have made official inquiries to Promise Keepers concerning establishing PK organizations in their own countries.[21] Several of them are well on their way toward meeting the requirements to have an affiliated organization within their own national borders.[22] By the end of 1997, PK had held more than thirty events in countries outside the United States with nearly 90,000 men participating.[23] Furthermore, as Newton acknowledges, U.S. leadership, despite the financial difficulties the organization has faced recently, announced its intention to launch an even more wide-reaching global initiative in the year 2000. Future studies will be able to examine this initiative to see how effectively PK's message and strategies were able to be transplanted into quite different cultural contexts and, if successful, how much the movements in these different contexts differed from the one based in North America.

In a very perceptive analysis of how PK leaders continued to develop their understanding of reconciliation in race relations, Newton suggests that an important discursive shift occurred in 1996 and that it was even more fully manifested at the 1997 Stand in the Gap assembly in Washington: she observed that the African American speakers made particularly effective appeals to connect that experience with themes from the 1963 march on Washington led by Martin Luther King Jr. This assessment contrasts with the dismissive way that Kimmel views PK's racial reconciliation efforts; he emphasizes its focus on personal life rather than on institutional remedies, perhaps in part because Kimmel wrote his essay in 1996 before it was possible to ascertain the significance of this developing discursive shift.

Also helping us place PK within today's wider cultural scene is the essay by Steven Jones and William Lockhart. They provide a somewhat less sweeping analysis to examine the similarities and differences between the Million Man March of 1995 and the Stand in the Gap gathering in 1997, both of which took place on the Mall in Washington, D.C. They believe that the two events shared several common themes, particularly the reality of the country's racial crisis, the importance of being a responsible father and husband, the condemnation of domestic violence and the degradation of women, and the need for repentance and atonement. But they insist that the basic frameworks within which these themes were developed were very different, with Million Man March goals oriented toward the good of the larger racial community, while PK's was based in a set of religious goals that are rooted in a personal faith in Jesus Christ. I wonder if this differentiation is overdrawn. On the one hand, it does not take into account sufficiently the ways in which the Million Man March was at the time and still is being interpreted by a number of black Christian clergy and theologians as an expression of God's activity in the world revealed in the actions of oppressed black men marching for their own liberation.[24] On the other hand, this way of viewing PK does not take into account the manner in which the African American speakers at Stand in the Gap invoked themes that harked back to the justice and liberation themes of the movement led by Dr. King, as Newton has carefully pointed out in her chapter.

Patriarchy, Homophobia, and Right-Wing Politics

Several chapters are at least partially related to these concerns. I want to begin by noting some similarities, but more important some differences, in the interpretations provided by two well-known feminist/pro-feminist male authors, Kimmel and Stoltenberg.

Kimmel views the PK agenda as a not-so-subtle reinscription of patriarchy and warns his readers of the movement's "ominous ties with fanatic right-wing organizations and their views on women, homosexuals, and non-Christians." This comment echoes Patricia Ireland's views when she wrote: "NOW opposes Promise Keepers because it is, in large part, a stealth political group formed by people who think the former Christian Coalition leader Ralph Reed is too liberal."[25]

Kimmel seems to agree with one of the most critical assessments, a cover story in the *Nation*, entitled "The Promise Keepers Are Coming: The Third Wave of the Religious Right," by Joe Conason, Alfred Ross, and Lee Cokorinos.[26] Paralleling in many respects a special report prepared by Sterling Research Associates,[27] the article by Conason et al. highlights the Religious Right connections of McCartney and several prominent figures who stand behind him, including James Dobson of Focus on the Family, Bill Bright of Campus Crusade for Christ, and Pat Robertson, who has given PK extensive exposure on the Christian Broadcasting Network.

These authors acknowledge, however, that at PK events and in PK literature, "strident cultural messages are muted to the point of inaudibility."[28] But, they conclude, "In conception and execution . . . Promise Keepers appears to be one of the most sophisticated creations of the religious right. It may come dressed in jeans and sound some themes reminiscent of the liberal left, but the movement lacks progressive content."[29] They view PK as the third wave of the conservative religious political movement, modernizing fundamentalism's public image. By "mobilizing hundreds of thousands of men into a disciplined, hierarchical, nationwide grass-roots formation with significant military connections but a subtle presentation, Promise Keepers poses a new challenge. Its promise may be our peril."[30]

Stoltenberg, who identifies himself as a radical feminist and who is as critical as Kimmel of the hierarchical view of the relationship between men and women that characterizes much of PK teachings, refutes a characterization of PK in right-wing political categories, whether such views are espoused by the National Organization for Women or others on the political Left. Stoltenberg is impressed by the delicate balancing that must be maintained to hold together the "big-tent coalition," a coalition that would be torn apart if PK were to become involved in overt partisan political activities (in contrast to the Christian Coalition, which has obviously been overtly political and partisan). Further, he points out that PK has deliberately not taken a stand on issues that are divisive in internal church politics, such as the ordination of women and even abortion, although abortion has been discussed among the highest levels of the organization's leadership and some of the movement's highly visible leaders have, in other contexts, been strongly identified with antiabortion politics.

As a gay man, Stoltenberg examines PK's policy opposing homosexuality, and he takes it on directly, with surprising results. In commenting on his interview with PK leader Glenn Wagner, he describes how he was personally touched by the compassionate way in which Wagner dealt with the question of homosexuality; Stoltenberg reports that he felt ministered to personally—he guessed that Wagner had sensed he was gay without his having mentioned it. Further, Stoltenberg appreciated how PK's policy would "head off intemperate and homophobic innuendoes at PK stadium conferences" and send a "signal to all men in attendance at its events in sports arenas—venues typically athrob with homophobia—that as a matter of policy, Promise Keepers would not countenance gay-baiting." Stoltenberg draws upon his previous writings and antipornography political activism as he demonstrates how he stands closer to PK than to NOW on the pornography issues. His strongest critique of PK is based on his belief (articulated in his earlier writings) that "manhood is a myth, a chimera, a delusional state of subjectivity that feels real only episodically in interactions that are unjust and/or injurious."

This radical "social constructionist" view of gender stands in dramatic contrast to the "essentialist" view held by Sears, for example; Sears grounds his interpretation of a Christian approach to homosexuality in a theological position, found in the first eleven chapters of Genesis, that the sexes are complementary. But this contrast is not all that surprising when one remembers that Stoltenberg identifies his own "faith" as radical feminism. Though most North American feminists and gender scholars hold social constructionist views of sexuality and gender (although seldom as radical as Stoltenberg's), a minority of theorists but probably the majority of the public at large would favor an essentialist perspective—whether or not they ground it in the conservative theological framework that Sears holds.

Women as (More Than) Suitable Helpers?

John Keeler, Ben Fraser, and William Brown attempt to interpret who the Promise Keepers are by examining what PK leaders and participants consider the movement to be. They state that they provide an overview of PK, based on an Internet survey of those actively involved; questions could be raised about this method (i.e., how representative it is of participants). But from what they have reported, criticisms such as those made by Kimmel and the other authors discussed above would leave many PK men bewildered because they do not regard themselves as advocating a politics of male domination. But I want to focus more on the part of this chapter that purports to provide the "Critics' Points of View" of who Promise Keepers are, because I think it has a significant bearing upon these authors' conclusions that a wide gap exists between the self-perceived identity of PK participants and the way in which those who are external to the movement see them.

They assert, for example, that "feminists seem certain PK is composed of angry, threatened, ultra-conservative, predominantly white men determined to destroy decades of women's political and civil rights gains." Although this may be true of some feminists, such as Ireland, whom they (and I) quote, it does not accurately describe all feminists (as Clella Jaffe illustrates). My reading is that feminists' reactions to PK have been mixed and that mass media have reported this.

Donna Minkowitz, a Jewish lesbian feminist, was asked by *Ms.* to attend a PK rally, which she did by squashing her breasts beneath layers of Ace bandages, putting on a tight running bra and an undershirt, placing a rolled-up sock between her legs, and donning male clothing and an artificial mustache to make her appear as a teenage boy into heavy metal. Though she reported that she was put on edge by some speakers' sexism, among her most insightful comments was a suggestion that PK men saw themselves as persons working counter to mainstream values; she even compared some of what she observed to ACT UP (AIDS Coalition to Unleash Power) meetings.

She suggested that many people in the United States look down on evangelical culture as strange and weird—in much the same way that they see, for example, lesbian and gay culture. Evangelicals of all political persuasions frequently see themselves as pariahs, scorned and stereotyped by the unbelieving majority. "More than anything," Minkowitz commented, "the in-your-face masculinity is an effort to stand up for the goodness of men as a class." But she wrote that it is a mistake to interpret PK as the Christian Right's stealth organization. "For one thing," she wrote, "Promise Keepers is a diverse group, both politically and culturally. Not all are right-wingers. Many aren't political at all and some are even progressive."[31]

Even Suzanne Pharr, a radical lesbian feminist quoted by Keeler, Fraser, and Brown, wrote an early article that was quite supportive of PK,[32] although she subsequently revised her position and described the Promise Keepers as a proto-Nazi movement in a keynote address at a summer 1997 men's studies conference.[33] Perhaps Priscilla Inkpen, a United Church of Christ pastor in Boulder, Colorado, has given the most balanced feminist response when she said: "It's difficult to be 100% critical of the Promise Keepers. I think they are speaking to an important need: for men to take responsibility. A lot of men need to learn that, and Promise Keepers seems to be touching a nerve with many. But . . . you have to ask: What nerve are they touching? Is it men's hunger to be present in the relationships with their wives and children? Or is it the hunger to be on top?"[34]

John Bartkowski's chapter can be read as a gloss upon these questions posed by Inkpen in his analysis of advice manuals written by two authors prominently associated with PK, Ed Cole and Gary Oliver, whom he views as providing significantly different views of Christian manhood. He interprets Cole as a purveyor of an instrumentalist masculinity, which emphasized radical differences between genders and a patriarchal family structure, whereas he interprets Oliver as a purveyor of expressive masculinity that is based on androgynous understandings of gender and egalitarianism in marriage. Bartkowski wisely suggests that future research needs to determine just how the advice in such manuals is accepted, rejected, or amended by those persons who are the intended readers of these books, that is the "rank-and-file Promise Keepers."

Valerie Bridgeman Davis, identifying herself as a womanist/feminist, gives one answer to how participants deal with the advice given by PK leaders. She draws upon her personal experience in attesting to the positive changes that have taken place in her husband and in their marriage as a result of his participation. She acknowledges that some PK literature that they have read is "conservative and sometimes restrictive," but she says that she and her husband "simply take the information" selectively into their lives as they need it and "discard" what they do not. The future research that Bartkowski suggests is needed would help us understand the extent to which others involved in PK "take" or "discard" the advice they are given in the concrete social practices of their daily lives. Judith Newton indicates she has conducted ethnographic analyses that show gaps between rhetoric and the day-to-day negotiations in life. To elaborate upon this further I now turn to the remaining authors.

Clella Jaffe and Lauren Winner provide contrasting interpretations of women closely related to PK men. It was helpful to learn that Claussen had asked Winner "to focus primarily on women who were generally negative about or skeptical toward PK because such women have so rarely been interviewed by the media or studied in other research."[35] Winner did not draw from most interviews with women who had positive assessment of PK's impact on their lives. Jaffe's report of the very positive assessment of PK's effects by Free Methodist Church women, who had men in their lives involved in the movement, is further supported by the "testimonials" provided by Jeanne Parrott and Marilyn Kenaga—who emphasize the benefits they have received from their husbands' PK participation as well as their own involvement in the corollary Suitable Helpers ministry. But the writer Anonymous, who was fired up by attending a Suitable Helpers conference and was disappointed when she realized that her husband and son were not comparably transformed by their attendance at Promise Keepers events, corroborates Winner's accounts, showing that not all women are happy with what happens when the men in their lives become involved in this movement.

Perhaps Jaffe's most important contribution, however, is her discussion about power relationships within PK men's households as she distinguishes between "social status," which may emphasize power in terms of hierarchy and control, and "rhetorical status," which emphasizes communicators, contexts, and outcomes in ways that the specific contexts in which communication is taking place make a difference. Jaffe believes that "rhetorical status" provides a more accurate interpretation of how power is shared in PK households than "social status," which fits more with the perspective of PK critics who believe that participation reinforces men's social status as holding power "over" their wives in a hierarchical fashion.

Concluding Personal Remarks

How do we make sense out of all of this? My view is that many critiques of Promise Keepers, though valid in important ways, fail to understand the impulses, often contradictory, that have brought millions of men swarming into stadiums. I would suggest that the process by which men grow into cultural manhood, at least in North America, is so repressive that Promise Keepers has tapped in to some deeply felt needs; the men who come together seek personal healing and self-growth. Progressives, including several pro-feminist men's organizations of which I am a member, have not been able to mobilize men in anything approaching these numbers for this kind of healing and change. The Promise Keepers stepped into this vacuum.

part 1

---

an evangelical men's movement on the world stage?

2

What the Media Missed
about the Promise Keepers

Dane S. Claussen

ounded by former Colorado University football coach Bill McCartney, Promise Keepers (PK) is a Denver-based international evangelical Christian organization—involving huge public meetings, clergy conferences, books, tapes, local chapters, and other products and services—that asks men in the United States to make and keep commitments. These include pacts with their God, themselves, their wives, their children, their parents, their friends, their worship and fellowship, their work, their neighbors and community, those in need, and for the future, all within the context of a literal reading of the Bible.

McCartney writes in his first autobiography that the movement began when his friend Dr. Dave Wardell asked him what he would do for the rest of his life if money were not an issue. McCartney remembers he said, "More than anything, God has put it in my heart to witness a tremendous outpouring of His Spirit upon men. I envision men coming together in huge numbers in the name of Jesus, worshipping and celebrating their faith together. I long to see men openly proclaiming their love for Christ and their commitment to their families."[1]

Four Possible Causes of the Attendance Drop

PK started with a summer 1991 meeting of 4,200 men, followed by a 22,500-man conference in 1992, and more than 50,000 in 1993. In 1994, PK brought a total of more than 230,000 men together at seven cities, and the numbers of meetings and attendees increased significantly again in 1995 and 1996 (twenty-two events with attendance of 1.1 million). Plans were made in 1995 for an event of 1 million men in Washington, D.C., but the idea was preempted by October 1995's Million Man March, and delayed by a wish to avoid appearing political during the 1996 election year. In 1996, PK grossed about $115 million and had more than three hundred employees and a national network of representatives and offices. In October 1997, PK finally held its Washington, D.C., event, Stand in the Gap, which brought together hundreds of thousands of men and received extensive media coverage.

In 1997, however, attendance at PK's regional stadium events dropped significantly—to 630,000 at eighteen events—and because PK received 72 percent of its 1997 revenues of about $85 million from those events, PK was forced to lay off more than one hundred employees in July 1997. At the time, McCartney promised no more layoffs, but later in 1997, the PK board adopted his proposal that PK no longer charge for its events. Admission generally had been sixty dollars per person.

In February 1998, PK announced that it would lay off its entire staff of 345 on March 31, and PK would be run entirely by volunteers until donations and other income allowed paid staff. It committed to holding nineteen events during 1998, but many observers were skeptical. As one conservative Christian told me without apparent sarcasm, for PK to survive relying only on volunteers, "it would take a miracle." However, about $4 million in donations were received shortly after the layoff announcement, and employees were rehired. But through the remainder of 1998 and then 1999, PK underwent "restructuring" and "downsizing."

The reasons why attendance declined at PK events in 1997 are unclear. PK officials attributed the drop to many men passing up regional PK events to save enough time and money for Stand in the Gap (SITG). But it is unlikely that this was the only reason; after all, PK had been growing quickly and steadily, and if recent growth levels were continuing, PK should have had a huge attendance at SITG and strong attendance at regional events as well, even if attendees did not overlap. Second, the decision to eliminate admissions fees may have been in part because potential attendees—whether new or returning—were becoming resistant to the cost. Third, McCartney, though optimistic about race relations, attributed the 1997 attendance drop to PK's racial reconciliation theme during the previous year:

> Of the 1996 conference participants who had a complaint, nearly 40 percent reacted negatively to the reconciliation theme. I personally believe it was a major factor in the significant fall-off in P.K.'s 1997 attendance—it is simply a hard teaching for many. But many in Jesus' day also turned back from His "hard teaching" and followed Him no more (John 6:66). In all actuality, I suspect that much of the criticism leveled at Promise Keepers from within the Christian community— typically cloaked in assorted, untested claims that we're an ecumenical movement, or that we preach a gospel palatable to Mormons or fringe cults—has at its true root a deep-seated cultural resistance to the message on reconciliation. It simply tells me we're on the right track.[2]

A fourth possible reason for the attendance decline was the lack of new content. An attendee of two PK events volunteered to me his opinion that the second year's event was just like the first and he assumed that the third year's would be yet the same. Not interested in the potential ritual value of attending annually, he was looking for new substantive content and not getting it. Mary Stewart van Leeuwen points out, "Like going to a Billy Graham crusade, once you've been to one PK rally you've pretty much been to all of them."[3]

Promise Keepers in Historical Context

Neither the PK organization nor mass media have placed the movement into a historical context. This task is important because it can provide media, scholars, critics, clergy, the public, and even PK members and leaders with some perspective on what a group such as PK can accomplish, what its weak spots are, and what its critics will likely say. Steve Rabey compared Promise Keepers to the Men and Religion Forward Movement (MRFM) of 1911–12, and added that PK is similar in various ways to Dwight Moody and his followers, Billy Sunday and his followers, and the Muscular Christianity movement generally, of which Sunday was a part.[4] One of Gustav Niebuhr's *New York Times* articles quoted an evangelism scholar:

> Randall Balmer, a professor of religion at Barnard College, likened the organization [Promise Keepers] to a broad religious movement aimed at men at the turn of the century, the "muscular-Christianity" movement. Citing a particularly famous evangelist of the time, he said, "You had Billy Sunday taunting men to stand up and be a 'real man' and give their hearts to Jesus."
>
> Nine decades later, Mr. Sunday's challenge found an echo at the meeting here, where scores of men wore T-shirts emblazoned with the slogan, "Real Men Love Jesus."[5]

David Halbrook's article in *New Man*, then the official PK magazine, was headlined "Is This Revival? How Does the Promise Keepers Movement Compare with the World's Historical Revivals?"[6] It described the overall nature of revivals and suggested that PK had not achieved revival status yet; the only specific revivals mentioned were the Great Awakening (1730s–40s), Charles Finney's 1830s revival, and the United Prayer Meetings Revival of 1858, none of which were compared to PK. But neither Rabey nor Halbrook got it quite right, and Niebuhr told only part of the story. Only some of PK's speakers and texts have strong flavors of Muscular Christianity; some are more similar to other revivalists, and PK has almost nothing in common with MRFM or the broader Social Gospel movement of which it was a part.

The Nature of Religious Movements in the United States

The first point that helps place PK into a broader historical context is the overall nature and history of religion in the United States. Contrary to the longtime "secularization hypothesis," which holds that religion is on the decline, church attendance in the 1990s is much higher than it was in the 1790s. Despite claims that science, technology, capitalism, and liberal democracy have carried the day in the United States, beliefs in a God, miracles, heaven, hell, angels, and even in creationism and rejection of evolution have remained remarkably persistent here. Moreover, the United States experiences periodic religious revivals; scholars agree on the First and Second Great Awakenings, and this country has recently been experiencing either a Third or a Fourth Great Awakening (depending on whether one recognizes an earlier third one) since about 1960 (or since about 1970 or since about 1980, again depending on which scholar's work one reads), which may or may not already be over. Thus, although the specific characteristics of organizations such as the Moral Majority, Christian Coalition, Focus on the Family, American Family Association, and Promise Keepers may be unique to our time, the impulse is not.

Moreover, numerous other Christian men's organizations exist, some predating Promise Keepers (such as the Christian Business Men's Committee, which was founded during the Great Depression). None are of PK's size, and none receive much media attention. Among them are Christian Men's Network, Dad's University, National Center for Fathering, Career Impact Ministries, Business Life Management, Men Reaching Men, Fathers and Brothers, Dad the Family Shepherd, and the Southern Baptist Convention Brotherhood Commission's Men's Ministries.[7]

While later evangelists targeted men who already strongly identified as Christian, Dwight Moody and Billy Sunday appealed to the unconverted.[8] Moody and his followers had numerous similarities to McCartney and his, although Moody's preaching has been categorized as "Victorian sentimentalism," and not Muscular Christianity.[9] Moody was the "first fundamentalist,"[10] a layman who had been successful in another field (Moody was a successful shoe/boot salesman; at least one longtime scholar claimed he also was a loan shark and bill collector) and was financially secure when he dedicated himself to church work.[11] Moody, like McCartney could be, was described as

> conservative in theology, a literalist in his interpretation of Scripture though never a bigot . . . often ungrammatical in speech, there was

never a moment when he was eloquent; that he cared not a whit for logic; that he murdered the English language; that he had never seen the inside of a geology; and yet he stated there was not another man in America that could have filled the vast auditorium day after day. He held, during these meetings, forty-eight thousand people in the hollow of his hand, and they wept and smiled as he willed. The attempts of sociologists and psychologists to explain him seem trite and foolish. Some have suggested that his "unusual earnestness and simplicity" were the things that kept his hearers enchained. The impression that he left was that there was truth behind the man greater than he.[12]

Moody's 1875–85 revival meetings for men were held in large cities and were overwhelmingly attended only by the native-born, white, Protestant, middle-class, disproportionately business owners. Although pessimistic about and critical of contemporary society and popular culture, Moody was optimistic about Christians, Christianity, democracy, and capitalism. William G. McLoughlin explained,

He was brought in to the cities in times of unemployment by middle-class churchgoers and businessmen precisely to tell the workers that the American dream was true, that the system was fundamentally sound. People should not grumble or complain in hard times, because, sooner or later, the laws of supply and demand would bring a readjustment in the market, business would pick up, the factories would hum, good times would return. Meanwhile, they should tighten their belts, take any work that was available, and have faith in God's laws of economics.[13]

When Moody finally confronted the fact that the poor were not attending his revivals, and that his stock message would not necessarily help them anyway, he supported Christian education but not social reform[14]—despite his earlier support of political reform.[15]

Muscular Christianity, which sought to "revitalize the image of Jesus and thus remasculinize the Church," traces its roots to the British novels of Charles Kingsley and Thomas Hughes that "fused a hardy physical manliness with ideals of Christian service."[16] Book critics applied the term—intended as a trivializing label—to volumes about what previously had been called "Christian manliness," a term that was itself the title of an 1867 book.[17] The philosophy was introduced to the United States through Thomas Wentworth Higginson's 1858–61 *Atlantic Monthly* articles. Over the next several decades the idea profoundly and permanently impacted both American and British culture,[18] eventually offering models of "physical manliness, chivalry and the gentleman, moral manliness."[19] And despite Ted Ownby's argument that at some places and times, evangelical Christianity and masculinity have been in tension with each other,[20] the theme of Jesus as manly and masculine, religion as a manly and masculine pursuit, and the church as properly dominated by men continued for about sixty years. Muscular Christianity eventually included the revival meetings of Billy Sunday and others, a related flurry of books that apparently peaked between 1904 and 1918,[21] and in some ways, Moody's revivals.

Sunday, the "most famous of all Muscular Christians," was a former center fielder for baseball teams in Chicago and Pittsburgh who left the sport not because it was immoral, but because it was amoral.[22] Like that of McCartney, his former sports affiliation remained part of his identity and perhaps a large part of his appeal. The first major biography of Sunday was subtitled *Famous Baseball Evangelist*,[23] as if to blur the lines between playing baseball and preaching Christianity. Like PK, Sunday was "able to appear to be both a leader of the old-time religion and a spokesman for twentieth century religion."[24] And like PK, which within its first few years was grossing hundreds of thousands and millions of dollars per event, Sunday's revivals included "great emphasis placed on highly organized machinery set up by business agents, who demanded that great sums of money be subscribed before the meetings could begin. . . . He utilized almost to perfection the techniques of big business in organizing his campaigns and very large sums of money were subscribed to carry them forward."[25]

Sunday, who started his revival career in 1902, was at his peak from 1908 to 1918,[26] and may have helped inspire MRFM if only because it was in part a reaction to Sunday. MRFM officially rejected Sunday's emotional appeals and was established as a national organization with a group of key speakers and no central charismatic leader. While MRFM and some other later evangelical leaders or groups opposed racism, Sunday was openly racist, commenting once on African Americans and Native Americans, "If they don't like it here, let 'em go back to the land where they were kenneled."[27] More fundamentally, Sunday sought "especially to bring men back into established churches,"[28] and he did not preach the progressive Social Gospel agenda. Sunday said that MRFM was a "lamentable failure" because it sought to "make a religion out of social service with Jesus Christ left out."[29]

The Social Gospel, launched by Walter Rauschenbusch and Washington Gladden, was a liberal movement in the late nineteenth century and early twentieth century that believed that Christian principles could be successfully applied to social problems caused by industrialization. Early Social Gospelers, under the influences of socialism, Darwinism, and scientific positivism generally, primarily worked with labor, believing that capitalism could be reformed from the inside rather than from the outside. They advocated more rights, profit sharing and higher wages, improved living conditions for the working class, and eventually better race relations and international peace and justice.

Although several scholars have either stated or implied that MRFM was a Muscular Christianity movement,[30] it is a textbook case of a Social Gospel group. MRFM's "primary goal was to educate Christians about social conditions in their own communities and to inspire and equip them to improve these conditions."[31] Managed by the YMCA and endorsed by eleven Protestant denominations, it was part of a movement to make individual churches, entire religions, government, and all aspects of the public sphere more businesslike and scientific. Between September 1911 and April 1912, the close-ended MRFM drew more than 1 million men to events in 76 cities and 1,083 towns; three books were published about the movement—*The Message and the Program, Making Religion Efficient,* and *Men and Religion Messages.*[32] It conducted general social surveys in every city in which it met, with questions centered on the health, education, and welfare of working-class citizens, and conducted apparently the first surveys on, and published the first volume about, press coverage of religion. One of its most active speakers was socialist leader Raymond Robins, one of its most active writers was labor leader Charles Stelzle, and one of its most tangible results was the launching of the Labor Forward movement, but MRFM also received significant donations from robber baron-philanthropists. Other MRFM speakers included Rauschenbusch, Booker T. Washington, Charles Jennings Bryan, *Toronto Globe* editor J. A. Macdonald, former Georgia Governor W. J. Northen, University of Kansas Chancellor Frank Strong, Congressman Richard P. Hobson and, significantly, Jane Addams.

PK always has claimed to intentionally and successfully avoid an overtly political agenda, but MRFM developed a specific agenda. Gary Smith reported that "the Movement's leaders encouraged Americans to promote peace, education and temperance, to improve municipal government, housing, food, recreation, the penal system, race relations, and the conditions of rural life, and to abolish prostitution"; "support the demands of the American Federation of Labor for collective bargaining, higher wages, unemployment and old age pensions, better treatment of female employees, the abolition of child labor, and shorter hours and a safer working environment"; and "aid women and alcoholics."[33] MRFM seems to have ignored the women's movement entirely, but did not take the next logical step, which would have been to oppose women's suffrage. Instead, MRFM's official position was that women could work outside the home if they needed to, and even Gail Bederman—who essentially calls MRFM a reactionary, sexist organization—was forced to admit that "most women approved" of the movement, although they had "mixed feelings about the move to masculinize the churches."[34] PK's media coverage also typically depicts wives, girlfriends, and daughters approving of men's involvement.

Smith concluded, "While most of contemporary observers applauded its achievements, later historians have regarded the Movement as insignificant" because it netted "few permanent results" and was not successful in its goal of recruiting three million men into regular church attendance and social work.[35] He explained that "the crusade failed to achieve its longer range goals in large part because its participants became increasingly preoccupied with intensifying debates over biblical authority, evolution and social Christianity," not to mention World War I.[36] Smith wrote that not only did MRFM fail to endure, but evangelicals' support of social action faded as they "became preoccupied with resisting efforts of theological liberals to control their denominational agencies," turned to "premillennial beliefs that evil would increasingly flourish until Christ returned," and continued "fighting against evolution and . . . enforcing prohibition."[37] He speculated that a modern-day version of MRFM would "combat the world's present social ills—the threat of nuclear war, world hunger, economic exploitation, racism, and the abridgment of human rights—and . . . provide moral direction for American society."[38] PK may be trying to provide moral direction and fight racism, but even its opposition to racism is not the same as advocating a civil rights bill or other substantive steps.

Men's Movements in the 1970s and 1980s

Modern men's movements, groups, and books interested in exploring and advancing men's personal development in various ways can be traced in the United States back to small, local meetings and "men's liberation" books—of either me-too or reactionary varieties—appearing in the early 1970s. Since then, thousands of people have attended annual national meetings to discuss men's issues, and hundreds of thousands of men have participated in local discussion and support groups, and conferences and conventions of various kinds. By 1981, at least thirty "men's centers" had been established, in addition to various publications, existing or forming national organizations, and service projects.[39]

During the 1970s and 1980s, men's movements consisted largely of pro-feminist men who wanted to support feminism (such as the National Organization for Changing Men, later the National Organization for Men Against Sexism [NOMAS]) and men's rights activists (such as Men's Rights Association and Men's Rights Incorporated). Both camps are still active, although they receive little media attention and apparently have a limited following (NOMAS has fewer than one thousand members). Pro-feminist men support feminist causes, oppose sexism, and usually support gay rights. Men's rights activists concern themselves primarily with helping men achieve more equality primarily in divorce settlements and child custody battles, although the more militant wing (such as the National Organization of Men) opposes preferential treatment of women in any sphere of U.S. life. Lists of men's movements sometimes also include a black men's movement, a gay men's movement, and a Marxist men's movement, although all three of them are part of or largely overlap with larger movements that include both sexes. Generally liberal men's movement groups probably would not acknowledge them—barely acknowledging the men's rights groups now—but it is arguable that various militia, skinhead, and similar radical right-wing organizations are in some sense a men's movement as well.

The news media gave little coverage to men's movements until the early 1990s, when at least two distinctive new branches—PK and mythopoetism—emerged, and one distinctive event—the Million Man March (MMM)—occurred. And these movements cannot be clearly connected with earlier men's movements,[40] primarily because the 1970s liberationists were divided into strongly pro-feminist and antifeminist camps. The responses of mythopoets and PK to feminism are mostly indirect. Mythopoets generally concede much of feminism's descriptions, but think that it tells only part of the story, and do not agree with feminism's prescriptions (at least not for men). PK texts and speakers claim that the feminist movement failed. Nor are mythopoetism, PK, and the MMM explicitly connected to each other although they are clearly related under a men's movements umbrella.[41]

Mythopoetism stems from mythopoesis, meaning "re-mythologizing, not merely repeating old stories," and not from any synthesis or coordinated usage of myths and poetry, as is commonly thought.[42] It evolved, in a disjointed and uncoordinated fashion, from philosophical, historical, poetic, mythological, and other writings and lectures by Robert Bly, Sam Keen, Michael Meade, Shepherd Bliss, James Hillman, and many others. In 1990, Bly—a most prolific U.S. poet—published *Iron John: A Book about Men*, which caused the media to draft the initially unwilling Bly as the movement's titular head. Briefly, Bly and *Iron John* are advocates for men and their need, in his view, to recover healthy and natural aspects of masculinity that have been lost through the complex process of industrialization and social change over the past two hundred years. As Richard Gilbert explained, mythopoetism resulted from a growing realization that existing models of adult masculinity (i.e., the traditional, macho male or the gentler, feminine-identified male of the 1970s and 1980s) are

> both psychologically limited. . . . Methodologically, the mythopoetic approach employs didactic instruction, readings of poetry, mythic storytelling, music and movement, personal testimonials, and enactments of ritual to explore the psychology of men. Conceptually, it

offers a compelling set of ideas about the nature and responsibilities of a new or revitalized masculinity . . . a call for a greater masculine presence in the socialization process, especially that involving male offspring, and a proposed archetypal model of a mature, integrated masculinity. These ideas form the most coherent expression of a post-patriarchal, postfeminist model of masculinity.[43]

Ted Solotaroff described mythopoetism as a "complex phenomenon that appears to derive from A.A., feminism, New Age religion and therapy, environmentalism and the culture and charisma of Robert Bly."[44]

Iron John was on the *New York Times* bestseller list for more than a year (according to the *Washington Post* it was the bestselling nonfiction book of 1991), a popularity attributed, incidentally, largely to word of mouth and Bly's thought-provoking appearance on a ninety-minute Bill Moyers's public television program in January 1990.[45] Resulting "men's gatherings" attempted to help men rediscover lost dimensions of their masculinity. In two years, such "wildman weekend retreats" attracted more than 100,000 men, at $300 to $600 per head.[46] Such gatherings have both followed and preceded the formation of local men's groups nationwide.

Numerous books, newspapers, journals, newsletters, and other publications have been written by and for the mythopoetic movement—including a semi-official journal, *Wingspan*[47]—but Bly's *Iron John* was by far the biggest seller and clearly the most influential, with Keen's bestselling *Fire in the Belly* a distant second.[48] *Iron John* has been mentioned frequently by U.S. print news media, even though it has received generally neutral to negative reviews,[49] it is surely difficult for many potential readers to understand, and it is an "unclassifiable volume of literary analysis, philosophy and cultural criticism"[50]—not typical bestseller fare. It is an explanation and analysis—through a filter of liberal U.S. politics and Jungian psychology—of the Grimm Brothers' fairy tale, Iron Hans, which Bly believes could be 10,000 to 20,000 years old.[51] The main text, running 249 pages in the Addison-Wesley hardcover edition, covers a large variety of subjects and ideas, some of them of general interest to the men's movement, others arguably of interest throughout U.S. society today, and some particular to Robert Bly. The book's critique of U.S. men, women, fathers, sons, masculinity, politics, economics, and culture is wide-ranging, but his most important messages appear to be that current U.S. models of manhood are not working—most men may be "more thoughtful, more gentle" than before but not "more free"; U.S. men are too distant from their fathers and their fathers' work; U.S. society has no initiation process for males; men benefit greatly from mentors; today's "soft males" are passive, naive, and emotionally numb; U.S. men have internalized too much criticism from women and themselves, and generally identify too much with their mothers and other women; and a set definition for "masculine" or "man" does not and should not exist, although the book glorifies a "Wild Man" archetype. The book also strongly implies, though does not emphasize, the possibility of men being closer friends with other men.

Iron John's list of prescriptions for U.S. men is equally lengthy and diverse: men need to be in contact with their inner "Wild Man," who "resembles a Zen priest, a shaman, or a woodsman more than a savage"; boys need to be initiated into adulthood by men, not women; society needs "Zeus energy," male authority accepted by, and for the sake of, community; a young man who knows a "great" older person should not miss the opportunity to adopt a mentor; a man's psychological "wounds" are his largest source of strength; men must experience disasters and celebrate them to properly handle successes; men need a passion; men lose too much of their childhood or playfulness (lest they become "copper wires" for charm and niceness) and should not "merge" too much with their spouses; and men must recognize males and females as opposites without rejecting the feminine.

Many of the other books commonly referred to as related to men's movements make similar points: men are being marginalized in the family by themselves or others; men are stereotyped in society; men are out of touch with themselves; there are problems in relationships between men and their fathers and/or sons; and men need to develop a healthier masculinity, which includes, but is not dominated by, their feminine sides.

Although mythopoets and PK have in common a large number of specific criticisms of U.S. men, women, masculinity, society, unbridled capitalism, and materialism, and even have many of the same goals, if not the same methods or philosophies, the two movements' leaders and literatures have said little about each other.

Bly made an effort to be fair to PK by writing one long paragraph about its strengths and several short ones about his reservations and criticisms. He praised PK for emphasizing commitments to wives and children; men's "spiritual energy"; interracial healing; small men's groups; and fixing society's "fatherlessness." Bly also noted that "many men tend to feel at home" in football stadiums and might feel emotionally comfortable and otherwise secure with thousands of other men around.[52] But clearly calling PK sexist or worse, Bly said it seems out of touch with what women have accomplished over the past thirty years; literalism, which PK espouses, tends to result in intolerance, in this case against "so-called pagans and homosexuals"; and PK is paying no attention to the "dark side of any missionary movement."[53]

Shepherd Bliss has addressed Promise Keepers:

Some of the untruths, fantasies, and fears regarding the mythopoetic men's movement presented in many of the essays in this book have come to unfortunate reality in another men's movement—called the PromiseKeepers. This right-wing Christian group has filled football stadiums with over 50,000 men to challenge feminism and gay rights. . . . Men are encouraged by this group to return to Jesus and the Biblical image of men who control, dominate, and lead their wives and families. Feminism is blamed for the world's problems. This grow-ing group is a serious threat to women, gay people, and all of us advocating changes in gender relations.[54]

PK has roots of its own that perhaps have not yet been fully explored. Despite the other Christian men's organizations, the current Christian men's movement has been traced back once to two books: *Straight Talk to Men and Their Wives* (1980), by James Dobson, founder/president of Focus on the Family; and *Maximized Manhood* (1982), by Edwin Louis Cole.[55] Dobson attributes this latest Christian movement to men "who are recognizing that success in business, achieving all their goals, and making huge amounts of money are not going to satisfy them." A Christian Business Men's Committee spokesman, Robert Tamasy, noted that "today's economic inse-curities, epitomized by corporate downsizing, look a lot like the Depression era, when CBNC began amid a heightened spiritual need." Historian Timothy Weber said the movement is an attempt to slow or stop trends seen as destructive, such as divorce and illegitimacy.[56]

Michael Chrasta links PK to the Vineyard, Calvary, and Jesus People movements,[57] and Lynne Isaacson expressly compared PK to the Jesus People in her study of gender and sexuality in Shiloh, one of Jesus People's sub-groups.[58] But this link is much more easily made with a few PK leaders than with typical PK participants. As the *Los Angeles Times* explained: "Although identified as a Catholic by the [Los Angeles archdiocese's weekly newspaper] *Tidings*, McCartney left that church to join a Vineyard congregation in Boulder, Colo. The coach's pastor, the Rev. James Ryle, and the president of Promise Keepers, former pastor Randy Phillips, are both associated with Vineyard churches, a charismatic denomination started in Anaheim."[59]

Churches, the Media, and Promise Keepers

The reactions to PK by women in particular are detailed at length in this volume, and thus need not be covered here, and parts of chapters 3, 4, and 7 concern issues of race and ethnicity. But this chapter is an appropriate place to summarize both reactions to PK by U.S. organized religion and the news media's coverage of PK.

An article in *Christianity Today* reported that PK is "spawning dozens of parachurch groups," that "increasing numbers of denominational leaders have been rethinking the way they minister to men," that PK is a major discussion topic at religious leaders' meetings, and that men are participating more in local congregations.[60] The Southern Baptist Convention, the largest Protestant denomination (15 million members) in the United States, has cooperative agreements with both PK and Dad the Family Shepherd, plus its own men's ministries. The Assemblies of God appointed a men's ministries secretary to work with PK, the Lutheran Church–Missouri Synod worked on an eleven-page study of PK, the Presbyterian Church (U.S.A.) decided to develop a men's Bible study series, and the Catholic Church developed two new groups—the Saint Joseph's Covenant Keepers and a Ministry to Black Catholic Men.

The reaction of U.S. organized religion to Promise Keepers was not entirely cooperative or otherwise positive, however. The Southern Baptist Convention's Jim Burton complained that "some of our guys come home wearing shirts and hats, and they want to start Promise Keepers groups rather than work as a member of their local church. Some of these guys identify themselves as Promise Keepers, and they see themselves as separate from other men's ministries in the church."[61]

Catholics expressed concern about what they view as PK's potential to lead men away from Catholicism, its teaching of male "headship," and its "prejudice and discrimination against homosexuals."[62] And Doug Haugen, director of Lutheran Men in Missions for the Evangelical Lutheran Church in America, and president of the North American Conference of Church Men's Staff, admitted that various church leaders' reactions to PK have included "bouts of resentment, defensiveness, and jealousy."[63] Significantly, considering PK's racial reconciliation efforts, the National Baptist Convention USA—a traditionally African American denomination—in September 1995 formed Trusted Partners as a black counterpart and response.[64] The convention's president, Henry J. Lyons, immediately called for a 25,000-man rally in Memphis two months later, and invited Baptist, Methodist, and Pentecostal men, although this organization apparently did not take root and Lyons soon had his own scandals to deal with.

Various theologically conservative Christian individuals and organizations have emerged that are criticizing PK for not being conservative enough or not reading the Bible literally enough or similarly enough to their readings. In addition to numerous critical Internet Web sites,[65] PK's critics from the Right have written several scathing books.[66]

Media coverage of Promise Keepers has been addressed at length elsewhere, and space does not permit a full examination here. But briefly, virtually all academic studies and trade press articles on media coverage of religion (and especially evangelism or fundamentalism), masculinity issues, feminism, and social movements generally would have predicted that media coverage of PK would be negative, increasingly negative as opponents emerged, inaccurate, incomplete, late, shallow, and otherwise inadequate.[67] And it is easy for PK's supporters and critics alike to remember negative articles such as John Spalding's article in *Christian Century*:

> After a brief account of the resistance he's encountered trying to sell his message about racism at Promise Keepers events (angry letters, eerily silent responses from largely white audiences), McCartney's talk suddenly becomes a breathless, nearly incomprehensible rant that prompts the guy next to me to observe that he's "never seen anyone so filled with the spirit as Coach Mac." . . .
>
> Neck bulging, arms flailing, spit flying, McCartney builds to his point. "What Almighty God is doin' is waitin' for the church to come together in harmony! He's got a whole backload of things up there he wants to do. He's got so much on his heart he's wanted to do for so long but the church is divided."[68]

Another easily remembered negative article, this one in GQ, described McCartney as looking like a junior high "shop" teacher with a "low forehead, meaty arms and thick, black-rimmed glasses." The article's author, Scott Raab, lampooned McCartney with observations of "fogged sincerity" and "perceptible goofiness," and a suspicion that McCartney is kept from the press by the handlers because he's a "raving lunatic." Raab decided that some American men's attraction to PK, meeting in stadiums, is the symbolic metaphor that "life is a football game. The opposing team is scary as hell, and pissed off to boot, but we've got a humdinger of a coach and God's own playbook." Moreover, he wrote, PK speakers—like some football coaches— simultaneously tell American men that they have become "feminized" and "sissified," and that they can and will be victorious. Raab also concluded that PK is less about Jesus Christ than it is about the devil; in other words, PK literature and speakers tell men that Satan is everywhere, especially in the men themselves, and that PK is their shield. Raab, who at one point compares a PK stadium conference with a Nazi Party rally, suggests that it is primarily PK's racial and interdenominational reconciliation rhetoric and its "feel-good goals" that have obtained for it "relatively hands-off" media coverage.[69]

But these were just two of scores of articles on PK in national magazines and hundreds of stories in local and national newspapers, local television news, national television networks, and cable stations. And reading and watching the overwhelming majority of stories across the United States reveal quite a different picture from that of articles in GQ and some in *Christian Century*.

PK has received almost entirely favorable media coverage.[70] Even a self-proclaimed feminist writer for *Ms.* was ultimately sold on PK (although other

Ms. writers have not been). Donna Minkowitz wrote that she had concluded that U.S. society cannot change in ways feminists want it to change unless men receive help in becoming "caring, loving, ethical, and nondominating." More specifically, she wrote that American manhood is so "repressive" that men require "active healing—not just women's understandable impatient suggestion that they cease their misdeeds." And she felt compelled to admit that PK has stepped into a "vacuum" that John Stoltenberg and other progressives had tried but been unable to fill. Ultimately, Minkowitz suggested that women not criticize PK men as "dupes or unmitigated reactionaries," but instead understand the "contradictory impulses" that draw men to PK and "tap into the very needs" that PK leaders already understand.[71]

Why Has Promise Keepers Fared Better?

Why has PK fared so much better with the media than other men's movement organizations, other conservative Christian groups, and other social movements? And why do so many men involved in PK still bitterly complain about their media coverage? These are complicated questions to answer, but many possible explanations emerge clearly.

Numerous reasons can help explain PK's overall favorable media coverage. One explanation is the journalistic practice of balance. It is responsible for commonly finding one negative-sounding quote from one source in so many articles on PK. PK men may not like this, but "balancing" content is time consuming to gather and reporters also have considerable latitude in implementing it. Frequently, as in the case of PK coverage, only one critic is quoted, although many different critics with many different points of view exist. Media often choose the most extreme critics because they are the most "interesting" and the easiest to identify. But PK supporters should remember that extreme critics do not always have the most credibility with the general public (or even with the media that quote them).[72] In short, if PK men have been unhappy with media coverage of NOW protests, they should be particularly happy that no single story on PK will ever quote representatives from the wide range of other Christian, non-Christian religious, feminist men's, mythopoetic, civil rights, civil liberties, gay rights and other feminist organizations, and the liberal theologians and fundamentalist Christians who all would make skeptical or hostile comments about PK.

A second explanation for the favorable coverage is that many media workers perhaps see conservative Christians as the status quo or part of the status quo rather than a threat to it.

Third, perhaps media workers have a difficult time being critical of an organization that grew quickly (is popular) and is public, Christian, antiracist and promoting racial reconciliation, causing men to renew family and community commitments, denying that it is sexist, and saying much less than it could against abortion and homosexuality.

Fourth, perhaps some moderate to liberal media workers were unaware of how conservative PK is.

Fifth, perhaps media workers believe that the state of society has become so grim that an organization such as PK—even if the media workers do not agree with all of the ways in which it has framed social problems, causes, consequences, and solutions—can do more good than harm.

Sixth, perhaps social movements' coverage (conservative Christian revivals in particular) is not as negative as is commonly believed and as research and commentary indicate. (Whether the reason is that the media have changed, the movements have changed, or both, is unknown.)

Seventh, perhaps media have been "primed" by their experiences covering mythopoetism to cover Promise Keepers more positively. In other words, media could have covered mythopoetism less often or more negatively on the assumption that it was an anomaly, and that men's issues really were not of any importance in society. But when PK emerged, media workers could have realized that men's movements and men's issues were not limited to one organization, philosophy, or theme and therefore must have broader support and be more important.

Eighth, perhaps some media workers would consciously avoid giving negative coverage to PK, even if they felt it justified, because they would simply prefer not to deal with angry letters, phone calls, E-mails, and visits to their offices that would result. For example, Nancy Novosod tells us, "The newspaper that ran the controversial Promise Keepers article received protest calls for more than two weeks after it appeared and subsequently ran a column indicating the callers were right, the paper should not have devoted so much space to the protesters."[73]

Finally, and I think most significantly, most U.S. general interest news media still are almost entirely incompetent at covering news concerning religion (of course, they are not much more competent in covering economics, science, and many other complex subjects). Almost no stories in any media have fully explained PK within any larger religious, historical, cultural, political, or economic context, and it is very easy to produce a list of story ideas about PK, of legitimate merit to professional journalists, that have rarely if ever been pursued.[74] In short, then, PK's media coverage has been overwhelmingly poor, regardless of whether one interprets its tone as positive, negative, or objective (mixed or neutral).

To help explain PK men's complaints about their media coverage, I have pointed out that how a reader interprets the extent to which news reporting is positive or negative depends mostly on how one defines those words and applies them to the coverage.[75] For instance, many PK men may be interpreting the parts of articles that provide substantial information about PK goals, history, positive effects, teachings, and speakers as "neutral" or "objective" information, and then a single critical quote (which is usually all that appears) from NOW or a liberal theologian seems to tip that article toward the negative for the reader who is supportive of PK. But this interpretation overlooks the fact that most of the facts and opinions about PK are presented without being questioned or commented on at all. This interpretation also overlooks the fact that the media chose to cover PK rather than to devote resources elsewhere, and there is never any question that news media have more story ideas than they possibly could ever cover.

Second, as Dean Allen points out, many conservative Christians engage in "dichotomous thinking," drawing distinct and polar opposite boundaries around "good" and "evil," "Christians" and "non-Christians," and so on.[76] This apparently results in a negative reaction by PK supporters to articles about PK that contain even one unfavorable fact or opinion. One can only wonder how such PK supporters would react to a continuous stream of articles about PK as negative as the coverage that most other U.S. social movements received during their first few years.

Third, Hillary Warren explains that many conservative Christians have been so conditioned to expect unfavorable media coverage of their beliefs and activities, when they receive favorable media coverage, they treat it as a fluke and the reporter as some sort of rebel within the media establishment.[77]

Fourth, it is easier to remember one vitriolic article attacking PK than it is to remember dozens of stories that did not.

Fifth, critics of PK's coverage generally have not compared and contrasted media coverage of PK with coverage of other current or past religious or social movements, evangelical or fundamentalist Christian organizations, other men's movements, and so on.

Finally, complaints about media coverage of PK seldom take into account that PK did not have a public relations agency to professionally handle media contacts until 1995, that Bill McCartney has revealed information about himself in his own books that reflects poorly on him for some people not involved in PK, and that even some PK participants have reservations or complaints about the organization.[78]

In sum, while the news media have not been particularly competent in covering PK, PK was not always the most competent in its dealings with the media, and friends and participants of PK have not been particularly competent in interpreting coverage of PK or in understanding how U.S. news media work on their stories or others' stories.

3

A Reaction to Declining Market
and Religious Influence

Judith L. Newton

The Promise Keepers is the story of the apostle becoming a citizen. Many Hollywood productions in the 1990s suggested that the decade was indeed marked by a sense of crisis over the dominant meanings of what it means to be a man. Two movies come to mind as a way of framing this assertion: *The Apostle*, a 1998 film that garnered an Oscar nomination for Robert Duvall; and *Falling Down*, a 1991 film.

The apostle is a white, middle-class hero—Euliss "Sonny" Dewey—who in rapid succession loses his wife, children, home, and accustomed means of employment (as a preacher in his own Pentecostal church). Stripped of almost everything that has defined his somewhat tenuous hold on his identity, as head of household and self-made man, Dewey finds himself in a limbo of economic and social dislocation.

Defens is the protagonist in *Falling Down*. Like Dewey, Defens is also a white, middle-class hero. Defens, however, mistakenly believes in the possibility of going home again. It takes a painful sojourn in the wilderness for him to learn that following the perceived rules of self-making, breadwinning, head-of-household masculinity has made him "the bad guy" and that, as a "bad guy," he cannot go home. In the end, Defens dies, fatherless and unfatherly. Like the middle-class black man, Prendergast, who mirrors the hero's plight, Defens is economically (and also socially) no longer "viable." The future, however, belongs to Prendergast, a paternal Los Angeles police detective who supports multiculturalism and advances for women and who duly takes back the job from which he has retired, his role as head of house and, implicitly, his status as protector of the nation.

Reinvention in the Wilderness of Late Capitalism

If in 1991 it takes the entire movie to learn this, Dewey, in *The Apostle*, learns early on that he is the bad guy. His womanizing, seen as an abuse of legitimate patriarchal power, has contributed to the breakdown of his marriage, and in a moment of rage, he also fatally injures his wife's lover with a baseball bat. Then Dewey, in an act of self-baptism duly witnessed and validated by an older, poor black man, transforms himself into the apostle, E. F. As a wandering evangelist, E. F. does not go home again, but empowered by the psychic certainty of his belief in a heavenly Parent, he is able to invent, and then reinvent, new forms of work, family, community, and identity. With the help of an assortment of other, variously marginalized, men—a retired black preacher (Brother Blackwell), a lonely white mechanic, and the white manager of a local religious radio station—E. F. rebuilds the preacher's church, gathers a following, and inherits Brother Blackwell's role as minister to a poor mixed-race congregation. When apprehended in the end for his bad guy behavior in the past, E. F. moves on, re-creating himself once more as the spiritual leader of a multicultural chain gang. The wilderness of late capitalism is full of displaced and marginalized persons with whom he may reinvent home, work, and community—with himself as fatherly, loving head.

Many components of E. F.'s reinvented life—psychic certainty in uncertain times, passionate communion with mixed-race communities, and faith in the possibility of miraculous transformations (E. F., with the help of his congregation, converts a white supremacist as he prepares to bulldoze their church)—unmistakably evoke the spirit of early Pentecostalism and, as I shall suggest, of Promise Keepers too. An outgrowth of the U.S. holiness movement and of nineteenth-century black religious traditions, Pentecostalism is often said to have originated in the 1906 Los Angeles–based Azusa Street revival, a mixed-race congregation headed by a black minister, William Joseph Seymour, which held to a gospel of racial reconciliation and entertained forms of gender equity within the church. Although by 1912, Pentecostalism had splintered somewhat along race lines, some cross-racial forms of Pentecostalism spread rapidly in the United States and then in Europe, Latin America, and Africa, enjoying a second revival in the post–World War II era. Today, Pentecostalism has an estimated 400 million adherents worldwide, may soon become the dominant religion in South Korea and in parts of Latin America, and is often said to be the fastest-growing religion in the world.[1]

Pentecostalism Fills New Voids

Although earlier accounts of the Pentecostal-charismatic movement sometimes attributed its rapid spread to the machinations of transnational corporations and the U.S. Religious Right, more recent accounts, from a range of political positions, see its growth, like the growth of other fundamentalist religions, as a series of semi-indigenous responses to the end of the cold war, the decline of Marxist-Leninist certainties, and the deleterious effects of transnational capitalism. The latter include a lowering of living standards for the nonwhite majority of the world's population, a widening of the already enormous gap between rich and poor, the uprooting of traditional occupations, identities, and communities, and the erosion of the state itself as a fulcrum of security and protection as well as an institutionalized epitome of masculinity.[2]

Pentecostalism, many scholars argue, interacts with indigenous religious traditions, filling in the voids left by the metamorphosis of old social contracts and providing an alternative basis for identity, for community, for making sense of rapid social change, and for feeling empowered in a wilderness in which the forces making for economic and social dislocation seem mysterious and impossible to control. For lower-class men who have often lost traditional forms of occupation without being fully integrated into the new, poorly paid, and largely female global workforce, Pentecostalism may offer particular consolations because it officially endorses men's leadership in the home.

Similar consolations may be afforded to "second tier" middle-class men whose economic and social powers have diminished, especially in relation to those of the transnational capitalist elite, and whose status as male citizens representing the "nation" has declined with the shrinking powers of some nation-states. Middle-class health and wealth Pentecostalisms, for example, are developing alongside Pentecostalisms that function largely to organize displaced persons of the lower classes.[3]

Opinions vary widely, however, about the impact of this apostolic religion. In the eyes of some, Pentecostalism paves the way for transnational capitalism because the psychic certainty it provides enables the individual to "assume his/her place in the irrational order of global consumerism."[4] For others, Pentecostalism's transracial, transnational ministry to the poor suggests promising new forms of global citizenship, involving transnational ethical traditions capable of promoting peace and human rights, new forms of liberation theology, and even improved gender relations.[5] Some interpreters, for example, see a gap between Pentecostal rhetoric about male leadership and everyday practices. Pentecostalism's emphasis upon masculine responsibility and its condemnation of drinking and violence toward women, they argue, have produced more egalitarian gender relations in poor Latin American homes.[6]

The last three decades in the United States have also seen the dramatic expansion of evangelical, fundamentalist, and Pentecostal ideas and organizations.[7] Promise Keepers, which combines elements of all three, is part of this expansion. Like Pentecostalisms, indeed, Promise Keepers enjoyed exponential growth from its beginnings in the early 1990s until 1997 and now numbers more than 2 million participants in the United States. The PK movement, moreover, has already spread to Canada, New Zealand, and other countries, and the U.S. leadership, despite PK's financial difficulties in late 1997 and early 1998, has announced its intention of launching a wider-reaching global initiative in the year 2000.

As with Pentecostalism, PK's growth may be linked partially to transnational capitalist development and economic restructuring. The deleterious effects of these processes are most evident in the United States, as elsewhere, in the increasing gap between rich and poor and in the expansion of a vast pool of low-paid workers of color. But the domestic consequences of transnational capitalism are also now experienced as a "crisis" for even white, middle-class men and therefore for dominant definitions of masculinity as well.

Crisis in Middle-Class Masculinity

Corporate downsizing, a decline in real wages, and the perceived necessity of two incomes to sustain a middle-class life have hit white male members of the middle class where they have undermined the identification of dominant masculinity with self-making, primary breadwinning, and authority as head of house. Coupled with the continued entry of women into the labor force, feminist challenges to traditional gender arrangements at work and at home, and critiques of white, straight, middle-class masculinity by identity movements on every front, dominant forms of masculinity have been deeply challenged and indeed changed. Being straight, white, middle class, and male has lost material and moral authority, leaving many men who followed the old self-making, head-of-household rules secretly protesting, with Defens, "I'm the bad guy?" The precipitous drop in wages and employment for black men of the middle and lower classes and, moreover, the related rise in black female-headed households, black feminist critiques of black masculinity, and the absence of a viable antiracist movement have contributed to an even greater loss of moral authority and social viability for black men. PK—like the mythopoetic movement, many black nationalisms, and Pentecostalism to boot—offers an alternative paradigm for masculine identity.

As a participant in the explosion of discourse on masculinities in the 1990s, PK draws upon and reinvents a host of themes that have characterized folklore, previous men's movements, media writing, and Hollywood films about male transformation such as, for example, male loss and wounding, entering the wilderness or woods, and being rebaptized or reborn through the power of masculine figures. The particular appeal of PK's reinvented masculinity, however, may lie partially in the fact that it addresses the material underpinning of this crisis more effectively than past men's movements. In an age when the masculinity-defining, single, primary, or even reliable breadwinner role has already been eroded, PK validates an alternative foundation for middle-class masculinity—putting God and family before career.

The shift from a masculinity based on competitive self-making and economic performance to one based on loving fathering and husbandhood has, as I argue elsewhere, distinct benefits for women and children as well as for men.[8] But one downside of this "focus on the family" lies in its tendency to direct attention away from economic issues and relations. PK rhetoric, like that of many spokespersons for "family values" on the Right, tends to obscure the role of corporate policy in producing the very crisis in masculinity to which PK ministers. (PK's blindness to this relationship is in stark contrast with the Social Gospel movement's attention to it during the time of the robber barons, muckraking, and trust busting.) In this sense, PK, like some Pentecostalisms, may function to "tailor the spirit" for a transnational capitalism as seemingly unstoppable as the juggernaut of, say, the Roman Empire.[9]

PK as Both Liberal and Conservative

PK is open to the charge that it substitutes one form of traditional masculine power for another—servant/leadership in the home for lost power and control in the public sphere. As I argue elsewhere, however, and as others argue in this book, PK publications and rally speeches interpret biblical injunctions about male leadership in both conservative and liberal ways. Most interpretations emphasize leadership as a form of servanthood and responsibility, both of which involve concrete forms of giving to women and children such as sharing child care, housework, and ironing and even taking on the notion that men too have a "second shift." My ethnographic work with Promise Keepers suggests a gap between their rhetoric and the actual negotiations of everyday life, as well as considerable regional variation. In California, for example, where the men I interviewed were in dual-career families, white and African American men and women regularly reported acting like a "team." Much of PK's appeal appears to stem from the fact that it responds to changes in the gender order and that it does not simply encourage men to believe that "going home again" means recapturing the patriarchal past.

In 1995 and 1996 conferences, nonetheless, men's commitment to their families became the basis on which they were invited to lay implicit claim to leadership and possession of the civil and the public sphere. Promise Keepers' national conferences, and particularly the "sacred assembly" in the nation's capital, effectively evoked the nation and its crises while the all-male crowds implicitly identified the national citizen as male. Like secular conservative and centrist spokespersons for "family values," and like Afrocentric black nationalists, PK speakers have claimed that fatherless families are at the core of our nation's ills and that fathers are the ticket to national recuperation.[10]

In identifying men as the leaders and protectors of the next generation, of course, PK conferences affirm long-held traditions of U.S. national culture. Among them are the symbolic tie of the nation's founding to masculine protection and the implicit identification of the citizen as male, but not simply male—also property-holding, white, and heterosexual. Vietnam, however, and the emergence of identity politics undermined the easy equation of U.S. citizens with straight white men just as they undermined any automatic support for national missions in which elite white men were in control. Immigration, demographic change, and postmodern notions of a fluid, nomadic subject have raised questions about the very notion of "a" model citizen, a national mission, or a national identity.

Redefining the United States

U.S. nationalism and national mission may be open to spiritualization and redefinition nowadays because the stockholders and officers of transnational corporations maintain loyalty largely to one another and no longer correlate their self-interest with that of the nation to the same degree as in the past.[11] Much of PK's cultural resonance, I would argue, stems from its articulation of a new national identity and mission, and from the fact that both resolve emblematically some of the tensions between what Lisa Lowe calls the abstract figure of the (implicitly white, male) citizen and the economic, social, and cultural limitations of its applications to, in this case, straight, nonwhite men.[12]

In casting men, aka citizens, as members of families rather than as economically competitive individuals, for example, PK de-emphasizes the unfriendly and unequal relations of the marketplace. The domestic sphere, after all, is a place in which all PK participants are invited to feel equal as servant/leaders (no matter how compromised by real arrangements this affirmation of men's leadership may be). The family is presumed to be private, natural, and God given, and to operate similarly despite different economic and social locations. Thus all (implicitly) heterosexual men, regardless of economic and social location, may be alike in being good family men. Citizenship becomes a cross-racial and, implicitly, a cross-class affair.

Since family units have historically served men of color as a means of survival and protection in a racist world, PK's family-man rhetoric may have particular resonance with them. The Nation of Islam and other black nationalisms speak a similar language. Men are leaders of family first, then leaders of community.[13] Although PK's message to men of color—"Christ, not culture"—directly challenges nationalist priorities, such as separatism and Afrocentricity, PK also rivals cultural nationalisms in positing an imagined community in which men of color (also) represent the nation.

In contrast to most white family values spokesmen, however, PK has increasingly urged its participants to move beyond a "focus on the family," to enlarge its circles of caring, and to engage in a more collective and potentially more progressive national project—that of racial reconciliation. PK conferences, for example, have been marked by highly orchestrated emphases on embracing difference. Black and Latin music, bilingual prayers, videos of men in mixed-race situations and relations, the generous representation of blacks and Latinos among the speakers (of six speakers in Los Angeles in 1996, only two were white), the PK logo of three hands or three bodies—white, brown, and black—create a ritual space in which the national and Christian community looks and sounds cross-racial. The sports arena setting in which men typically enter a cross-racial community and cheer for mixed-race teams reinforces the multicultural message.

PK conferences in 1995, however, staged racial difference, by and large, as a matter of skin color and cultural variation. In essence, all men were alike, which is to say that, in essence, PK men were white-defined. Conference patter about cultural difference leaned heavily toward metaphors of culinary or linguistic exploration, and racism was defined, by and large, as attitude. As attitude, its resolution could be imagined as individual and ritually performed. In Oakland, for example, where enough men of color were in attendance to make this feasible, attendees were urged to cross the aisles, embrace a man of a different race, and repeat the words, "I have failed you; things are going to be different." The moment was moving and impressive, but the assumed mutuality of racism symbolically canceled out the structural inequalities of race and white domination. In its early conferences, therefore, PK might evoke those familiar American narratives in which men of color witness and implicitly validate the self-redeeming rituals of white men or in which emotional bonding with a man of color functions largely as a form of justification for the continuation of white male headship in a reinvented national community and home.

Shifts in PK's Rhetoric

In 1996, in a significant discursive shift, owing in large part, I believe, to the greater prominence of men of color on the PK board of directors, PK's racial mission was somewhat differently defined. If in 1995, for example, PK men were invited to an unrealistic mutual forgiveness, in 1996 white brothers were forgiven and then urged to give up privilege for the sake of racial justice. The African American minister Wellington Boone, significantly, did not pray for black forgiveness but called for a spiritually based race awakening. Like the Pentecostal Azusa Street revival, which began with a mixed-race congregation in Los Angeles almost a century ago, so the next revival movement, race reconciliation, with its beginning there in the Coliseum of South Central Los Angeles, would sweep the nation. It was no accident that PK's first conference in 1996 was scheduled for the same month as, and housed near the site of, the Los Angeles uprising four years before.

The call for reconciliation became a call for antiracist action at the 1997 Stand in the Gap assembly on the Washington, D.C., Mall, where the rhetoric of African American speakers, in particular, seemed haunted by the 1963 march on Washington and by reminders of King's disappointment in the failure of white Christian churches to support civil rights. African Americans constituted 13 percent of the crowd, according to a *Washington Post* poll, but many of the men I interviewed had come "out of curiosity"— the same reason many black men gave for attending the Million Man March. And several men of color who had recently joined the PK stable of conference speakers and intermediaries testified to having joined the organization after great deliberation. Having closely observed the movement for at least a year, they reported noting that, at clergy conferences, a meaningful opening toward clergy of color had occurred. For them as for men of color on the PK staff, the antiracist project represents the possibility of a mixed-race movement against racism able to reverse some of the failures of white (and black) churches actively to support the civil rights movement. Unlike Brother Blackwell, however, PK men of color see themselves as also leading this movement, not as fading gracefully into the role of witness and suppliers of moral support to white apostles.

It would be unwise, therefore, to dismiss PK's antiracist project as yet another instance of white men rebaptizing themselves in the wilderness, and it would be insulting as well once again to cast men of color as always the hapless witnesses to white male rebirth or the perpetual victims of white men's envious attempts to co-opt their virtues. The shift within PK discourse toward a more structural reading of racism owes much to the fact that men of color in the PK leadership have agendas of their own just as PK's effort to make antiracism a central feature of godly masculinity owes much to the way progressive men of color have traditionally defined what it means to be "a man." Despite PK's generally conservative politics, its definition of masculinity represents a considerable intervention into far Right and conservative understandings of masculinity in the past and has begun to verge on what some pro-feminist men have defined as socially engaged or "democratic manhood."[14]

Having attended a half dozen Promise Keeper conferences and having interviewed some fifty men, I would find it difficult to question the passion and sincerity of the racially mixed speakers when they talk of seeing racism as a sin and of wanting to end racism in the church by the year 2000. But the meanings and possible effects of social movements must be gauged within larger contexts, within relationships of power that intentions, no matter how worthy, do not control. The potential effects of PK's antiracist project, for example, must be speculated about within the context of the overtly politicized Christian Right and of the new Right as a whole. The former has been eager to ally with conservative black and Latino churches in relation to its stance against abortion and homosexuality, a stance that PK shares.

New Right Benefits from Alliance with Men of Color

The new Right as a whole has much to gain from an enlarged alliance with men of color. Conservatives such as Clarence Thomas have been routinely marshaled to demonstrate that affirmative action, for example, is no longer needed or that the economy can be left to run itself. Without a greater emphasis on structural change, PK's antiracist project could function largely as a form of corporate multiculturalism, helping to produce a more harmonious workforce but one that fails to understand, much less protest, the role of corporate practice in perpetuating race and class injustice.

PK's antiracist project must also be seen as part of a larger movement by historically white evangelical organizations to apologize publicly for their racism and, at times, for their failure to act on civil rights.[15] While it seems clear that for many evangelicals racism really is a sin and that personal transformations are taking place—and as a feminist I cannot dismiss the importance of the personal as political—it seems equally clear that racism is also perceived to be a barrier to evangelizing the world and that some evangelicals see themselves in a struggle both with secular humanism and with other religions, particularly Islam, not only for souls but for dominion over secular institutions. PK, after all, implicitly defines the citizen as Christian in the context of an economic wilderness in which Islam appears to be replacing communism as the enemy of conservative Christianity and of mainstream transnational corporate interests as well.

On the domestic front, the rapid growth of Islam has raised conservative (and some progressive) white and black fears that it could become the dominant religion in U.S. urban areas by 2020. Certainly one reading of race reconciliation on the part of evangelical U.S. churches is that the effort is bent on keeping black men, in particular, within the Christian fold, a fold that—in the United States at least—is still largely white-dominated and white-centered in its understanding of race relations and race progress.

PK's Silence on Sexism

Domestically and globally, a cross-race alliance of men that lays rhetorical claim to being in charge of race reconciliation is in danger, despite the nobility of its purpose, of strengthening the exclusion of women from citizenship and of rendering gender inequality invisible as a social issue. As one feminist Promise Keeper I interviewed pointed out, PK has never taken a stance against, or asked forgiveness for, sexism. Any organization that condemns homosexuality as sin inevitably contributes to a climate in which discrimination and violence against gays can and do easily flourish. PK's recent embrace of a masculinity more firmly grounded in social justice and attention to structural inequality, of course, raises the issue of social justice for gay men (not to mention women of all persuasions), and PK's "love the sinner" rhetoric is less harsh than the "condemn the sinner" rhetoric of many fundamentalist groups.[16] Nonetheless, PK has yet to follow more liberal religious groups in extending love for the sinner to an endorsement of gay civil rights.

It would be simplistic, however, to read racial reconciliation as a conspiracy of the Religious Right bound only to make conservative social and economic policies look less racist or to unify voters against abortion and homosexuality, although each of these outcomes is a possibility. The racial reconciliation movement, for one thing, is larger than its conservative evangelical constituency and includes many progressive individuals and groups, such as those involved in the Call to Renewal that vigorously support gender, race, and economic justice along with gay civil rights.[17] Some members of the Call identify themselves as Promise Keepers.

Promise Keepers continues to reinvent itself and decided to make all 1998 and 1999 conferences free of charge, a move that could have opened its membership to greater class and race diversity, but did not.[18] Whatever direction Promise Keepers takes, it is a movement well worth watching, most particularly as it enters the global scene. Now that it has begun to urge its participants, 90 percent of whom are born-again Christians, to bring with them skeptical and non-Christian friends, it moves ever more in the direction of producing the citizen as apostle—the citizen as apostle of the world. It will be interesting to see how this figure interacts with those other apostolic citizens of the world, Pentecostal and Islamic, who are largely poor, nonwhite, non-American—and often female.

4

Race and Religion at the Million Man March and the Promise Keepers' Stand in the Gap

Steven L. Jones and William H. Lockhart

Aerial photographs of both the Million Man March (MMM) and Promise Keepers' Stand in the Gap (SITG) rally show hundreds of thousands of men gathered in one location and appear somewhat similar. However, while both events were held for men, the groups sponsoring these events affected the sort of men who attended. The MMM was specifically for black men. Planners of the event sought to transcend the religious diversity of the audience by promoting race as the common bond for participants. PK, on the other hand, invited evangelical Christian men to Washington and tried to transcend racial and ethnic diversities in an effort to find religious unity.

Many people expressed opinions about what happened during those two days in Washington, D.C. Some social critics lambasted both events.[1] Others viewed the events as large-scale group therapy.[2] Nevertheless, detailed comparisons of two of the largest social demonstrations in U.S. history have yet to surface. Some media articles, noting that both events were for men only, were limited in scope to responses by feminist groups;[3] a substantial majority of media coverage was overwhelmingly favorable, yet it was superficial.[4] One journalist even suggested that the MMM and PK activities should be understood as "two wings to one mass men's movement,"[5] although it has been more common to link PK with the mythopoetic men's movement, and even more common to cover each men's organization without any context at all.

Although the Million Man March and the Stand in the Gap events were for men only, they attracted different men and led the men in different directions. And because the audiences were distinct, the events themselves further separated the movements. Accordingly, while comparisons are in order, a more thorough approach leads to the conclusion that these are separate movements.

In this chapter we analyze the promotional material, speeches, and published reflections of event participants. We realize that numerous possible perspectives exist from which to analyze these events. However, given that each event was attended by hundreds of thousands of men, it is impossible to learn what each participant thought of the rallies. How then can we make sense of the events? Emile Durkheim provides an often used framework for understanding social gatherings.[6] Randall Collins has formulated this framework into four aspects of social assemblies.[7] First, these events, which Durkheim calls rituals, bring like-minded people together where they can see and communicate with others they may not encounter every day. Second, rituals encourage group members to participate in common activities. These activities result in the generation of common emotions, which is the third aspect of a ritual. Finally, an emotionally charged symbol grows out of the ritual that reminds participants of the event and allows them to remember the powerful experience they have shared. The meanings attached to these experiences take on the air of authority in the lives of participants, but are actually "social constructs," created by the ritual process.

Yet these mass gatherings do not happen in a vacuum. They both shape and are shaped by the social movements that call them into existence. Nancy Whittier defined social movements as "clusters of organizations, overlapping networks, and individuals that share goals and are bound together by a collective identity, and cultural events."[8] Understanding the MMM and SITG as shared cultural events, we will focus on how the events illuminate the sources of collective identity and shared goals.

Collective identity is crucial for the life of a social movement. Christian Smith has noted that "social movements must also construct and maintain collective identities that signify to themselves and the world who they are. . . . Movements lacking coherent shared identities are likely to be culturally and politically ineffectual."[9] But how does a social movement construct a collective identity among separate individuals? Whittier suggests that collective identity has been achieved when participants internalize a new self-definition as part of the larger collective. She identified three processes involved in the construction of this new self-definition. First, group boundaries are delineated and demarcated by the adoption of a label that signals affiliation with the group. This label need not be new as long as there is a common understanding of what it means to adopt it among members of the group. Second, social movements construct an "oppositional consciousness." This consciousness serves as the central interpretive framework group members use to diagnose the events of their lives. Thus, even matters only tangentially related to the social movement are understood from the group's perspective. Finally, social movements encourage the "politicization of everyday life." Certain actions and attitudes become central to what it means to be a member of the group. This results in a set of defining attitudes and actions that identify group members.

Clearly, social movements seek to modify individuals' notions of themselves in an effort to gain their loyalty. Ultimately to be successful, the effect needs to be long lasting—which presents another difficulty for social movements. Recent literature questions the possibility, or even the desirability, of an individual's maintaining a permanent sense of self, one that remains intact across situations.[10] We conclude that both movements challenge that idea by reasserting the need for a sense of permanence in terms of personal identity. We call this the anchor identity. For instance, the leaders of the MMM exalted black manhood as the anchor identity that attracted men to Washington, D.C. Similarly, SITG stressed Christian manhood as the anchor identity that called men to the nation's capital.

The Million Man March

How did it happen that on October 16, 1995, hundreds of thousands of African American men filled the Mall in Washington, D.C.? Participants went because the call by Minister Louis Farrakhan of the Nation of Islam resonated with their experiences. Of course, the march itself then became part of their experience and was thus both a display and a product of the movement's unity. This unity resulted in an increased capacity for collective action—solidarity—toward the goals of the movement.

The first attribute of social gatherings that contributes to solidarity is the mere fact that such events draw participants together in one place and time. Called copresence, this is partly the realization that there is power in numbers. One man wrote of his sense of amazement at the march: "People, beautiful people, stretching as far as the eye could or camera could see. A living sea of blackness."[11] These gatherings also spur a sense of collective energy that emanates from the group. This was captured perceptively by Wayne Wilson, a participant from Los Angeles: "For the first two hours all I did was stand in the middle of the crowd near the reflecting pool to absorb the spiritual energy that was in the air and enjoy the moment."[12]

Since the very act of coming together contains power for the movement, it matters a great deal who is actually present to share in the experience. The invitation to the MMM was extended only to black men. Whittier identified the demarcation of group boundaries as the first step in building a collective identity. This demarcation is evidenced by the adoption of a self-label that announces membership in the movement. Although no new term was coined at the MMM, a sense developed that the event challenged participants' understanding of themselves as black men. In fact, the pre-march publicity packet specified that the march was intended to "convey to the world a vastly different picture of the black male."[13] Jeremiah Wright, who was scheduled to speak at the MMM but did not do so, reflected in a series of sermons that the event spawned a "regenerated" identity for black men.[14] At the march, black men were asked to abandon old habits and stereotypes, such as violence and profanity. The preferred image of the black man as a productive, politically active, caring father figure is very different from the popular image the march planners disavowed.

Perhaps more interesting is the way that MMM participants declared what they are not. Wright stressed the need for black men to abandon old methods used to ingratiate themselves into white society. He reflected on what he termed the "Negro leaders" or "Uncle Toms" who did not support the MMM. This older label seems to apply to African Americans who do not embrace the ideals represented by the MMM. Clearly, the march challenged the United States, and the participants themselves, to concentrate on a new image of the black man.

The second aspect of rituals identified by Durkheim is that they provide chances for common activity. Numerous activities oriented the attention of marchers in one direction. Songs and chants were designed to bring participants together in verbal declarations of unity and hope for the future. For instance, Ben Chavis, the national coordinator of the MMM, led the crowd in a repeating chant, "Long live the spirit of the Million Man March!" Similarly, the recitation of the pledge at the end of Minister Farrakhan's speech provided an opportunity for all those gathered to do the same thing at the same time. These common actions offered powerful memories to participants and a rallying point for future activity.

While the march itself was an activity shared by participants, it comprised a cluster of activities. Several men noted the trek to Washington as a common experience that bonded the sojourners. References to the procession of cars that took shape along the highways are filled with the realization that everyone was having similar experiences. Eric Hill observed that the caravan itself was very uplifting and noted that a rest stop outside Pittsburgh provided the site for a spontaneous gathering of men on their way to Washington. Even in the small congregation, Hill found that it was hard not to cry.[15] Although Durkheim's analysis focuses on activities within the context of the ritual, Whittier's notion of how social movements encourage participation in common activities in everyday life complements Durkheim's findings.

A host of new activities were encouraged by the sponsors of the MMM, all of which were designed to show the world a different image of the black man in the United States. The MMM Mission Statement identified four paths of action that black men will be encouraged to pursue. Mentoring younger black men, supporting the "black economy," strengthening the black family, and engaging in greater participation in civic life (voting) were held up as the activities that will be at the front of the new image for the black man in the United States. The MMM pledge contains numerous references to such activities, particularly participating in the black economy and strengthening the black family. Participants promised to "build businesses . . . houses . . . hospitals . . . factories . . . [to] support black newspapers, radio, television." They further promised to stop domestic and sexual abuse and to stop using the "B word" to describe women. Clearly, the MMM was designed to change the daily activities of black men.

Did it work? In *Atonement*, edited by Kim Martin Sadler, fifty participants reflected on the day and provided examples of how their lives changed after the MMM. Numerous contributors mentioned their efforts to mentor young or imprisoned black men. Others stressed ways of supporting the black economy. Still others participated in voter registration drives after the MMM. At the very least, the event brought attention to several avenues of action available to those seeking to emulate the new model of the black man in the United States.[16] Ivory Lyons notes that the MMM will continue to have "spiritual ramifications which will become evident as those that heard the call . . . act on the call."[17]

These common activities contributed to, and are reinforced by, emotional bonds that grow out of social rituals. The realization that they were not alone often overpowered MMM participants. Some of the men wept for joy, others over the misery they had caused their loved ones, but all seemed to experience a powerful emotional moment at the MMM. One anonymous author suggested that the "euphoria of Black pride and connectedness generated by the March" was enough for many participants to look past their personal dislike for Farrakhan.[18] Indeed, pride and a sense of unity were the most often mentioned emotional sentiments in the collection of reflections on the march.

This realization that they were not alone also contributed to the development of a central interpretive framework that group members use to analyze their lives. The sense of unity fostered by common activities and common emotions provides the realization that only those individuals who have "seen what I have seen" can understand me. References to the inability of those outside the black community to understand "black experience" are evidence of this phenomenon, which Whittier calls oppositional consciousness. Again, Jeremiah Wright provides examples. In his attempt to clear up a misunderstanding on the part of a colleague he stresses that the MMM was about "the social order under which we live, under which we suffer, and under which we are killed."[19] Apparently, his unnamed colleague was concerned about Christians participating in the event with followers of a different faith. Wright points out that blacks' experiences have less to do with religion than with color. He goes on to say that men such as Ted Turner and President Clinton could not understand the appeal of the MMM because they have not lived the black experience.

In a similar vein, Minister Farrakhan made numerous references to "white supremacy" as the cause of African American suffering. Farrakhan claimed that white supremacy has poisoned everything about our society and that it is the "real evil that undergirds the Western world."[20] These references amount to the idea that the discrimination experienced by African Americans is the result of white supremacy. Furthermore, the pervasive nature of white supremacy means that any sort of discrimination, whether professional or interpersonal, is to be understood by African Americans as the result of a deep-rooted problem in the Western world. Thus, race serves as the central category through which African Americans understand their life situation.

Finally, social rituals result in emotionally charged symbols that reinforce the experience of the event by reminding participants of its power. We contend that the number one million, visible on T-shirts and banners, is the most emotionally charged symbol of the march. Particularly in light of the conflict over the number of participants, the number became a rallying cry after the march. The visual representation of the symbol, namely, the picture of the march, took on significance as participants reflected on what it meant to be part of history in the making. One man wished that the picture could be placed in the homes of all the participants to remind them of their experience.[21] The question about how many men were actually present may never be answered to everyone's satisfaction. When the official count placed the number well under one million, Farrakhan decried it as a racist plot.[22] Precisely because the number is a symbol, the debate over whether the goal of one million men was actually reached took on dimensions greater than anyone had anticipated.

We do not mean to suggest that race is the only source of identity at the MMM. Of course, personal identity is the product of a complicated web of interactions among race, gender, religion, class, and a host of other characteristics. But the MMM was an event that shaped a collective identity for participants based primarily on race and gender. In *Politics of Masculinities: Men in Movements*, Michael Messner plots the location of several men's movements on his chart, "Terrain of the Politics of Masculinity." In the case of the MMM, Messner correctly identifies it as an example of racial/sexual identity politics. While he laments the lack of enthusiasm at the event for the progressive causes in which he is interested, he notes that the concerns of the MMM dealt with issues specific to men of color. Thus, for Messner, their racial identity connected participants at the MMM. Similarly, we hold that race was elevated over religion as the key to the collective identity so crucial to the movement. In light of the fact that most participants were not part of the Nation of Islam, the principal personality behind the march, organizers appealed to the one bond participants shared: race. Thus, the

MMM is not an example of a general men's movement; it is an example of a movement for black men in particular and is accordingly not related to PK.

Stand in the Gap

In 1994, PK began to organize a massive prayer rally in Washington, D.C. Beyond PK's base in white evangelicalism, PK had been reaching out to Christian men in other racial and ethnic groups.[23] For SITG, PK leaders urged participants to "invite a man of another race or denominational background to come with you"[24] to a massive event where the men would be "praying on our knees in humility; rising on our feet in unity."[25] This phrase symbolized both the idea of humility and repentance before God and the unified worship with Christians across racial and denominational barriers.

Four shared goals of the PK leadership for the event may be identified from public statements and promotional materials. They sought to (1) counter the moral and social problems of today by urging men to return to active roles in the church, family, and community; (2) present a massive public repentance of sins so that God might put aside divine righteous anger at the sins of the men and the church and instead bring revival to the church and an awakening among the lost; (3) in an increasingly religiously pluralistic society, proclaim the Jesus of the Bible; and (4) counter divisions in the church by creating attitudes of mutual love and forbearance and the promotion of faith in Jesus Christ as the preeminent identity. By exalting personal faith in Jesus Christ as the center of identity for every Christian— as opposed to denomination, race, or ethnicity—barriers associated with these sources of identity could be overcome; the church could be united and its impact on the world magnified.

The result was attendance by a massive and diverse crowd of people. On Saturday, October 4, 1997, an estimated 600,000 men from all over the United States gathered in Washington, D.C.[26] According to the *Washington Post*'s survey of SITG participants, 14 percent considered themselves black, 80 percent white, 2 percent Asian, and the remaining 4 percent "other" or refused to answer. In addition, 5 percent also considered themselves "Hispanic."[27] These numbers reflect the demographics of the U.S. population: 12.1 percent black, 80.3 percent white, 2.9 percent Asian, 9 percent Hispanic, and 3.9 percent other.[28] The *Post* survey was not very helpful in revealing denominational backgrounds because it lumped together all Protestants. PK Web surveys in 1996 showed that one-sixth of the participants were from one of four mainline denominations, and that almost 4 percent were Roman Catholic (akin to the *Post*'s results for Catholics). Yet theologically broad similarities emerged: 90 percent of the *Post*'s sample declared that they were "born again, evangelical or charismatic Christians."

They attended a massive Durkheimian ritual event and experienced not only copresence, but also involvement in common activities that promoted a common identity and common emotions, and resulted in "sacred" symbols. SITG was designed to be a much more interactive event than the MMM, with activities to promote the participants interacting face-to-face with each other in prayer groups and prayer triads. They listened to speakers, laughed together, repeated words together in response to the speakers, and read along as the speakers read aloud from the Bible. Together, they responded to the instructions of the speakers with singing, clapping, waving their hands in the air, prostrating themselves on the ground (as nearly as possible), and with prayer.

Whittier mentions that social movements create a common identity by using group boundaries, oppositional consciousness, and "the politicization of all of life." Personal faith in Jesus Christ created the group boundary at SITG. Those who had faith in Jesus were "in," regardless of race, ethnicity, or class. Yet as the beginning altar call and later prayers for mission outreach illustrate, those without faith in Christ were outside and needed to be brought in and saved.

Oppositional consciousness was also established through a focus on faith in Jesus Christ, which served as a symbol of an interpretive framework for understanding the world. PK's Promise Six is "A Promise Keeper is committed to reaching beyond any racial and denominational barriers to demonstrate the power of biblical unity," and much of the programming of PK has revolved around this goal.[29] Large portions of SITG were also spent specifically dealing with these barriers. The solution was always the same: PK does not deny distinctions, but transcends them by unity in Christ.

Time and time again, representatives of different racial or ethnic groups announced how being a Christian took priority over their racial identity. "I used to hold up my fist and say, 'Red Power,'" said one Native American speaker, "but now I say there is 'power in the blood of Jesus.'"[30] During an extended period of repentance for racial and ethnic division, participants at the podium stood and spoke on behalf of Christian whites, African Americans, Native Americans, Asian Americans, Hispanic Americans, Deaf people, and messianic Jews. They led the participants in confessing sins of fear and distrust, pain and bitterness. They demonstrated the granting of forgiveness and symbolized new bonds of peace. Several participants commented on how at first they were fearful of initiating relationships with people of other races or classes at SITG. But during and after SITG they realized that their unity in Christ bonded them more with one another than with those of their same class or race who did not have such faith.[31]

Although Christianity provided a common source of identity and unity, three clarifications need to be noted. First, racial diversity remains and was even celebrated. SITG was not an effort toward cultural homogenization.

Instead, it sought a transcendent unity that recognized diversity. Second, pain resulting from oppression was not denied or assumed to have been quickly overcome in one day. The men were encouraged to build relationships with men of other backgrounds, living a lifestyle of repentance, learning to be sensitive and caring with one another. Third, there was a serious call to continue the reconciliation demonstrated at SITG with intentional cross-barrier relationships between churches in the community. How serious and costly these relationships prove to be will either confirm or disprove the power of this movement toward racial reconciliation.[32]

Last, akin to Whittier's concept of the "politicization of all of life," the speakers urged that real Christian faith should affect all aspects of a participant's life. He is to be "a godly man" demonstrating Christ's love and personal integrity in his family, workplace, church, and community. This lived-out aspect of faith was highlighted during the main part of the day, which focused on "our extraordinary response." This time followed a pattern of proclamation, confession, and declaration. Speakers proclaimed what the sin was and how terrible it was in God's eyes. Then a multiethnic team led prayers of repentance. Finally, speakers challenged the men to make a difference in this area of their lives and practically exhorted them on how to avoid the sin in the future. Thus, an evangelical faith in Christ defined the SITG boundaries, centered their oppositional consciousness, and exhorted them to live their lives as men of integrity.

The event was for men because women, on the whole, were seen as those who did not need to repent. They were assumed to have faith in Jesus and to be "already standing in the gap."[33] PK sought to use SITG to counter criticisms made by some feminists that they were sexist and antiwomen. Michael Messner describes PK as an "essentialist retreat" from modern feminism and locates the organization at the heart of the terrain of "antifeminist backlash" among modern masculinity movements.[34] As John Bartkowski's chapter in this book and research by William Lockhart[35] illustrate, not all PK participants are essentialists, and several express progressive egalitarianism. From PK President Randy Phillips's opening remarks to the words of the concluding D.C. Covenant, SITG speakers sought to make it clear that they were not exalting masculinity or any essentialist construction of it, but seeking to help men become more like Jesus, who "came not to be served but to serve." Masculinity is still an important characteristic for PK, but not one to be used for oppression. Domestic abuse and family abandonment were clearly condemned. Tony Evans's controversial remarks at earlier PK events and in a major PK text about men not needing to ask permission from their wives to lead in their households—among other issues—had created friction with some women's groups. At SITG, he sought to clarify his comments, speaking of husbands and wives working together as "equal partners," with the man serving his wife and family. His comments and those of others balanced the previous rhetoric, yet ambiguity still exists about the proper role of women according to PK.[36]

The participants at SITG not only shared one another's company and participated in common activities, but also shared emotions. The dominant shared emotions of the event appeared to be the following: humility, knowing that we are not perfect and have contributed to problems in this world—and that God was not pleased; thankfulness and joy toward God for forgiveness and the indwelling power of the Holy Spirit, which enable us to live better lives; love for our families, for other Christians (particularly the brothers at SITG), and for "the lost," who either do not know any better or have made the same mistakes we have; hope that God will send revival and spiritual awakening, that reconciliation seen today will really happen in the body of Christ, and that the moral problems in the United States will end.

The result of this emotionally charged experience was, as Durkheim might have predicted, the creation of emotionally charged symbols. Publicized photographs of SITG had great symbolic power, particularly if they combined four key aspects: the great number of men, the diversity of the men, the fact that they were obviously worshiping God, and the fact that they were doing it in the heart of Washington, D.C. Similar to the Million Man March, the sheer size of the crowd was a major element of the image of SITG. Whenever aerial shots filled the Jumbotron screens, men would respond with applause and shouts. Also especially valued were photos emphasizing the diversity of the people there—motorbikers, messianic Jews, American Indians in traditional garb, men of different races of different generations together. The third element was of men prostrating themselves before God or raising their hands in praise. A graphic representation of three ethnically diverse men in prayer was an official logo for SITG, and posters featuring this logo were distributed to all those on PK mailing lists. The fourth aspect of this image was that it was in "the nation's soul," in Washington, D.C., surrounded by iconic government buildings. In an era when many conservative Christians believe the government is pushing Christianity out of public discourse, hundreds of thousands of men filled the symbolic heart of the country, very visibly worshiping God. For many conservative Protestants, the image of men praying in the country's "soul" meant there was still hope for the United States.

Beyond the photos, other cultural products produced by PK for the event as symbolic reminders included a Bible, music, clothing, and the D.C. Covenant. One million SITG Commemorative New Testaments were distributed at the event, comprising an easy-to-read translation and including thirteen weeks of daily devotionals highlighting PK themes, masculine-oriented evangelistic material, and envelopes for contributions. In response to requests from the podium, the Bibles were raised up by all the participants several times during SITG. Most of the songs sung at the event were available prior to SITG on a prerecorded cassette and compact disc.[37] Although the language was not gender inclusive toward God, beyond a reference to men praying and to evangelizing men, all the references to people were gender inclusive. The focus was not on gender, but on repentance, worship, and unity with other Christians. An official SITG T-shirt with the call of 2 Chronicles 7:14 to national repentance printed on the back was also made available prior to the event. The D.C. Covenant was a public prayer to God reaffirming the commitments made that day. Similar to the Million Man March pledge, it was read during the last few minutes of the program, sought to summarize the day's activities, and was later made available free to all participants.

Thus, as a ritual, SITG powerfully communicated an image of hundreds of thousands of racially diverse Christian men gathering in Washington to repent of sins and worship God. The shared identity was faith in Jesus Christ and living out that faith in everyday life. A major theme was humility and repentance for past mistakes, including the failure to live and love as God desires. The hope was that this reconciliation and rededication would continue and permeate every church in the United States. Furthermore, PK hoped God would send revival to the churches and a spiritual awakening to transform the country. PK and the evangelical Christian men involved were portrayed as those now ready to serve God for the work of religious revival advanced by SITG.

Conclusion

We contend that the MMM and SITG are expressions of two different social movements, one focused on race, the other on religion. But how do we explain the fact that two massive demonstrations took place for men relatively close together in time and space, even utilizing the same verse from the Hebrew Scriptures as their guiding principle, if they are not two parts to one movement? In other words, in light of everything they have in common, how can we claim they are separate phenomena? Both events stress the need for atonement and repentance. Both talk about men playing a higher profile role in the home. How is this much overlap possible if they are different movements?

Steve Nock[38] and others have shown that throughout the world, the "oughts" of masculinity, although socially constructed, are very similar. They include practicing responsible fatherhood, protecting women and children, and being better providers. Thus, much of the rhetoric about fatherhood and "being a man" merely draws upon culturally available notions that surround both movements. When the leadership of both movements cite 2 Chronicles

7:14 and speak of repentance and atonement, they are merely drawing upon a common cultural reservoir. In fact, drawing from themes in the surrounding culture has been noted to be a common practice of social movements.[39]

Both MMM and SITG condemn domestic violence and the degradation of women. In fact, one may substitute the word "Christian" for the word "black" in this excerpt from the MMM National Organizing Committee information packet and remain true to the intentions of both groups. The event was intended to "enable and encourage black men in the US to take a greater responsibility and play a greater role in caring for, and uplifting the status of, the black family." Nevertheless, one should never lose sight of the fact that the pro-family sentiments and resources of both groups are specific to either black or Christian families, however much overlap there may be between these two groups.

Both denounce "white supremacy," but Farrakhan finds the solution in black empowerment. He calls for black men to participate in the black economy and to be more politically active. Taking these steps will result in changing the conditions under which African Americans live, and thus, the assumptions of white supremacy will prove unfounded. On the other hand, PK counters white supremacy by calling for white humility and the development of healthy interpersonal relationships between Christian white men and Christian minority men. One movement visualizes greater independence for the black community as the key to race relations while the other calls for an increase in interpersonal relationships across racial lines. One cannot but suspect that the inward focus of activity Farrakhan calls for within the black community may be counterproductive to McCartney's vision of a larger circle of fellowship and, conversely, that PK's lack of interest in civil rights legislation or affirmative action programs will make its reconciliation effort sound hollow to many blacks.

Although both groups talk about race relations and family responsibility, we find they are saying different things. Furthermore, we find that the collective identities so crucial to the life of a social movement differ. Both groups utilize massive rallies as a means for building solidarity, but the identities and symbols produced are very different. At the MMM, race is the cornerstone of the movement, and the goals of the movement are for the good of the larger racial community. For PK, a personal faith in Jesus Christ anchors the sense of collective identity and its religious goals for the United States.[40]

5

Biblical Interpretations
That Influence Promise Keepers

Marianne Ferguson

henever sacred writings are used to promote ideas that regulate the behavior of individuals, one must carefully examine the method of interpretation used. When Promise Keepers use phrases that imply or require keeping women submissive to male leadership, and appeal to the Bible as the authority for their premises, some women are impressed either negatively or positively, depending upon what method of biblical interpretation is relied upon.

Literal versus Historical-Critical Interpretations

If one ascribes to the literal interpretation of Scripture, one believes that each word conveys a truth that can be applied today in the same way that one imagines it was applied at the time it was written. Since Scripture is believed to be inspired by God, it must be inerrant and cannot make a mistake, either in its message or in its application. This inerrancy would apply to "history, and science as well as faith and doctrine."[1] Literal interpretation allows for no contradictions so, although John 3:22 says that Jesus baptized and John 4:2 says Jesus did not baptize anyone, a fundamentalist would ignore the contradiction. When Paul said, "Women are to remain quiet in the assemblies, since she has no permission to speak, theirs is the subordinate part as the law itself says" (1 Cor. 14:35), the literal interpretation would be that women should neither preach nor lead church services today.

Most "mainline" Protestant denominations subscribe to the historical-critical method of scriptural interpretation. They look at a sentence in the context of other statements that would be consistent with the whole Christian message. Consideration is given to the identity of the speaker (was it Jesus or Paul?); the audience (were they followers or Pharisees?); and the circumstances in which the message was given. For example, in that quote from Paul (1 Cor. 14:35) scriptural scholars would point out that the law to which he refers is the Jewish law, since no Christian law had been codified at that time. They would note the obvious contradictions, such as Paul's appointing Phoebe to lead the church at Cenchreae (Rom. 16:1) and in the same chapter the greetings he sent to other women leaders of the community. The house churches that were led by the women in the Acts of the Apostles, Lydia and the mother of John Mark, also provide contradictions for that one statement of Paul. Finally, the historical evidence of the Corinthians and the female oracle who prophesied at Delphi near Corinth may have influenced this harsh statement against female leadership in the church as stated in Paul's letter. The general message of the Christian Scriptures, if staying consistent with the teachings of Jesus, would include and uphold women in all places. For example, in Luke 7, Jesus praised the unnamed woman who washed his feet with her tears and wiped them with her hair. Jesus healed women on the Sabbath, spoke to them in public, and allowed them to be his disciples (Luke 8:1–3). Paul respected this example of Jesus in his letter to the Galatians when he said, "There is no difference between Jews and Gentiles, slaves and free, men and women; you are all one in union with Christ Jesus" (Gal. 3:28).

Much of PK rhetoric about the dominance of men over women is based on the Creation stories in Genesis. Fundamentalists prefer the second Creation story where Adam is created first and Eve created later as a helpmate (Gen. 2:5–24). In this story, Adam gets to name Eve as he does the animals, which indicates that he has power over her. PK participants who follow the fundamentalist approach ignore the first Creation story where God, after creating the cosmos, created men and women simultaneously as the pinnacle of the Divine's work: "God created humankind in his image, in the image of God he created them; male and female he created them" (Gen. 1:27).

Rather than seeing men and women as both created in the image of God and therefore equal, fundamentalists organize a hierarchy in creation, starting with God, then Christ, then man, and finally woman. They base their assumptions on Paul: "The head of every man is Christ, the head of woman is man, and the head of Christ is God" (1 Cor. 11:3). If she is inferior to man, then she should be submissive to him and the man submissive to God, just as PK teaches.

A fundamentalist interpretation of the story of the Fall has more disastrous implications for the relationship between man and woman than the Creation stories. The woman is blamed for succumbing to the temptation to learn more about good and evil. For this she is cursed by God (Gen. 3:16): "To the woman He said: 'I shall give you intense pain in childbearing you will give birth to your children in pain. Your yearning will be for your husband and he will dominate you.'"

Putting the Seal of Approval on Women's Maltreatment

Unfortunately, a literal interpretation of this passage has put God's seal of approval on any maltreatment of women by men. Marian Hetherly and other feminists fear that PK's philosophy justifies domestic violence against women and children.[2] Patricia Ireland, president of the National Organization for Women, warned, "Promise Keepers has created a false veneer of men taking responsibility, when they really mean men taking charge. Their targets are women, lesbians, gay men and anyone who supports abortion rights or opposes authoritarian religiously based government."[3] The feminist laments the years of effort expended to make progress against this abuse, and fears that her efforts may be sabotaged by PK rhetoric. Political delays in equal opportunity initiatives to improve conditions for women may also be influenced by a literal interpretation that justifies male dominance. Pamela Coukos, public policy director for the National Coalition against Domestic Violence, said, "The apparent goal of the Promise Keepers is reinforcing a sense of men's entitlement within the home and family, and strengthening men's authority over women and children are incompatible with our nation's continued progress to eliminate violence against women and children."[4]

When PK leaders say that man should be head of the household, they have a champion in Paul who said, "Wives should be subject to their husbands as to the Lord, since, as Christ is head of the church saves the whole body, so is the husband head of his wife, and as the Church is subject to Christ, so should wives be subject to their husbands in everything" (Eph. 5:22–24). Most scriptural scholars say that Paul did not write this letter and that one must look at the context of the whole letter, which is trying to highlight the priesthood of Christ, not subjugate women.

The Protestant Reformation in the sixteenth century did not bring much relief to women. Martin Luther perpetuated these myths of inferiority as just punishment for the sin of Eve: "The rule remains with the husband, and the wife is compelled to obey him by God's command. He wages wars, defends his possessions, tills the soil, builds, plants, etc. The woman on the other hand is like a nail driven into the wall, she sits at home . . . and looks after the affairs of the household."[5]

What better way to justify gender-assigned roles than to keep the woman in the home and allow the man to deal with affairs of the world? John Calvin, the "reformer," also supported the double standard as applied to women, saying that women should remain within the domestic sphere. He resurrected biblical laws that said adulterous wives should be stoned to death, although unfaithful husbands should not be punished.

The Puritans reinforced the gender roles, stating that the household should be organized with the husband as the little minister and the wife and children as the obedient congregation. PK can look to religious teaching to support its strong stance on gender roles in the family that enhance the position of the man at the expense of the woman. The fourth promise made by PK men is to commit themselves to building strong marriages and families through love, protection, and biblical values. Not all women would agree with some of the interpretations of these biblical values that oppress women. John Spalding, a writer for *Christian Century*, described a speech by Ed Cole at the PK rally held in Oakland, California: "Today's males are pathetic. Men have become so weak, so insensitive, so uncommunicative, irresponsible, and unreliable that woman—the weaker vessel—has had to assume man's God-given roles as leaders of the family. If your wife no longer trusts you, she can no longer respect you or submit to you."[6]

Nostalgia for the Old Days

PK represents a faction in the United States today that seems to long for the security of the days of the middle of this century when gender roles were more easily defined. The present times of instability and insecurity cause some people to yearn for a time when values seemed more stable because everyone knew what he or she was expected to do. Fathers were the bread-winners, and mothers stayed at home to care for the children. We have fond memories of the times when doors were left unlocked, parents disciplined their children, apparently honest officials held public office, and more credible media presented newsworthy facts. We compare that stable, gracious era to the current times in which drugs, crime, moral dereliction, divorce, abortion, and political upheaval seem most salient. This comparison instills feelings of regret that societal conditions are not as good as they were then and that it must be our fault. PK then suggests that the way to right the situation is to go back to the family values of that era. These family values are identified with biblical values that defined morality and gender roles that did not favor women.

Unfortunately for PK, there is no way to return to the subjection of women. Once women are educated, they are not content to stay at home and sacrifice their own fulfillment for some vague family value. Economically, the situation of the working class and most of the middle class in our country demands two breadwinners per family, which makes a nostalgic return to earlier times an impossibility.

PK shows some characteristics of sect mentality that capitalizes on disagreement with the values of the dominant culture. Rather than basing their teachings on doctrine, sects usually emphasize action. Instead of involved religious rituals led by an educated clergy, sects maintain group experiences that mark them as separate from the outside society. PK holds its rallies in stadiums instead of churches; its adherents dress alike and maintain a stance against dominant cultural values. John Higgins describes his visit to the PK rally at Rich Stadium in Buffalo, New York: "Most, but not all of the participants were in uniform. If they were not already decked out in PK wear, they had on other shirts and caps of a religious nature."[7] PK organizes a team spirit to protest society's current values, which PK perceives as corrupt. Higgins describes a video he saw at the rally: "This video stressed the idea that, behind the secure walls of the stadium, the nation was in turmoil. So efforts must be made against the common enemies of feminism, homosexuals, and anyone else who seem opposed to their values."[8]

When these values can be justified by appealing to Scripture, their teaching can be more effective because they seem to represent the Word of God. In their literal interpretation of Scripture, PK participants find certainty that God is on their side and will help them in their fight against societal values, portrayed as currently dominant, that will destroy our civilization.

The appeal to responsibility for men appears virtuous, and they expect to be rewarded by God and their families. Perhaps some feminist teachings on partnership in marriage, where responsibilities are shared by both parents and the children, would be more helpful to every member of the family. Even a few classes in scriptural interpretation might help these men to evaluate the slogans, teachings, and easy solutions to the problems of their self-esteem. They could learn from the women's movement, which tries to boost the self-esteem of women without downgrading the experiences of men.

Women and men scriptural scholars have studied the Bible using the more sophisticated historical-critical method and found conclusions more inclusive of all people. These scholars have found the Christian message to be more egalitarian and balanced rather than the oppressive ideas of the Promise Keepers, which are based on a literal interpretation of the Bible.

6

The Need to Develop Male Friendship

George E. Sears

God intended that men have a positive view of male friendship. This can be seen in Scripture through the relationships that exist there. The strength of the biblical model has been watered down in recent centuries through the influences of culture and people's sinful condition. Men do not "do friendship" the way they did centuries ago. Many influences must be analyzed in order to develop strategies to foster and encourage men in search of male friendships. Men need also to believe again that male friendship is an asset as the century turns over.

The Theology of Friendship

To come to a theology of friendship, one needs the wisdom of God, for in this age men have not benefited from God's desire for men to have male friends and enjoy intimacy. In our day, intimate male friendship is viewed with suspicion. But even prior to the sense that male friendship was suspect in the latter part of this century, there had been a decrease in interest in and time for male friendships. Work, its need, and pleasure had replaced the friendship of the Greek and Roman period. Gilbert Meilaender writes, "Friendship appears to have fallen to a lower . . . estate." He continues, "The reasons for this are no doubt many. Ours is a world in which work has become dominant, and we identify ourselves in terms of what we do (for pay), not who our friends are."[1]

Deep within the hearts of men today, I believe there exists a desire for friendship, but the circumstances of our living will not allow for the craving to be conspicuous. Nonetheless, the Promise Keepers (PK) movement has made serious and public attempts to affect this resistance to male friendship. Its second promise is: "A Promise Keeper is committed to pursuing vital relationships with a few other men, understanding that he needs brothers to help him keep his promises." It is within God's nature to demonstrate love.

God is love (1 John 4:16). Friendship is a by-product of love, and it will take an understanding of God's wisdom to release men to be close friends in the context of our society. Friendship is most rewarding, satisfying, and adequate when love is free to flow.

Before "in the beginning" (Gen. 1:1), both love and communication existed.[2] These two basic attributes of relationship existed in the Godhead between the persons of the Trinity. Thus, friendship also existed. It was God's wise choice to impart that friendship to those whom God created. Jesus said, "I have called you friends, for all that I have heard from my Father I have made known to you" (John 15:15). We have the freedom, when we understand God's grace and the depth of God's love for us, to love horizontally, man-to-man, person-to-person; for we have discovered vertical love, the friendship of Christ to man. It was demonstrated in the most obvious of friendship; he died for us: "Greater love has no one than this; that one lay down their life for their friends" (John 15:13). Jesus further commented: "This command I give you to love one another" (John 15:17). Promise Keepers from the outset has attempted to deal with male friendship along the lines of Jesus' emphasis on relationships. This has been healthy. It gives a solid reason for men who know Christ in a personal way to at least consider a deeper relationship with some other men, even in our culture.

Losing Components of Friendship

John Reisman defined a friend as "a person who likes and wishes to do well for someone else and who believes that these feelings and good intentions are reciprocated by the other party."[3] The authors of *Habits of the Heart* wrote that three essential components of friendship are "friends must enjoy each other's company, they must be useful to one another, and they must share a common commitment to the good."[4] Although the first two components, with a priority of the first, are understandable and in line with our experience of friendship today, the last component is less likely to get our attention and understanding in a society with an individualistic orientation. But in the past, "it was precisely the moral component of friendship that made it the indispensable basis of a good society." For those who lived in an earlier era, which would have tended to be collectivistic, friends had an obligation to help one another become better persons. Modeled on the Godhead, in the life of Christ on earth is a friendship that men need in the latter part of the twentieth century.

Promise Keeper rallies have brought together thousands of men who have experienced deeper levels of communication. As a tool of the church, this movement could develop and contribute in a more constructive way to the state of male relationships and male mentoring. While PK was not initially intended to foster male friendships over a longer period of time, it is possible that some aspects of the two-day conference or rally format could be altered to facilitate the forming of lasting friendships.

At this time in history, the church must pick up on the lack of participation in male friendship and address the need. Robert Bly, the poet and de facto leader of the mythopoetic men's movement, writes, "The love unit most damaged by the Industrial Revolution has been the father-son bond."[5] As much as the Industrial Revolution in Europe played a significant role in the development of the Western world, as much as it influenced business and the economy for generations after, it also had a profoundly negative effect on the family and eventually upon the relationship of male friendships.

In the biblical record and in history are clear indications that male friendships once were healthy, heterosexual, and uplifting to the male gender, with male bonding occurring at puberty. But a great upheaval in the dynamics of men's search for male friendship has occurred since and because of the Industrial Revolution. I believe that the fledgling Promise Keepers movement, if it intends to continue beyond the early part of this next century, could reverse this trend that has all but eliminated male mentoring by fathers and jeopardized significantly the male rites of passage or male initiation of earlier Western history. As it is, men in our society are generally separated from one another. If PK rallies, in cooperation with the churches, could contribute to males coming closer together in the months after a rally, some major contribution could be noted in time. What an influence that could be!

Several developments have resulted in that upheaval of male relationships. One is that fathers were no longer around the home during and after the Industrial Revolution. They were away for most of the day at "work," and sons no longer understood what their dads did most of the day because they could not directly observe them. Up to the time of the Industrial Revolution, fathers generally took their boys out with them to the mines and farms and introduced them to the work that they did. As industry began to dominate in Europe, men left the farms and mines and moved to the city to work. They would bring their families to the city to live, but they would no longer be with them during the day. Boys came to be under the tutelage of the mother for all things, and honest work was being demonstrated by their mother during the day. What the father did when he was away for long hours each day was an unknown. A mistrust of the father's work developed, and the relationship between fathers and sons generally has continued to deteriorate for several generations.

A clear idea that physical work was wrong also developed. Work at a desk was more wholesome, but the father had nothing to show his son in terms of what he did during the day. The deterioration of the relationship between fathers and sons, and between older men and younger men in society, also contributed to this breakdown in trust. In commenting about the effect of the distancing between children and fathers, Jack Balswick notes: "It may very well be that, because of the separation of work and family brought about by the Industrial Revolution, fathers are less emotionally bonded with their children today than they were in the past."[6] The distancing of fathers and sons, consistent since the mid-nineteenth century, has been transferred to the relationships between male friends.

More recently, this mistrust was compounded by the role of government, which in the '60s sent men to a war that is still considered unjust. If what fathers did in their absence was not to be trusted, men in high places doing what they did was not to be trusted either. In the 1960s in the United States, the result was student unrest and takeovers. The students' fear of their own fathers' evil was transferred to all authority. The by-product of this confusion of male roles has been generations of young males who do not glean a clear idea of a male role from men in their experience. The way men, fathers, and male leaders act has been altered, and confusion has been passed on.

Friendship in the Modern Economy and Culture

In recent decades, with the advent of high divorce rates and greater mobility, the relationship between fathers and sons has deteriorated even further. The lack of involvement between fathers and sons and the amount of time that boys spend with only female models in the classroom, the home, and society seem to have nurtured a mistrust of men and fathers in particular. Adequate fathering is severely lacking. Sons cannot see the role they are to take on. Adequate models for their roles are absent. Fathers are needed who know their role, and "functional" (as opposed to dysfunctional) men are needed to be big brothers to boys who have no fathers.

PK rallies can and have contributed in some measure to the reestablishment of role models and healthier relationships, as fathers and sons have joined in worship and praise of one another and of God's love. At my first rally, in 1995, I encouraged my sons-in-law to attend with me. I benefited greatly from those days of travel and togetherness. Recently, the "calling of the young men" to the front of the stadium during a rally so that the larger group may celebrate young men's uniqueness could also become a significant "initiative" experience.

Male friendship has also been undermined by increased competition for jobs, which developed as many men worked together at tasks where performance and ability contributed to job advancement. Men were pitted against one another for advancement, and friendship was the loser. This also contributed to the loss of friendship among men at different levels of employment due to the status connected with a particular vocation or type of employment. Promise Keepers rallies have contributed some to ameliorate this major problem by encouraging men who attend to identify themselves by means other than what they do for a living.

Male inexpressiveness has also developed during this period of history. "Social structural changes resulting from the Industrial Revolution, such as the removal of the father from the home for long periods of time during the day, has probably resulted in increased male inexpressiveness."[7] The lack of consistent male role modeling by fathers has contributed to males being less expressive of their feelings. Male inexpressiveness has become acceptable although, in recent years, it has been viewed increasingly as contradictory to male gender expectations. More recently, males have been expected to communicate their feelings to those with whom they are intimate, including spouses. Rallies have encouraged men to be expressive of their feelings in small groups. They have been encouraged to sing together—something men do not typically do.

Mobility also influences the formation and continuation of friendship. People are constantly on the move in our society; between one-fifth and one-fourth of all Americans and Canadians move each year. Stresses on friendship deepen as a result of mobility in that we hesitate to develop friendships because we will lose so much when inevitably we must move away, particularly for a job change. It is one of the most difficult events to which friendship has had to adapt.

Male friendship is influenced by vocational demands. A vocation exacts time, and our society has, over several generations, developed the notion that vocation and calling are more significant to human happiness than friendship. What we have is a result due, in part, to a Puritan work ethic that has developed into a full-blown workaholism, a phrase coined by Dr. Wayne Oates in the 1960s. Stressing the importance of work, based on the scriptural justification that one needs to be responsible with his talents, has somehow expanded to mean that it must become the joy in a man's life, with a resulting loss of friendships. The loss of friendship because of workaholism is not the only price man has paid in these recent generations: "To suggest that we live to work—and to cloak this in the religious garb of the calling— is to try to have work play a similar role in our lives. It is to make work as central in our sense of who we are as friendship was for the Greeks."[8] Work has become the justification for men's absence from the home and for the fathers' absenteeism when it comes to rearing and disciplining children. This concept has become so significant in recent years that industry in the 1970s began to look for men who were not happy in the home so that they could devote more quality time to their jobs.[9]

Further, many men in our culture work because they are still trying to prove themselves to some mentor who failed them in the past. "Many men use work to prove something to themselves, their fathers, or early mentors about their own manhood."[10] This attitude contributes to their perceived need to live to work rather than to work to live.

Male Friendship and Sexuality

Another barrier to the full development and enjoyment of male friendship revolves around the area of male sexuality. Of all the areas of life that involve people who deal with one another on a day-to-day basis, sexuality is one of the most significant. An adequate biblical understanding of human sexuality and, in particular, male sexuality is essential to enable the church to deal with barriers to friendship.

All of theology is influenced by the first eleven chapters of Genesis. This thesis is apparent in the teaching I have encountered at PK rallies. To come to some understanding of sexuality itself, we need to consider in particular chapters 1–3 of Genesis. Here we find a viewpoint on human sexuality that influences and sheds light on other passages of Scripture that articulate a theology of sexuality.

On the sixth day of creation God created man: "Male and female God created them" (Gen. 1:27 NRSV). The essence of this passage and theme is that God created man, and mankind is defined as male and female. In his excellent work, Don Williams states, "Man is created for another. That other is woman."[11] To be in the image of God is to be male and female. In this deep and clear understanding of what it means to be made in the image of God, one finds an understanding of the place of heterosexuality in God's definition of man and God's expectations of the family as it practices human sexuality. Neither male nor female alone represents the divine image in Genesis 1–3. Sexuality as it is addressed in the Bible must always be seen in this context.

While Genesis 1 and 2 describe the cosmos as God intended for us to understand it, Genesis 3 describes chaos. This chapter describes the fall of humankind from God's expectations of human sexuality to the reality of the abuse of that behavior. In this context we find some understanding of the Bible's view on homosexuality. It is an abuse, a sinful result of man's disobedience of God's divine initiative of human sexuality: fellowship of "man" as male and female. God reveals how procreation will take place in this beautiful context: "Be fruitful and multiply" (Gen. 1:28 NRSV). This is the definition of "man" as male and female and how the creation, which was "good," would be able to fill the earth and care for it. "To be human is to share humanity with the opposite sex."[12] This is the message of human sexuality as first understood in Genesis 1–3.

The purpose for considering Genesis 1–3 is that the "presuppositions of human sexuality are established here and that homosexuality cannot be understood apart from these presuppositions."[13] From my perspective of pastoral experience of thirty years, the main causes of stress in marriage include in-laws, finances, time, and sexuality—and not necessarily in that order. Living as we all do in the West, influenced by two generations of a "playboy" philosophy, we find ourselves confused and bewildered about male sexuality. Roles seem ultimately to be defined almost exclusively from their sexual perspective. In 1995, Promise Keepers published *The Power of a Promise Kept.*[14] Chapter 8 of that work deals very skillfully with this subject.

In earlier times, little risk existed that close male friends would be viewed as suspect. God intended that we love one another, as discussed earlier. God intended that we work together to bring about a society in which the Divine would be understood, worshiped, and revered. Our society has moved far from this "corporate" goal because of some of the factors already suggested.

In order for men once again to seek male friendship, this matter of our sexuality needs to be clearly and forthrightly stated. Consider several concepts that influence our male sexual views, including homophobia and homosexuality.

Recent secular literature develops a concept that is in league with a hard line that a conservative biblical view of sexuality contributes to prejudice against a chosen homosexual lifestyle. Some writers on this subject appear quite eager to label as homophobic those who generally adhere to the teaching of an exclusive biblical monogamy and sex for procreation. The expressed views of homophobia are bringing division between the beliefs of some biblical Christians and some secular writers, who concern themselves with the issue of homosexuality and its causes.

Even as I consider male sexuality and place it in the context of our current society, it is to be understood that I do not write from a perspective of a "homophobic" fear of those who have learned to practice their sexuality in a homosexual format. I believe this is a learned behavior that is strongly influenced by society, environment, and dysfunctional families.

Many have commented on understandings of the rather new term "homophobia," which I believe generally refers to fear of being homosexual. It is often used in the same accusatory tone as is "fundamentalist." Homophobia may be seen as someone else's private abnormality. A biblical view that sexuality is expressed exclusively within the context of marriage would also reinforce homophobia, according to those who have developed the term.

Homophobia "refers to deep and irrational fears of same-sex attraction and expression or, in the case of lesbians and gay men, internalized self-rejection."[15] And "homophobia is the fear of being close to a person of the same sex."[16] The personal sense of homophobia is often broadened to an understanding of society's wider view of homosexuality from the point of view of those who continue an accusatory platform.

Homophobia within the context of the church family is a severe problem today. No reasonable explanation exists for the fear that persons who practice homosexuality will in any way cause heterosexual persons, whose sexuality is mature and understood, to become homosexual or to be threatened by this particular form of eroticism. Literature that addresses this matter is quick to point out that the roots of homophobia may be traced to male dominance in the historical church, to hatred of women or misogyny,[17] or to a belief that femininity is inferior so that men who express feminine characteristics are less than men. All of these irrational assumptions contribute to the fear called homophobia.

A Christian approach to homosexuality needs to begin with the Genesis view of God's creation and a theology indicating that man means man/woman.[18] This foundational approach then helps believers to interpret the rest of Scripture with some sense of consistency. It also enables Christians to open up their hearts and homes to those who suffer as a result of their sexual preferences, whether they are homosexual or heterosexual sinners. Sin does not have categories of seriousness. In other words, no sin is worse than any other. We come to those with sexual sin and deal with them as we do with others who sin, including ourselves; this approach will eliminate homophobia.

Homophobia in our society can work against the development of men's friendships because few, if any, role models exist that help men in terms of seeking and being sought by male friends. The warm format of Promise Keepers rallies and the encouragement of the development of triads of friendship when men return to their communities can play a significant role in reversing the homophobic trends in our society. This is true in part because of the large and positive media coverage that this movement is getting. In the church I pastored when our children were in their teens, I had several male friends. We sought out each other regularly. I am grateful today that our family saw me spend time with these men and model male friendship. They were the men I called when there was a crisis in our family or when I was stressed out. Our children saw me make time, occasionally and not nearly enough, for the men who were my friends.

The Role of Men's Inexpressiveness

Friendship involves being truthful and open about areas of interest and commonality among closest friends. Dr. Archibald Hart points out, that like a number of factors in our twentieth-century society, male sexuality is in a state of confusion. This confusion contributes to the weakening of male strength and the male ego. It negatively influences friendships. Hart noted: "Men talk to no one about their deep, sexual feelings, least of all their own wives or friends."[19] Such important aspects of our being are to be shared in order for friendship to be legitimate and reciprocal. God likely never intended male sexuality to be as feared and distorted as it seems to be today. A by-product of this scenario is the undermining of the development of male friendships.

The sexual male is further confused today because, according to Hart, any "tenderness, for the male, becomes synonymous with sexuality."[20] Many men feel awkward hugging each other or expressing care in any other physical manner such as touch or kiss because they fear it may be perceived as sexual. Boys in our current culture may in their earlier years develop a lack of appreciation for sensuality. This tendency predisposes them to later shy away from sensual experience and therefore to be inhibited when it comes to expressing their sexuality in marriage. The basic building blocks of sensuality are physical expressions such as hugging, kissing, touching, stroking, and being close to each other. These expressions of tenderness, which can be legitimate signs of the expression of one's senses, are taboo because they are viewed as sexual and are therefore repressed in boys and deemed not for exploration, even in a healthy family. "Physical contact of a nonsexual nature helps to open up sexual touching later,"[21] and this modeling in a healthy family is crucial to the development of healthy sexuality in boys and girls as they mature.

A comment made by our daughter-in-law several years ago was that she was very impressed with the outward signs of affection between our son and me. We have always been demonstrative in our affections and always look forward to seeing each other again.

One of the key behaviors a sexually healthy father can engage in for his children is to be able to express himself sensually without any hint or suggestion of a sexual nature. This is the only safe environment in our society, within the protection of the family, that sensual expression may be carried out in trust; where daughters as well as sons can learn that their feelings and expressions of sensuality are properly and safely expressed without a risk of sexual innuendo. A sexually healthy parent can give this gift to the members of his or her healthy family, even in a sexually dysfunctional society that is so confused about the sexual male. This particular gift that fathers can give to their children needs to be more clearly communicated in the milieu of a PK weekend.

The Downside of Individualism

Probably nothing has contributed more to the breakdown of men's desire to seek friendships in recent centuries than the powerful force of Western society's move toward individualization. To be a "man's man," in some sense, means to be an individual apart from the rest of humankind, not influenced by other men and certainly not influenced by the female! The move of societies from collectivism to individualism has had a negative impact on men's search for male friendship.

A strong correlation exists between the onset of individualism and the deterioration of male friendship. Bruce Melina described individualism in this way: "the belief that persons are each and singly an end in themselves, and as such ought to realize their 'self' and cultivate their own judgment, notwithstanding the push of pervasive social pressures in the direction of conformity."[22] The need or desire for male companionship has fallen prey to the demands of individualism in the Western world, yet another development intensified by the Industrial Revolution. Though individualism is a relatively recent phenomenon, it is well established in Western cultures. It plays into the hands of those who would do their "own thing" as has been noted in music lyrics sung in these last several decades.

Individualism's influence is strong and will continue as the dominant social model in Western societies for the foreseeable future. It will be a formidable challenge to the suggestion that men need to be searching for male friendship in spite of the factors that have undermined its development. Such is the challenge that PK rallies offer. When we live in a materialistically oriented society, one in which each person is encouraged to do his own thing to get himself through life—no one will do it for him—then individualism is just the thing. It is influencing women who have moved into the workforce in recent decades as well as men. And it is discouraging development of their friendship for the same reasons.

Men must once again seek to renew the friendships of their earlier years, such as those in school. Due to mobility and other factors, they more realistically may need to start fresh with men of like mind and interest. It is for the sake of our health that we develop friendships that can last and stand the test of disagreement and competition: "The most decisive step is to want friends and to be willing to do what may be necessary to attract them. Once that decision has been made and that step taken, there are other steps, easy to find and perhaps less easy to follow, which inevitably lead to making friends."[23]

Conclusion

I have endeavored to suggest the barriers to the development and maintenance of male friendship in our society. My much deeper study indicates that many other barriers persist.[24] A source that, in my opinion, is available to foster healthy male friendships is the Christian church in North America. But for the purpose of this book, the phenomenon known as Promise

Keepers is the tool we are considering as one that could make male friendship "more friendly."

Promise Keepers has had many purposes since it was instigated through the power of the Holy Spirit and prayer at the beginning of this decade. Those purposes are commendable and are being demonstrated at rallies all across our continent. PK with its rallies and enthusiastic environment, men spending quality time with other men and their sons outside of business, can be used to foster lasting friendships.

PK can and has been communicating with churches about study material, men's Bible study groups, and small group fellowships in homes and restaurants across the land. Making information available through the speakers and literature about father/son mentoring strategies and the development and maintenance of triads (groups of three men meeting weekly with purpose, covenant, and commitment) would encourage those who are seeking male friendship on a long-term basis, despite all the barriers.

Finally, in coming to a fuller understanding of the many pressures that inhibit the surfacing of male friendships today, Promise Keepers may find that its role will continue beyond the end of this century. The rally format may permit men to seek more intimate male friendships at home. The very nature of the rallies, with the hype and enthusiasm, suggests that they could become a unique tool of God that would positively encourage and influence the role of male friendship in our society, and invest in the role men can more effectively play in promoting healthy families in the future.

part 2

---

patriarchy, homophobia, and right-wing politics

7

How Promise Keepers
See Themselves as Men Behaving Goodly

John D. Keeler, Ben Fraser, and William J. Brown

Who are the Promise Keepers? Numerous individuals, organizations, special interest groups, news professionals, and political commentators have offered their opinions. National interest in this question has grown as large rallies, educational seminars, and other activities of the Promise Keepers (PK) attracted more than one million participants in 1996 and extensive media coverage in 1997 and 1998. Visibility of the PK movement reached new highs at the Stand in the Gap rally in October 1997 in Washington, D.C., which attracted several hundred thousand men representing diverse denominational and cultural backgrounds. Even prior to the gathering in the nation's capital, PK was hailed as the "largest and most important men's movement in the United States today."[1] In the wake of this event and public pronouncements of the organization's founder, Bill McCartney, of a broadening agenda and probable global expansion,[2] the movement's ability to simultaneously elicit great hope and excitement among its supporters, and fear and alarm among its opponents, appears to have skyrocketed.

PK leaders and participants have made concerted efforts to proclaim publicly who they are and who they are not. Little doubt exists that the primary themes embedded in official PK descriptions of organizational purpose and in the declarations of its leaders have a special, burgeoning appeal to many in contemporary U.S. culture. PK has multiple goals, including promoting unity and accountability among Christian men; racial reconciliation; and servant leadership in the home, church, and society. As one journalist suggests, the growth of PK indicates "that hundreds of thousands of men throughout our nation desire to commit their lives to Christian-style principles."[3]

Yet this same basic vision and message have been challenged by some outside observers of PK and have aroused considerable suspicion, volatile rhetorical attacks, and organized campaigns by critics. Through the often limited perspectives of their own worldviews, traditions, beliefs, and causes, these critics have provided anyone who may agree with them vague, often distorted images of PK. The rationale and evidence used to support various images of PK have not been carefully and systematically assessed.

Lost in this flood of competing perspectives is an accurate description of those who are involved with this movement. The opinions, beliefs, and behavior of PK founder Bill McCartney have been publicly scrutinized; but beyond occasional anecdotal references, other PK leaders have not been examined, and the perceptions of the typical PK adherent have not been widely explored. Little meaningful empirical evidence exists in this respect.

This chapter examines what the leaders and participants of Promise Keepers consider their movement to be. Then based on preliminary findings of an Internet survey of those who are most actively involved with PK, the present chapter examines some of the characteristics, perceptions, and beliefs of those within it.[4] By comparing this study's results with the perceptions of PK leaders and critics, we seek to provide a clearer picture of the movement.

The Critics' Points of View

Some individuals representing organizations that are highly critical of PK have diverse ideas about who comprises this growing men's movement and why it is a threat to our contemporary culture. Some feminists seem certain PK is composed of angry, threatened, ultra-conservative, predominantly white men determined to destroy decades of women's political and civil rights gains. From their point of view, PK leaders and their followers are determined to establish a male-dominated society that will force women into abject subservience in the workplace, the home, and other spheres of life. The National Organization for Women (NOW) officially resolved that PK is "the greatest danger to women's rights." In an "Open Letter to Activists" about its Promise Keepers Mobilization Project, the leaders of NOW vowed "to change public opinion and to create a true and accurate portrait of the Promise Keepers."[5]

One PK supporter provides a common perception of how he sees the movement. PK is

> a renaissance for many who have lost the meaning and the example of what it means to be a man. . . . It is hard because often we do not receive the support of those who should be supporting us most: women. The feminist movement, while empowering women, has had a negative effect on many men. The pervasive mentality that men are no longer truly needed to raise a child or to be the protectors and providers in society has severely weakened the position of men and women.[6]

Many critics contend that PK poses a threat to the feminist idea "that mothers and fathers are somehow interchangeable."[7]

Some PK leaders have expressed the belief that local churches are disproportionately filled with women and that men need to become more involved in their local churches. Dedicated feminists may find it difficult to reconcile the emphasis on men's leadership in the church and home with PK's intent to model the spiritual, self-sacrificial, servant leadership of Jesus Christ.[8] They find it equally hard to fathom that wives of Promise Keepers, or any woman for that matter, might actively support an exclusively men's leadership movement (e.g., 30 percent of Promise Keepers' voluntary workforce is reportedly female).[9] Some feminists are also disturbed that the PK message is so thoroughly entrenched in Christian beliefs and rhetoric. In their minds, PK participants misuse biblical doctrine in applying it to their relationships with women. Said one critic,

> In Christianity, I've experienced "leadership" attitudes from men that had been of the dominating perspective rather than of the understanding guidance perspective. I know many men who have taken "Christian" teachings and used them as their God-given authority to "keep a woman in the place" and maintain their leadership role. They refuse to let their wives get a job, to go to college, have their own friends, dress the way they want, etc. They want to control a person in order to be the "leader." And guess what a lot of Christian men do when their wives won't do what they tell them to—a little verbal hollering, a few slaps, a little hitting, to show them who's in charge because God said so in the Bible.[10]

Although PK is not a political movement, its leaders have publicly declared a pro-life stance on the issue of abortion. Feminists who have long supported a pro-choice political agenda have another strong reason to perceive PK as a threat. Some feminists believe that PK has a destructive political and social agenda. NOW leader Patricia Ireland stated, "We know, from our firsthand experience at firebombed clinics, the political Molotov cocktail that the radical right can concoct out of fanaticism and intolerance. The arch foes of women's rights and civil rights behind the Promise Keepers cannot quit claiming they are all about Godly male bonding and not about political organizing."[11]

Emerging amidst what many have described as a "culture war" in the United States based on conflicting moral visions,[12] God-centered versus human-centered perspectives of life,[13] and heated rhetoric and propaganda rather than meaningful dialogue,[14] PK also has provoked suspicion and wrath among some political groups and elements of society who have long battled against conservative forces. Convinced that Promise Keepers represents the "third wave of the Religious Right" (Jerry Falwell's Moral Majority and Pat Robertson's Christian Coalition represent the first two waves), liberal political groups view PK members as basically "Christian reconstructionists," espousing and actively seeking political power through a particular version of the Christian religion. "Although PK leaders have denied that it has a political agenda, their various public statements and their list of enemies clearly define them as the army of the far right," states one critic.[15]

PK rhetoric, especially repeated publicly stated goals such as living solely in accordance with biblical standards, being part of an "army of God," or decrying the evils of such organizations as the American Civil Liberties Union (ACLU), engenders animosity toward the movement among those who have pushed liberal agendas for many years. The ability of PK leaders to organize followers with considerable success is therefore perceived to be no more than the result of effective political or "military" tactics. PK efforts to organize men into small accountability groups have drawn suspicion from both political liberals and feminists. So has its leaders' use of sports to promote its message to men.[16] PK entreaties for reconciliation among men of different races and denominational backgrounds are viewed as just a concerted attempt at "the dismantling of the old New Deal Democratic coalition."[17] In addition, the movement and its members are considered by many to be a serious threat to religious freedom by organizations and elements of the culture that champion the separation of religion and state.

The homosexual community may be counted among PK's most vocal critics. PK leader Bill McCartney is well known for his ties to past legislative efforts in Colorado designed to curb civil rights gains for homosexuals. "Where are the queers?" asked a contributor to the *Village Voice*, who concluded that a PK gathering at New York's Shea Stadium was "terrifying, like some demented pep rally"[18]—even though he also realized that several homosexual men were in attendance. McCartney and other Promise Keepers have publicly denounced homosexual behavior but have stated that homosexuals should be the recipients of Christian love and respect. PK participants are encouraged to practice sexual purity in accordance with biblical standards. At the heart of this issue, observed one representative of the homosexual community, appear to be basic differences among those who view the Bible as literal truth, those who perceive it as a great "historic record with spiritual content," and those whose views fall somewhere between these positions.[19]

Despite its call for racial reconciliation and the participation of greater numbers of African American and Latino men, PK has its detractors within those communities. Although the movement has recently attracted more African Americans, including pastors, many view it as merely a conservative,

Republican strategy for uniting black and white Christians on specific social issues in order to undermine the efforts of more ethnically diverse, liberal Democrats.[20] Columnist John Leo suggests that PK's condemnation of racism and its efforts to attract minority group followers confuse political liberals and liberal journalists. Critics who equate the movement with the political Right, writes Leo, "show a very crude understanding of the men's movement in evangelical churches."[21] PK's commitment to the Great Commission (Matt. 28:19–20)—Christian evangelism—may also kindle the political fears of some who are critical of the movement and threatened by its expansion.

Some PK critics are of religious faiths other than Christianity. To them, the movement is intolerant of other faiths that do not believe God may be reached only and worshiped through the redeeming work of Jesus Christ. Some liberal Christians are also concerned about PK, especially the denominations that have embraced liberal causes such as legalized homosexuality, sexual practices outside marriage, no-fault divorce, and abortion rights. They are uneasy about the conservative Christian perspective on biblical truths promoted by PK. Although some Catholics have participated in the movement, a few Catholic leaders fear PK may ultimately cause many Catholics to reevaluate their commitment to the Catholic Church.[22]

Christian conservatives have questioned and attacked PK. Reformed leaders and others fear it will pull people away from the institutional church or create some sort of popular "new age" church. This fear exists despite the official proclamations of PK leaders that the movement is intended to work in cooperation with local clergy in revitalizing men spiritually and encouraging their meaningful involvement in the local church setting. Others criticize the strong ties of PK's origins and leaders to the charismatic elements of the Christian community and, particularly, the controversial Vineyard movement.[23]

In an extensive, highly critical assessment of PK, Phil Arms—a conservative Christian—seems basically to represent much of the thinking of a few Christian conservatives. He challenges the movement on the grounds that (1) it is a threat to the authority and biblically stated purposes of the institutionalized church and the local church; (2) it has compromised biblical standards with its ecumenical willingness to include liberal Protestants, Catholics, Mormons, and others who interpret Scripture more liberally; (3) it is linked to the Vineyard movement and the questionable doctrinal influence of its founder, John Wimber; (4) it emphasizes seven "promises" that all Promise Keepers should make and strive to keep rather than stressing the more important scriptural truths and self-sufficiency of the Bible; (5) it focuses on self-effort as a means of modeling the life and teachings of Jesus Christ rather than total reliance on God's grace through faith in Jesus

Christ; and (6) it incorporates modern psychology and New Age philosophy in its men's accountability groups, seminars and other vehicles for teaching and counseling rather than relying solely on the Bible.[24] A number of pamphlets and Internet Web sites make similar arguments.

The perceptions of these many different critical views of the PK movement serve as points of comparison with the perceptions of the movement's leaders, followers, and critics.

The View of the Movement's Leaders

An examination of official statements of Promise Keepers reveals the perceptions of its leaders about those involved in the movement. A "fact sheet" available at its national headquarters' Internet Web site declares that PK is

> Christian outreach to men. Through stadium conferences, educational seminars, resource materials, and local churches, PK encourages men to live godly lives and to keep seven basic promises of commitment to God, their families, and fellow man. Promise Keepers seeks to unite Christian men of all races, denominations, ages, cultures, and socio-economic groups, believing that accountable relationships among men are critical in helping one another become promise keepers in their relationships with God, their wives, their children, and each other.[25]

The movement's leaders are interested in attracting those who fit this general description and are amenable to these basic ideas.

In the same "fact sheet," PK has tried to explain who its participants are not. They make it clear that they are a movement of Christian men "becoming more active in their local churches" and involved in encouraging "men to commit every aspect of their lives to Jesus Christ." They try to allay the fears of critics by declaring that they are not (1) an organization that has membership and collects dues; (2) affiliated with any specific denomination; (3) a political organization; or (4) a proponent of self-help philosophy, an advocate of having psychology supersede biblical principles and revelation. They note that the "seven promises" of Promise Keepers are "commitments to grow, rather than a set of rules to be followed." The organization has tried to appease conservative Christian critics by declaring that it believes that eternal, spiritual salvation is gained through the grace of God rather than through works.

For PK leaders, the ideal participant understands and shares these views, although the fact that PK has felt compelled to clarify what it is not suggests that many supporters may misunderstand what it is. It is a movement open to anyone, says McCartney, who believes men should be godly and committed to fundamental biblical principles to which a large spectrum of the Christian community already adheres.[26]

Despite efforts to make their purposes clear and to explain their movement, PK leaders have not always clearly and consistently communicated their mission and vision. The movement also had to further define its mission and purpose as it grew quickly and criticism abounded. At conferences or in statements provided to the news media, leaders have sometimes been misunderstood.

Several surveys have been taken of PK participants. *USA Today* reported in the summer of 1995 that PK men were 88 percent married, 7 percent single, and 5 percent divorced or separated (with 21 percent having been divorced at some point); and 84 percent white, 7 percent black, 5 percent Hispanic, 2 percent Asian, and 2 percent Native American. By religious affiliation, the men self-identified as 23.9 percent Baptist, 13.5 percent no affiliation, 10.2 percent Southern Baptist, 5.9 percent Assembly of God, 5.2 percent United Methodist, 4.5 percent Nazarene, 3.6 percent Presbyterian, 3.5 percent Christian Church, 3.5 percent Bible Church, 2.6 percent Evangelical Free, 2.4 percent Lutheran, 2.4 percent Reformed, and 2.2 percent Roman Catholic.[27]

A series of surveys conducted by PK through its national Web site gives some indication of the attitudes, beliefs, and demographics of those involved in the movement. The surveys confirmed a *Washington Post* poll taken at the Stand in the Gap rally in Washington, D.C., that indicated the participants were predominantly white (i.e., 80 percent white, 14 percent black, 2 percent Asian American). Most respondents to PK surveys had been Christians for many years and are active in their local churches. About half were lay leaders, and about 9 percent were part of paid pastoral staff. Common church affiliations of survey respondents included Baptist, Assemblies of God, and nondenominational, although many other denominations were represented. The majority of respondents reported that they regularly read the Bible and meditated on God's Word, prayed, and shared their faith with others. Most stated they were willing to be involved in more outreach activities in the local community.

More than half were currently involved in men's accountability groups, but more than 80 percent believed their local church lacked a "vibrant men's ministry." Three-fourths indicated they believed themselves "more confident and secure in [their] sense of masculinity than five years ago." Nearly 70 percent of those who were married thought their wives would say they had changed for the better since becoming involved with PK. Most believed strongly in the need for interdenominational unity, racial reconciliation, and reconciliation between men and women in the church and in society.[28]

Views of the Movement's Participants

To gather more information from PK participants, an 84-item survey questionnaire was administered by posting it on the World Wide Web and linking it to search engines frequented by Christian men. The questionnaire assessed levels of involvement in PK; perceptions of the movement, its leaders, critics, and media coverage; benefits of Promise Keepers; the perceived impact of the movement on individuals within the movement; the basic Christian doctrinal beliefs of participants; and other demographic and psychographic characteristics of participants. Most questions were in statement form with participants responding to a five-point, agree to disagree, Likert scale. Two open-ended questions were included, one asking the respondents how PK had most affected their lives and the other asking them to describe their greatest disappointment with PK.

The questionnaire was posted in early 1998, and initial results of the survey, in which more than one hundred very detailed, completed questionnaires were analyzed, revealed several important findings.

Characteristics of Promise Keepers

Men participating in this survey were overwhelmingly white (nearly 90 percent), were married (90 percent), and had children (more than 80 percent). They were primarily between the ages of thirty and forty-nine, and were well educated (i.e., nearly all had attended college and nearly half had gone to graduate school). Nearly all major Protestant denominations were represented, but no Roman Catholics participated in the survey. As was discovered in previous surveys, those who identified themselves as Assemblies of God, Baptist, or nondenominational were best represented (nearly 70 percent).

The respondents tended to be very active in their local churches. About 40 percent described themselves as lay leaders, while about 40 percent more were church members. Four percent were paid church employees. Nearly 75 percent identified themselves as religious conservatives while the rest were moderates. About 67 percent were affiliated with the Republican Party, and about 25 percent considered themselves political independents.

For the most part, respondents appeared to be quite actively involved with Promise Keepers. More than 60 percent had been involved for three years or more. Asked to rate how rewarding were a variety of PK activities on a seven-point scale (1–7), mean ratings were all 4.3 or higher. Attending PK rallies appeared to be the most rewarding activity for the group as a whole, followed by attending PK seminars and workshops at a local church and using PK teaching and reading materials. Asked to indicate on a scale of 1 to 7 the relative difficulty of keeping each of the PK's seven promises, mean scores suggested that all were equally difficult to keep, although supporting the mission of the local church and building strong marriages and families were deemed slightly less difficult.

Theological Beliefs of Promise Keepers

Almost all respondents reported traditional Christian beliefs consistent with those found in the major church creeds. These beliefs include one Creator God; the doctrine of the Trinity; the deity of Christ; the virgin birth; the inspiration of Scripture (the Bible); the physical death, burial, and resurrection of Christ; salvation through faith in Christ; and the judgment of God. Other beliefs held by some respondents but not by others were belief in the present-day gifts of the Holy Spirit (e.g., speaking in tongues), belief in infant baptism, belief in the rapture before the great tribulation, and belief that one may lose one's salvation. Other beliefs strongly held by respondents included God's ability to communicate directly with people, belief in God's direct involvement in the lives of individuals, and belief that divorce is not supported by Scripture.

Promise Keepers' Perceptions of the Movement and Its Leaders

Despite considerable public criticism of PK and its leaders, most (about 80 percent) "agreed" or "strongly agreed" with the statement, "I completely support what Promise Keepers believes in." In addition, more than 90 percent agreed that they "trust the leaders of Promise Keepers," and nearly 75 percent of the respondents believed that these leaders "practice what they preach." For the most part, the respondents viewed PK as a movement rather than an organization. In accordance with official statements by PK and in conflict with the views of many critics of the organization, more than 90 percent of the respondents "strongly disagreed" or "disagreed" with statements that PK is "primarily a conservative political movement" or "endorses political candidates and parties." PK has denied being "primarily a self-help or self-improvement group," and nearly 60 percent of the survey participants agreed it was not. However, approximately 25 percent appeared to believe this was its main purpose.

The respondents as a whole clearly perceived PK as an ecumenical movement. Nearly 90 percent "strongly disagreed" or "disagreed" with the idea that PK "attracts too many people from different Christian faiths." A similar number agreed that "liberals should be encouraged to become involved." Seventy-five percent "strongly disagreed" that the movement should be "limited to Protestant Christians," and about 80 percent did not think it should "exclude non-Christians." More than 90 percent "strongly agreed" or "agreed" that PK "should include all racial and ethnic groups." There was less consensus that "women should become more involved in the activities of Promise Keepers"; some agreed, some disagreed, and some were uncertain. But respondents overwhelmingly agreed that the movement "benefits women as much as it does men." Most of the respondents also agreed that PK is "Christian men becoming more involved in local churches," one of the main, officially stated purposes of the movement, but apparently not understood by many critics.

Criticisms of Promise Keepers by its participants varied widely but can generally be divided into six main areas: (1) disappointment with the homogeneity of the organization's participants ("overwhelming number of middle-aged white men"); (2) difficulty with the "vital relationships" promise ("My priorities place my family above pursuing vital relationships with other men"); (3) PK's national rather than local focus ("not enough . . . concerted, local follow-up effort"); (4) overzealous marketing or financial requests ("too commercialized . . . selling all kinds of stuff" or "almost routine" requests for additional contributions from regular donors); (5) poor management ("too heavy in chiefs and not enough Indians"); and (6) content concerns ("theologically simplistic and short-sighted pronouncements from the undereducated leadership"). But many men said PK had not disappointed them in any way, and others were disappointed with the behavior and/or lack of sustained commitment of other attendees, but not with PK's leaders.

What Men Seek from Promise Keepers

The survey respondents were generally divided with regard to the benefits they were seeking by becoming involved in PK. About one-third agreed that they became involved to "become a better leader in my local church," but approximately one-third disagreed with this statement. About one-fourth "strongly agreed" or "agreed" that they became involved "to become more aware of issues of racial conciliation," but many did not and some (14 percent) "strongly disagreed." They were evenly divided in responding to the idea that they had become involved "to interact with those from other backgrounds." About one-third agreed that they participated because they wanted "to become more aware of issues of racial conciliation"; one-third did not; the rest were neutral. There was a similar distribution of responses to becoming involved in order to "find men I could be accountable to." Only about 10 percent of the study participants apparently got involved with PK to "solve my marriage struggles."

The Impact of Promise Keepers on Men's Lives

There was a high level of agreement with nearly all statements included in the survey intended to measure the relative impact of PK on the lives of its active participants. More than 90 percent of the respondents "strongly agreed" or "agreed" that PK "has brought my family closer together." More than 70 percent agreed with the statement that my "wife or fiancee sees a positive difference in me since I became involved with Promise Keepers." About the same number "strongly agreed" or "agreed" it "has made me a better father." About 75 percent had "developed closer friendships," and 84 percent agreed their "personal relationship of God has improved" because of PK. About 70 percent thought they had become "a more moral person."

More than 80 percent of those who completed the survey "strongly agreed" or "agreed" that PK had "made me more sensitive to issues of racial injustice," and more than three-fifths believed they "have a greater respect for the beliefs of other Christians." PK also caused many (approximately 70 percent) "to better support my local pastor and church" and about the same number to "become much more open with other men about my problems in being a better man." There was less agreement (slightly more than 50 percent) with the statement that "Promise Keepers has helped me see that men should be the head of the household," but there was not strong disagreement.

Perceptions of Critics and the Media

The perceptions of those involved with PK of their critics were dealt with in the survey. More than 50 percent of the respondents disagreed with the statement, "I understand why many Christians and Christian organizations are critical of Promise Keepers." About 30 percent indicated they did understand. More than 75 percent did not understand "why some people believe Promise Keepers is a threat to freedom of religion and speech." Although about 10 percent agreed that "women's groups that are critical of Promise Keepers have some legitimate complaints," more than 80 percent disagreed. Approximately one-third agreed that they "often pay attention to what critics say about Promise Keepers," but another third did not.

The survey participants generally disagreed (85 percent) that PK "is understood by the media," but were divided in their responses to the statement that the "media seem to be trying to destroy Promise Keepers." Perhaps these results may be explained if respondents sense that media coverage even neutral to favorable in tone usually has been superficial.

Conclusion

The results of our study indicate there is a wide gap between the way in which PK insiders view themselves and the perceptions of those outside the movement. Perhaps much of the criticism of PK is based on deep-rooted fears that a group of men galvanized by religious values might weaken the rights of women and minority groups, particularly groups based on religious, moral, or lifestyle beliefs inconsistent with moderate to conservative interpretations of Judeo-Christian values. Contrary to the common misconceptions about PK, both the leaders and the participants in the movement are open to men of diverse religious and political affiliations. Promise Keepers conceive of themselves not as a religious, political, or even social organization, but as a network of men with common concerns and values within the context of traditional Judeo-Christian beliefs, emphasizing personal faith, responsibility, and commitment to family, church, and community.

Most Promise Keepers find it difficult to comprehend that some people see them as a threat. They want to be regarded as men who empower women and more effectively relate to women, citing changes in their own behavior and beliefs to make them better husbands and fathers. Regarding their relationships to their local churches, Promise Keepers perceive their involvement in the movement as strengthening their commitment to individual church communities. They cite evidence that indicates they have become more involved in their own church congregations as a result of being involved in PK.

Our research indicates many men become involved with PK not because they think they have failed in their marriages or are failures as fathers, but because they want to improve their marriages and become better husbands and fathers through spiritual growth and fellowship with other Christian men. There is no indication that those involved in the movement are motivated by feeling threatened by other groups or by a desire for consolidating political or social power. Although external groups may fear the potential influence of PK, Promise Keepers themselves do not exhibit an "us against them" mentality or groupthink tendencies.

Yet despite their desire to be an open and inclusive movement, Promise Keepers have not gained the widespread participation of some minority groups, Catholics, and several mainline denominations, and those who consider themselves to be politically liberal. This is a dilemma for the PK leaders. As they seek to "widen the net" of the movement across religious, social, and racial barriers, they will likely draw the criticism of certain conservative Christian groups who are concerned about the purity of the Christian foundation upon which the movement is based. And it is not foreseeable what kind of new challenges PK will face as it expands outside the United States and Canada.

Our study suggests that most participants in PK think the external criticisms are not warranted and are based on erroneous perceptions of their movement. To bridge the gap between the self-perceptions of PK and the perceptions of those outside the movement, those involved in PK will need to more effectively articulate their inclusive mission and vision.

PK's participants strongly express its ecumenical perspective. The goal of reconciliation across social and cultural divides seems to be more important to PK participants than is the commitment to certain theological perspectives.

The cynical view that Promise Keepers are seeking to gain political capital based on racial reconciliation is not supported in light of the genuine desire expressed by many of those involved in the movement to develop intercultural friendships.[29]

Promise Keepers exhibit a strong evangelical motivation to share the gospel with others, but do not conceive of creating a religious organization that would detract from participants' involvement in local churches. Our study indicates the fear of PK by some denominations as a rival religious organization is not based on the actual beliefs or goals of those involved in the movement. On the contrary, Promise Keepers state they have become more committed to their local churches as a result of their involvement in PK.

PK is being criticized from within the movement. A major complaint is that PK places much more emphasis on large events than on local efforts. One respondent stated the large events "do not have a lasting impact." These critics are apparently unaware that PK's leaders already understand this. Bill McCartney admitted, "We realize that [stadium] conferences might produce a lot of heat, but not much light,"[30] and explained, "After the white-knuckle excitement and adrenaline wore off, many who sported PK T-shirts, made vows of purity and lifted hands in worship returned home to resume their carnal, less-than-promise-keeping lifestyles."[31] And PK spokesman Jim Jewell said, "You just can't fill up stadiums forever. The only way that this will have a lasting impact is if it becomes grounded in local churches involved in the community. It needs to change devotion and faith into a lifestyle and commitment to social change."[32] PK has announced that it will discontinue the stadium rallies, although it will continue to hold other large events.

Another respondent perceived a "breakdown of the district and regional organization; everything is at the national level." Closely related to this issue is a concern with PK's structure. While PK leaders have placed an emphasis on the mass movement, the lack of organizational structure has disappointed many involved in the movement. For example, respondents complained of "the lack of correspondence from Promise Keepers," "the lack of proper communication between the organization and its constituents," that PK "expanded too fast" and "they do not know what they are doing."

A third criticism by PK participants is poor public relations responses to criticism of the movement by, or reported in, the mass media. Indicative of the many comments made, one respondent stated, "Promise Keepers does not defend itself against unfair attacks from outside forces." Another lamented the movement's "bad marketing to liberal critics," and a common concern is that many "have misinterpreted what Promise Keepers is all about." Even positive public relations opportunities seem to be squandered. One respondent noted "the failure of Promise Keeper leadership to exploit the Stand in the Gap" rally in the nation's capital in 1997.

A number of other concerns that were expressed reveal the tensions within PK. Some respondents wanted the movement to put a greater emphasis on the "acceptance of other subcultures" and to become more ecumenical, while others felt the organization was too inclusive, for example, welcoming the involvement of "Catholics and Mormons" or promoting "women pastors." A group within PK wanted the movement to become much more organized, to further develop its financial base, and to exert more influence, while others complained that it was "too commercialized" and that there was "too much emphasis on hype."

Finally, our study indicates that the influence of Promise Keepers on those involved with the movement is considerable. Those surveyed stated that their involvement has improved their relationships with their wives, their children, and other men in their churches and communities. Respondents reported being spiritually encouraged by "seeing so many men in one place . . . focusing on God." One respondent said he could provide "lots of testimonies about good men set free from the chains of bondage by Promise Keepers."

Promise Keepers have stated the movement has "strengthened my commitment to my family and Christian values" and "made me a better all around Christian." In addition to improving their relationships with their wives, several Promise Keepers indicated other interpersonal relationships had improved. One respondent indicated PK had "improved my relationship with my father," and another stated his relationship with God was now "stronger and more intimate" as a result of his PK participation.

Many respondents reported they had changed their views of cultural and religious groups with which they were unfamiliar. One respondent indicated that PK had "given me a better understanding of the Body of Christ across denominations and races." Another noted, "I am genuinely more interested in my Christian brothers from different denominations and races." A third respondent reported, "Promise Keepers has taught me to respect those who are different and have different beliefs." In summary, Promise Keepers is a complex movement whose image will continue to evolve, both positively and negatively, depending upon the efforts of the movement's leaders and participants in making their mission and goals better known.

8

Christianity, Feminism, and the Manhood Crisis

John Stoltenberg

Interview with a Man Peer

I covered a Promise Keepers conference in Texas Stadium near Dallas, and while there I asked a media representative if I could interview someone high up in Promise Keepers about the theological underpinnings of its organizing work with men. I identified myself as a lapsed but religion-literate seminary graduate, author of several books on ethics and masculinity from a secular perspective, and executive editor of a magazine whose readers were mostly women.[1] Soon a private appointment was arranged for me with Dr. E. Glenn Wagner, vice-president for national ministries, who is personally in charge of Promise Keepers' outreach to men in all the 400,000 churches in the United States.

At the designated time, Wagner's assistant, a briskly efficient, fiftyish woman, intercepted me outside closed doors to a conference room where I was to find him; he was inside conducting a leadership-training session, she explained, which was running late. When it let out, he greeted me, apologized for the delay; then he and I sat down together at a table for a wide-ranging, in-depth, on-the-record talk.[2]

Wagner appeared forty-something, slightly graying, warmly handsome, and I found him gracious, engaging, smart, and likable. At times he reminded me of someone I might once have wanted to become. Something in his quiet moral suasion seemed familiar—a fervor that might have been mine had I grown up straight, stayed devout, and gotten ordained.

Wagner's thoughtful answers to my questions were often couched in the language of the New Testament, as might be expected from this former parish pastor with a Ph.D. in divinity. Because of my religious upbringing— I was raised in Lutheranism but left the church in my late teens—I followed Wagner's sometimes specialized sectarian language easily. And perhaps because our exchange never got heated, it shed intriguing light on the relationship between one Christian man's beliefs about sexual sin and for-giveness and one male feminist's faith in sexual equality.

As has been widely reported, Promise Keepers conferences pack athletic stadiums with great numbers of men—this one drew 45,000—and a mass outpouring of emotion results. I asked Wagner why what happens in such gatherings could not happen if women were present. He replied that there are "mixed signals" in society about "what is a man . . . there's this defini-tion, that definition—get in touch with the feminine side, with Jungianism, be more sensitive yet strong—and the guy, he's absolutely confused. Yet in a context with just men, he is safe to discern what a man is, without anyone looking over his shoulder, without misperceived ideas."

"Surely you're familiar with contexts where only men gather where men don't feel safe at all," I offered. "They're afraid what *other men* will think of them."

"Right."

"How does what's happening here differ from that?"

Wagner explained that because of Promise Keepers' emphasis on worship, "there is more of an abandonment to God taking place," and because the context is worship, "the concerns about the guy sitting next to him are less-ened." Many men attend Promise Keepers in groups, he said, "on buses from their own church or community, so they all know each other," and some men attend by themselves, "because they want the anonymity—but more often than not they leave with several new friendships, because they come to a point where now they're comfortable, where they can experience a nonsex-ual intimate relationship with another man."

Having observed within the mammoth stadium thousands of men hug-ging tearfully in pairs or in prayer circles of five or six, I had a picture in my mind of what Wagner meant by that phrase "nonsexual intimate relationship with another man." "So are you saying," I said, "that the depth of emotion that's released in that huge gathering couldn't happen *with* women and couldn't happen *without* God?"

"Correct."

As I had indicated to Wagner, I graduated from Union Theological Seminary in New York City, a liberal, interdenominational school well known for emphasizing both Christian ethics and social-justice activism. I was therefore puzzled by one of Promise Keepers' official statements in the press kit: "Biblical reconciliation is greater than humanistic unification and more powerful than political equality."[3] I recognized *humanistic* as a neg-ative buzzword for conservative Christians, but I could not fathom what this statement meant as a whole, so I asked Wagner, "Tell me how to understand what your movement means by *reconciliation* and how you think it's better than *equality*."

"Okay," he began, "we are for equality. That's not the issue, okay?" This was news to me, but I did not interrupt.

> What we're teaching men is "You can vote all the legislation you want, but if the heart of a man is not changed, the issue will remain, no matter what programs you put in place." God is in the reconciliation business, and we're called to be ministers of reconciliation (Paul's letter to the Corinthians). God wants me to be reconciled to Him, and then God wants me to be reconciled to my brothers—and to my sisters, in marriage, families, et cetera. I cannot look at another man if he knows Christ and be at war with him; I cannot think less of him, because biblically he's my brother, he's family. What we're saying is "I may or may not be able to change things politically—I need to vote with a biblical conscience (Paul tells us in Romans we're to be active in the government that we've been placed in)—but I *can* build relationships with other men, and I can change what's going on *there*."

Wagner had come round again, in so many words, to the theme of "nonsexual intimate relationship with another man." And while greater harmony among men as men would surely reduce much male–male warfare (leaving aside Wagner's presumption that such camaraderie obtains only if all parties "know Christ"), I wanted to press him further on the point of *sexual* equality. I quoted to him a passage from Paul's letter to the Galatians: "In Christ there is no male or female"[4]—words that to me express a very profound reconciliation and words that inspire many people who are reimagining the gender of God. "Would you speak to what that verse means to you and to Promise Keepers?"

> I really can't speak to what it means for Promise Keepers, because the verse, especially in Evangelicalism, is utilized in a variety of ways—as a proof text for the ordination of women, for the feminization of men, in the sense that there should be no difference, et cetera. I think that where Paul says "neither male nor female, neither bond [slave] nor free," the context seems to be very clear that salvation is offered to everyone. Remember, in that day and age, women were not viewed as being savable; even in Jewish culture they were pretty much on the outskirts of what was happening. Their word was not taken seriously, they were not taught, they were not mentioned in the scriptures, et cetera. And so now St. Paul is saying: It doesn't matter whether you're rich or poor, it doesn't matter whether you're male or female; salvation is granted through the grace of God through faith in Christ. I think to take that verse into issues of the godhead, into issues of

ecclesiology, is misrepresenting what the verse is for. A verse out of
context—I can take it anywhere I want. So, trying to keep it within
the context and culture of the day—what Paul was speaking to in
Galatians—I think he was simply trying to say: You cannot have
second-class citizens in the Kingdom.

I knew that by "Kingdom," Wagner was using one of Christians' terms for
the assemblage of all baptized and saved believers now alive and in their
afterlife ("the Body of Christ" is another). But I did not think to ask why, if
there were not to be second-class citizens in heaven, wives should submit to
their husbands on earth. I know from my seminary studies that the historical Jesus' teachings were not at all as bifurcated by social gender as the
message of Promise Keepers is today. The reason Jesus' followers included so
many women to begin with was that within their male-supremacist cultural
milieu, this itinerant prophet's ministry stood out as stunningly inclusive,
nondiscriminatory, and egalitarian.

"There's a strong emphasis in Promise Keepers preaching about sin and
confession," I said instead, moving on. "I want to ask you about sin in particular. How specifically does it get talked about in Promise Keepers? There's
talk about sexual purity and adultery, but, for instance, is pornography on
the map of sins that are discussed—?"

"Yes."

"—consumption of it and masturbation to it?"

"Correct."

"And sexual harassment, or any kind of forced sex—do those count as sin
that a man can come to Promise Keepers and confess?"

"Right, absolutely. One of the seven promises is to practice 'spiritual,
moral, ethical, and sexual purity.'"

"Have sexual harassment and date rape ever come up?"

Oh, absolutely. With sexual harassment, the main thing we've been
teaching men is that they're to honor and esteem women—whether it
is their wife within the home or women within the workplace—that
they are not objects, they're not toys, they are individuals to be
esteemed and respected as God's creation, and so you have no right to
demean anyone. One of the seven promises is "Maintain sexual purity."
Very often a single man will say, "Well, gee, I can't be a Promise Keeper
because I'm not married." But I say, "Well, as a single man I can still
make that promise, because I'm going to be so committed to the family
that I will not mess with another man's daughter, and I will not mess
with another man's wife, in an inappropriate manner—I am not going
to do that." Most of the more heart-to-heart discussions come in the

small groups, in the prayer times that happen out there, when men come forward for every issue under the sun. As you go through the seven promises, they touch on every area of life, every social issue.

"Is *shame* a meaningful word here?" I asked.

No, I don't think so. I would probably use the word *conviction*. In the Gospel of John we're told that the Holy Spirit's job is to convict the world's sin. I think proclaiming what God's righteous standard is, and allowing men the process of conviction—that leads to an action. Guilt from the outside—yeah, I may feel bad, remorseful, but I will not be empowered in any way to do anything. But a conviction that's wrought by the Spirit of God—that connects me to the very One that helps me make significant change.

"I think I understand your theological reasoning," I told him, "but I'm trying to understand the emotion. I'm trying to attach a name to it. And I concede *shame* isn't it—but there's something happening in that stadium in the tears welling up, at the point of confession—"

I would call that being convicted. I'm being convicted, it's being wrought in me, I've heard a message. The Spirit of God then takes that message, applies it to my particular area of life, and out of that I am then being moved to make a decision based upon my need of God and my dependency upon Him—to live differently, to make a change, to seek forgiveness, to be restored, to be reconciled—whatever that is in my life.

Then he told this story:

I dealt with a man who came to a conference last year who was absolutely convicted that although he had never hit his wife he had abused her emotionally, spiritually, just had really beaten her down. We prayed about it; he confessed it to the men around him; he said, "I can't change unless somebody holds me accountable for this. I need help." So they covenanted with him—they prayed with him. He goes home and his wife hears this story, and with tears he asks for forgiveness. And she says, "That's great, I'm excited, but I don't trust you; I still need to have you move out." He told me that that was the very first test of his commitment—because he could have verbally overpowered her, reasoned her into a corner, manipulated her, et cetera. He made the decision almost instantaneously and said, "I'll honor that," and moved out. Then she began saying, "Would you take the kids to school? . . . cut the grass? . . . fix the house?" About six months went by, and finally she called him one day and said, "Will you move back home?—because this is real; there is such a change." And he said, "You know, I still am tempted to control you through words— but that's not what I want to do."

There's an emotion but it's not just human emotion. There are guys here, John—that's all it is, human emotion. And I believe that when they get home they'll try, but it will be like a New Year's resolution; it really won't last. What convinces us that we're in the midst of something that is a movement of the Spirit of God is the fact that by and large, the changes are continuing on; they're significant and ongoing. It's not just the emotion. When the emotion's over, what have you got? Well, if you've got the Lord and you've got some brothers around you you can trust, then you're going to be able to make those significant changes.

Here was that which set Promise Keepers apart from any secular men's-movement organizing I was familiar with: an emphasis on effectively and dramatically transforming men's everyday ethics, particularly in relation to women, with an honest acknowledgment that the emotion of the moment with other men—that ephemeral swoon of all those ostensibly nonsexual intimate relationships—was insufficient. Some deeper, more profound change of heart was necessary.

Many of the ethical standards Promise Keepers teaches would be, if more universally acted upon, a marked improvement on most men's behavior: Don't break your promises, don't cheat, don't lie—not in your relationship to your wife, to your children, to your work associates, even to your country. At the same time, Promise Keepers promises a renewed sense of male sexual identity as a *godly* man. Promise Keepers' explicit emphases on everyday ethics, on a redemptive theology, and on a divinely bestowed gender identity are not neatly divisible.

"I want to get to a couple of hard questions," I told Wagner. "Is it fair to assume that you believe abortion is in the category of sin, if not crime?"

"I would personally state that—as sin, because I believe it's the taking of a human life."

"*Whose* sin? Is it the mother's? Is it the physician's? In what sense is the inseminating partner's responsibility implicated?"

"I believe that both the man and the woman bear responsibility for the child they've conceived."

"How do you parse the problem of whose sin it is when an abortion is performed? Is there distributive responsibility?"

"There's always responsibility," he said, "and again I'm speaking personally, because I don't know if we have an official policy on it; I know we've had discussions about it. A doctor who chooses to take human life, whether within the womb, outside the womb, regardless of age—I think there is a consequence to that."

"What would the consequence be?"

"The consequence is an individual's relationship to God," Wagner said, "and that consequence they have to deal with. All sin is forgivable. I believe that God has offered to us eternal life and forgiveness of sin through faith in His Son Jesus Christ." Then suddenly he interjected a disclosure about himself:

I personally came out of drug addiction in the sixties and seventies, okay?—for another guy it's he's abusing his wife. To understand what my sin is and to seek a biblical solution to that sin is what we're calling men to. The ultimate consequence, to not receive God's grace and forgiveness, that I believe is eternal separation from God and literal hell. I do not want anyone there, okay? There are things that I disagree with, but there is no one that I do not want to see come to faith in Christ and receive His gift of eternal life. No matter where you've been, no matter what you've done, you can experience the forgiveness of God and new life in Him.

"So I hear you saying," I went on, "that what the physician does falls under the category of sin, what the pregnant woman does you would also cast into a sin category, and the man who bore responsibility for the insemination—would you say that some sin is on him even if he didn't choose to abort?"

"Yeah."

"Is his sin that he conceived an unwanted child, or a child that couldn't be raised?"

"Right, and now he's refusing responsibility—"

"And his sin is not exonerated because of whatever sin falls on her, right, or on the physician? There's some sin he carries, yes?"

"Yes."

So far as I know, Wagner had accurately articulated a position consistent with literalist, Bible-based theology: The inseminating partner is as much culpable as the pregnant woman and the abortion provider. Strictly speaking, if ever Bible-based Christian conservatives succeed in making the sin of abortion a crime, there would need to be contact tracing through DNA obtained from fetal tissue in order to prosecute biological fathers as well. That's where criminalizing the sin of abortion would logically lead.

"I was thinking through the enormous sense of responsibility on the man for his own sexuality," I continued.

"Correct."

"It's a rather absolute responsibility—"

"Right."

"—that goes so far as virginity, too, till marriage."

"Correct."

Wagner, the author of a best-selling Promise Keepers marriage manual,[5] then gave me this example from his experience counseling men:

> What does a man do if he *hasn't* been sexually pure? Well, virginity in principle from this point on *until* marriage. And then in marriage, maintain a monogamous relationship. If a man has sinned against a woman by having sexual relationships with her outside of marriage, I believe he needs to ask her forgiveness for that. He does not hold up the standard for her that God wants. What we're saying is that there is a righteous standard, not just for me but for the woman I'm dating: She is God's daughter—how do you want someone to treat your daughter?—therefore treat God's daughter that way, with respect, esteem; therefore I'm not going to make demands or seek to lead her down a path that is not right; it's not God's standard.

And again, he told a personal story:

> I have a daughter and I have a son. I tell my daughter—she's fifteen— if a man loves you, he's not going to ask you to do that which violates your conscience, or violates your relationship with God. Otherwise it's not love. If he really cares about you, he's going to want you to maintain your values and convictions. To not do that, then he has sinned against her.
>
> I find in the breakdown of marriages that when couples have had sex before marriage, somewhere along the line it comes to haunt the relationship, and I'm not exactly sure why. I'm not a psychologist, but I've seen that a lot; and I've seen healing in relationships when they've gone back and they've made that right. Even though the couple may have married, for some reason it [their premarital sex] seems to hinder their physical relationship and their emotional relationships somewhere down the road. So we challenge men to go back and sit down with your wife and say, you know, "We did that, I sinned against you"—and just clarify that, to be free from that, so that's not a hindrance in their relationship.

"One last question," I said, "and it relates to the Promise Keepers policy statement on homosexuality." With evident precision, Wagner had been telling me about the sin of heterosexual premarital and extramarital sex, and I was curious to know whether he could be so exacting about the sin of homosexuality. "I take as a given that you view homosexual activity as sinful," I began, "but is there a boundary in your own mind as to when it goes into sin? Is holding hands sin? Is kissing sin? Is anal intercourse the sin? Do you have a notion of where the sin begins and ends?"

I was surprised by his answer:

To me, in my mind, it would be the same place where it would be sin for me with another woman apart from my wife. In my mind, as soon as I begin to be emotionally attached to someone who is not my wife, then I'm in sin. Jesus said, "If you lust after a woman you've committed adultery." So I would venture to say that it would be similar in the homosexual relationship: As soon as that emotional attachment goes beyond a friendship, I would say sin would begin to enter there. I talk with a lot of men about their marriage relationships because, you know, flirtations are dangerous, and it's not long before the flirtation takes hold of the heart and the soul.

"During the worship services I was listening very carefully to the message about virginity and sexual purity," I said, "and I noted that there was a kind of relief with which that message was received."

What we're trying to tell them is that masculinity, and manhood, is not defined by how many people you've slept with, either male or female. And men are finally saying, "Oh, thank God!" Sexual prowess should have nothing to do with one's personhood or self-esteem, and yet our culture has made it that way.

We're not opposed to sex, we're all for it. God basically says that any man and woman married can have all the sex they can physically stand, and that's holy in His sight. The marriage bed, Paul says, is holy; it's undefiled before God. And so I think that there are homosexuals who have come [to Promise Keepers gatherings] who have not felt comfortable, but there are also heterosexuals who have come who have not felt comfortable, and I don't think their lack of comfort has been because of their sexuality; I think it's other issues, because I know of no one who's made derogatory remarks [against homosexuals]. We do view homosexuality as sin—

"Do you mean the act or the condition?" I interrupted.

"I'd say the act at this point. The condition is still being debated." Looking at me steadily, he went on:

> But from my understanding of the Scriptures, God has ordained that marriage is between a man and a woman, and sex outside of that marriage relationship is wrong. So we are praying that men who are in that sin also understand that there is a place here, and there is a place with Christ for every man, and that I don't view them any less than I view myself and the despicable things that I did: sticking needles in [myself in] the sixties—it's no worse.
>
> You know, it's become a cliché, John, "Hate the sin and love the sinner"; it's a cliché in Evangelical and fundamentalist circles. But it is the essence of truth. It's a lot of what much political activism has forgotten, whether on the prolife or the prochoice side. Jesus spoke very forcefully; He drove the money changers out of the temple, but He also took the prostitute and showed her a better way and didn't deride her and didn't malign her. So we speak forcefully, we speak straightforward about things, but not with the intent of deriding or maligning—because we want everyone to be able to experience the love and forgiveness of Christ that we believe enhances an understanding of masculinity rather than detracting from it.

I had not mentioned my being queer, but as Wagner pronounced that last answer, I sensed he had guessed, and was more ministering to me personally than talking for the sake of the tape recorder between us. I have to admit I was touched. I felt he deeply meant me well, and I suspected this obligatory press interview may have become for him, in some sense, a good-faith act of Christlike love. After we parted, I even found myself wondering whether, had I heard such compassionate counsel in my teens when I first deduced not only my homosexuality but my religion's condemnation of it, I would have quit the church as I did. I regret neither my lack of heterosexuality nor my lapsed religiosity; in fact I now look back on that anguished time in my life and thank the god I don't believe in for granting me apostasy. But if I had met Glenn Wagner then, when I was young, and were he as he seems now (not, as he confided to me, shooting up), would his gentle, pastoral demeanor have forestalled my secularity? Would his welcoming warmth have brought me the solace of an accepting, nonflirtatious embrace? I honestly do not know.

Glenn Wagner's faith is clearly fundamentalist Christian. He believes not only in the Christian godhead but in Christian manhood. My faith, by contrast (if I can be said to have one), is radical feminism. I no longer believe in manhood, much less a gendered deity. Indeed I am on record saying that "'the male sex' requires injustice in order to exist,"[6] that "manhood is the *paradigm* of injustice,"[7] and that "refusing to believe in manhood is the hot big bang of human freedom."[8] Ironically, though, Glenn Wagner and I share a common concern, for we both care urgently about the crisis of everyday ethics in men's behavior. He is deeply intuitive, insightful, and empathic about the interior processes by which one's morals, emotions, and relational acts connect oneself to others and to who one fundamentally is. We both understand that men as men commit grievous wrongs for which they are morally accountable. And we both understand that if a man honestly owns up to his personal responsibility for those wrongs, he is likely to experience enormous and warranted guilt (he will be convicted by the Spirit of God, as Wagner would say). The difference is that Wagner believes this moral dilemma is resolvable religiously, without anatomizing manhood, and I don't. I view the problem of masculinist ethics politically, as a problem endemic to gender polarity. Wagner believes that a man must confess his sin, then be redeemed through faith and thereby find the moral resolve to live in the world as a godly influence. I don't believe that this goes far enough; I don't believe that this reaches to the root of the problem, because it leaves gender polarity and hierarchy in place, and it leaves someone raised to be a man still stuck in all his relationships trying to be the man there—an identity that can be fully inhabited only in contradistinction to someone lower down in a hierarchy. It may well be true, as Wagner says, that there will be no second-class status for anyone in the kingdom of heaven. If indeed there is a heaven, I should expect no less. But for me what happens in the hereafter is moot, because for the notion of manhood to exist here and now as a subjective and social identity, there must be second-class status for nonmales on earth. There can be no "men" otherwise. And that is a moral and political problem of awesome proportions.

NOW and Them

In the United States today, pornography is the primary form of sex education for young men. Each year more and more of them become consumers in pornographers' target market; and each year more and more young women, many of them slipping into self-hatred and eating disorders to meet the body standards those young men expect, become fair game for the alienating, objectifying, and often violative sex that men learn from pornography to demand. At this point in U.S. history, pornography plays a far more deleterious role in propagandizing for the sexual subordination of women than does any religious movement.

Nearly every society on the globe has a distinctive set of historically specific, institutionalized practices that both re-create and maintain the subordinate status of females. In China, where once that function was served by foot-binding, it is done today through sex-selective abortion. (Married couples, allowed by law to have only one child, clandestinely abort female fetuses to ensure that they have a boy.) In much of Africa and some Arab nations, the subordinate status of females is institutionally instilled through female genital mutilation. (Approximately two million girls a year have part or all of their clitoris and labia removed, their vulva often sutured shut as well, such that for intercourse and childbirth the sutures are ripped out and restitched after.) In the United States, the practice that operates most similarly is pornography. Women are hurt in the making and use of it. The production, trafficking, and consumption of pornography keep the ideology of male supremacy embodied in a way that will have subjective and social continuity from generation to generation.

The economics of the institution of heterosexual marriage no longer embody male supremacy in the United States efficiently. Until recently, if a penised person possessed a wife's body and labor in marriage, his manhood was beyond doubt, both socially and subjectively. But thanks largely to feminist activism dating back to the Married Woman's Property Act of 1860 and extending to no-fault divorce laws, marital-rape laws, and shelters for battered women, wives now have more opportunity to opt out of bad marriages, and they are doing so by the millions. This trend has not only significantly reduced husbands' proprietary prerogatives; it has seriously undercut heterosexual marriage as a serviceable prop for male sexual identity. Compounding matters, the economics of the labor market no longer reliably embody male supremacy either. Again thanks to feminist activism and women's unprecedented influx into the paid work force, the workplace is no longer as sex-segregated and female-unfriendly as it was in the fifties. Few jobs anymore bestow on a man the sensorial subjectivity of his supremacy to women—not airline pilot, not cop, not soldier, not CEO—and if any penised employee sexually acts out his embodied presumption of male supremacy in the workplace, there are now sexual-harassment laws to swiftly disabuse him of it. These two trends converge in the dual-income heterosexual marriage, increasingly common because the standard of living once afforded by a husband's paycheck can be had today only if wife and husband are employed.

Over the last three decades, as both marriage and the labor market have precipitously lost their patriarchal potency—their power to implant in male bodies the gendered hubris without which male supremacy would collapse— the pornography industry has burgeoned, as though to fill the void. A technologized form of prostitution, pornography democratizes the sensorial presumption of limitless access to any orifice of any woman's body. Repetitive masturbation to it imprints in penised people, as if at a subcellular level, a sense of sexual identity that, for many men, is beyond compare. It is a sense of self that can be experienced and reckoned neither in one's job title and pay stub nor in possessing a wife as one's indentured, chattel property. Meanwhile on the liberal left, if anyone assails the pornography industry for its systematic violations of women's human rights, if anyone advocates for legal redress for those harmed in the making or consumption of pornography, a broad coalition of civil libertarians, sexual liberals, media pundits, and pornography publishers will ally to shut up objectors in the name of free speech. Pornography is defended on the political left in the United States with the same parochialism that foot-binding once was in China and female genital mutilation is now in Africa.

In summer 1984 the national convention of the National Organization for Women passed this resolution:[9]

> Resolved, that NOW finds that pornography is a factor in creating and maintaining sex as a basis for discrimination. Pornography, as distinct from erotica, is a systematic practice of exploitation and subordination based on sex which differentially harms women and children. This harm includes dehumanization, sexual exploitation, forced sex, forced prostitution, physical injury, and social and sexual terrorism and inferiority presented as entertainment. Pornography violates the civil rights of women and children. Be it further resolved that NOW supports education and action by the chapters on this issue.

Several months later, a NOW official testified before a federal judiciary sub-committee about the impact of pornography on women, and in 1986 representatives of national NOW traveled to several cities to conduct fact-finding hearings on the harm of pornography. But the final report of that trek was left to collect dust, and the national board took no more official action on NOW's 1984 resolution. Although some local NOW chapters kept active on the issue, a tacit policy of remaining silent and noncommittal about pornography emerged at the national level.[10] By 1998, if one searched NOW's Web site for the word *pornography*, one found not a single sentence put forth on the subject by anyone representing national leadership.

By contrast, at its national convention in summer 1997, NOW passed a resolution denouncing Promise Keepers as "a militaristic, anti-women organization." Promise Keepers' agenda, according to the resolution, "is to subordinate women and overturn the gains that women have made in the last century." Moreover, "Promise Keepers is the fastest growing and a well-financed segment of the religious right wing and presents the greatest danger to women's rights." The resolution vowed "to expose the Promise Keepers misogynist agenda, and actively campaign to defeat that agenda."[11] A flurry of articles demonizing Promise Keepers appeared on op-ed pages, in NOW publications, and on NOW's Web site; NOW staged a protest at Promise Keepers' fall 1997 "Stand in the Gap" rally in Washington, D.C.; and NOW president Patricia Ireland was a frequent talking head on TV, criticizing Promise Keepers for its danger to women in one sound bite after another.

The entire liberal left was in high dudgeon. Its anti–Promise Keepers rhetoric was riddled with anti-right demagoguery, and it threw its voice like a ventriloquist from behind NOW's skirts. But hard evidence linking Promise Keepers to the extreme right turned out to be scanty, because the Promise Keepers organization had an explicit policy of not endorsing political candidates, not lobbying, and not supporting any political party. Unlike the Christian Coalition, which had been specifically formed to do *all* those electoral things, Promise Keepers erected a fire wall against even the appearance of political influence peddling. The delicate task of building a big-tent coalition among Charismatics, Pentecostals, and Evangelicals (Southern Baptists, Southern Methodists, and such) plus a sizable contingent of Roman Catholics depended upon keeping Promise Keepers a personalist, revivalist movement. There would have been a massive rift in its inner circle, and a mass defection from its touchy-feely conferences, had Promise Keepers embarked on overtly partisan moves. For the same reason, the Promise Keepers organization deliberately did not take positions on a host of divisive issues of church polity, such as the ordination of women. Leadership decided early on not to permit any elected official to speak from the platform at a Promise Keepers event. Promise Keepers never even issued a position on abortion, despite deliberations on the subject at high levels of leadership. Homosexuality is the only "social issue" on which Promise Keepers officially took a stand, and the wording of this policy statement[12] is worth a close look:

> Promise Keepers shares the same historic stance taken by Evangelicals and Catholics: that sex is a good gift from God to be enjoyed in the context of heterosexual marriage. We believe that the Bible clearly teaches that homosexuality violates God's creative design for a husband and a wife and that it is a sin (Leviticus 18:22; Romans 1:24–27; 1 Corinthians 6:9–10).
>
> Because we have experienced the love of Christ, we desire to share His love with all men. While we have clear convictions regarding the issue of homosexuality, we invite homosexuals to be recipients of God's mercy, grace, and forgiveness, available to everyone through a personal relationship with Jesus Christ. We therefore support their being included and welcomed in all our events.

This policy was initiated by leadership not to lobby for or against any legislation but to head off intemperate homophobic innuendos at Promise
Keepers stadium conferences. Railing from the stage at suspected homosexuals would have proved toxic to the physically intimate male bonding that
leaders were trying to encourage. In the first paragraph, this statement situated same-sex sex acts in the category of sex acts outside heterosexual
marriage, all of which (including adultery and sex with prostituted women)
are deemed sinful in the standard orthodox Christian reading of biblical
texts. But the practical effect of the second paragraph was to signal to all
men in attendance at its events in sports arenas—venues typically athrob
with homophobia—that as a matter of policy, Promise Keepers would not
countenance gay-baiting. Thus the subtextual function of this policy was to
assure men that they had complete permission to hug, weep into one
another's arms, and pair off into prayerful, sustained, full-body embrace
without fear of censure, either from without or from within.

The impetus for Promise Keepers was not any electoral-political agenda;
it was the skyrocketing failure rate of heterosexual marriage. Not only secular, liberal, and non-Christian husbands and wives were going their separate
ways. Among orthodox Christians, too, tremors set in motion by second-
wave feminists' critique of men's bad behavior had become a groundswell.
One speaker at a Promise Keepers rally, urging his audience of husbands,
ex-husbands, and future husbands to clean up their act, declaimed: "In our
world today, many times divorce occurs simply because the man promises,
promises, promises, promises, but unlike God—Who watches over His word
to perform It—never performs it. Never performing his word teaches his wife
not to trust him."[13] Wives' distrust was vast. For at least a decade, women's
sorrows about being badly treated by men—and women's resolve to dump
men who hurt them—had become commonplace themes in country music,
whose consumer market overlapped the culture of conservative Christians.
Promise Keepers would never have needed to exist, would never have been
embraced by fundamentalist Christian clergy and churchgoers, and would
never have garnered near unanimous acclaim from wives of its male participants and throngs of female volunteers had not right-wing women's
resentment about men's epic fecklessness reached critical mass.

"A Promise Keeper is committed to practicing spiritual, moral, ethical,
and sexual purity" said the third of Promise Keepers' seven promises. "A
Promise Keeper is committed to building strong marriages and families
through love, protection, and biblical values" said the fourth.[14] Both were key
components of Promise Keepers' agenda to resurrect heterosexual marriage as
an institution that would again reliably embody men's status as paterfamilias.
That status, in Promise Keepers' orthodox reading of Scripture, was based
in a theory of patriarchal gender identity: God commands man, and man

submits; but in that submission, man is not feminized, for he in turn gets to command his wife; and she, in turn, is instructed by St. Paul to "submit" to her husband.[15] Thus does divinely ordained manhood trickle down from God without miring males in the muck of the feminine.

Significantly, under the rubric of sexual purity, Promise Keepers explicitly exhorted men not to be consumers of the sex industry—the very institution that in secular America happened to be supplanting the diminished patriarchal potency of heterosexual marriage. The best-selling handbook *Seven Promises of a Promise Keeper*,[16] for instance, contained among other preachments practical strategies for avoiding the temptation of pornography, as when traveling alone:

> When you stay in a hotel, request at check-in that the staff block the pornographic movies from your room. . . . In addition, you should offer a polite but firm word of protest at every hotel that carries those movies. It will strengthen you, and if enough men do it, the hotels might stop showing them.

This argument was not antismut, it was proloyalty; it was based on the harm of pornography to a man's capacity for a steadfast relationship to one woman as his wife—the moral linchpin without which the patriarchal potency of heterosexual marriage could never be restored:[17]

> Adultery can take many forms. Watching racy movies on a business trip in an airport hotel, with or without masturbation, is a form of emotional adultery that will eventually weaken the marriage.

New Man magazine—for three years the official magazine of Promise Keepers (whose leadership vetted its editorial contents until April 1998)—published numerous articles, both confessional and practical, about married men's struggle to overcome their addiction to pornography. One typical tip, from an article titled "Virtual Immorality": "Consider locating your computer in a common area of your home, rather than in a private den or office. Working in the rec room or family room, where your wife and children can see or hear you, helps build accountability."[18] According to surveys conducted among men attending Promise Keepers stadium conferences, 16 percent acknowledged they had "purchased pornographic material in the past year," and another 16 percent refused to answer the question. Compared with those who said they had not bought any pornography the previous year, self-identified purchasers reported "significantly lower marital, fathering and family-life satisfaction." Offering Promise Keepers' spin on this finding, an editor's note in *New Man* magazine summed up: "The implication is that exposure to pornographic materials negatively affects family life."[19]

There was a serious fallacy in NOW's depiction of Promise Keepers as having a right-wing "misogynist agenda." It would actually have been strategically more astute (and truer) to claim the Promise Keepers phenomenon as a measure of success: "Look, men by the hundreds of thousands are finally fessing up to the rotten behaviors that feminists have been accusing them of for the past two decades! This is a significant victory for feminism (even if the Promise Keepers don't know it)!" Instead, in order to keep faith with NOW's prochoice allies on the sexual-liberal left (the American Civil Liberties Union, various Democratic party bigwigs, the proporn and pro-S&M gay-rights movement), NOW engaged in hollow anti-right mudslinging, all the while keeping conspicuously mum about the misogynist agenda being propagandized by the sex industry.

From the point of view of right-wing women, NOW's obliviousness to the moral renewal going on among men in Promise Keepers made no sense whatsoever. The hundreds of thousands of grateful Promise Keepers wives would not have been wrong to wonder: Exactly where, anywhere else on the political spectrum, were men gathering, even on a tiny scale, to acknowledge anything resembling such personal accountability for their interpersonal acts? Most pointedly, from those right-wing women's perspective, so-called feminists' defense of pornography looked no better for women's welfare than Promise Keepers' patriarchal model of marriage looked to NOW. At least Promise Keepers, in its earnest efforts to restore the institution of heterosexual marriage as the sine qua non of male sexual identity, was forthright about citing the scriptural chapters and verses that authorized its views. Equivalent candor was not forthcoming from NOW. Indeed it would have been rather awkward for NOW officials to display in public the actual pornography that, behind the scenes, reliably incarnated male sexual identity for men on the secular left. Violent, misogynist, and degrading pornography had become, in its own way, sacrosanct to sexual liberals, whose sole faith was First Amendment fundamentalism. But unlike orthodox Christians, who prayerfully turned to the Bible for patriarchal potency, sexual liberals, when they meditated over their own holy writ, tended to pray with one hand. Whether manhood was to be embodied in reverence for heterosexual marriage (as the right wing would have it) or in ejaculating to pornography (as sexual liberals defended it), the civil status of women stayed exactly the same: subordinate, which is the only way that male supremacy can be made flesh. Hypocritically, NOW denounced Promise Keepers for its male-dominant model of marriage while remaining silent, in deference to its left-wing bedfellows, about the far more devastating sexual subordination of women in and through pornography. With the exception of a small fringe

group of so-called feminists who were propornography, proprostitution, and
pro-S&M (whom NOW bizarrely kept faith with), women across the country hate pornography, hate what it does to the men they love (including
their sons and brothers), hate what it does to their intimate relationships,
hate the hostility that it engenders and graphically exposes in their workplace, schools, and community. Had NOW vocally denounced the
objectifying, misogynist values in pornography, it might have reached out
meaningfully to a vast constituency of women all across the political spectrum. In speaking truth to the pornography industry's power over millions of
men's sexuality, NOW might actually have pitched a bigger tent among
women than the partisan pup tent it had put up by kowtowing to propornography coalitions. Instead, NOW acted no differently than wives in
patriarchal marriages who are told by their husbands what not to say.

The Apocalypse of an Apostate

For as long as there has been religion, aspects of its mysteries have been
gradually peeled off and become explicable. Science, in particular, has dealt
fundamentalist faith some serious blows, not least when Copernicus said that
the earth revolves around the sun and when Darwin hypothesized evolution.
But patriarchal faith has generally recovered from scientific setbacks. God in
His Heaven and the Creation of Man have maintained, rather miraculously,
their metaphoric force. Still there are mysteries, ineffable facts of life—birth
and death, growth and senescence, time and space—that have not yet
yielded their secrets to scientific explanation; and recently some cosmologists
and particle physicists, full of supersophisticated awe, say they are moving
ever closer to personal belief in the Divine. Religious believers hold fast, in
faith, trusting in some Higher Power where mere human understanding necessarily leaves off. And life goes on, fact after fact.

Today, however, radical feminism has exposed religious fundamentalism's
most influential con job: the ideological smoke and mirrors whereby the fic-
tion of gender polarity fools people, almost all of them, almost all the time.
Belief in the existence of "men" and "women"—as if gender polarity were a
metaphysical fact of life—has been sustained so persistently by patriarchal
monotheism, throughout recorded history, that one might well wonder how
else the normative categories "men" and "women" could have come to seem
so socially real. How else could the proper power relations have been
instilled in the human population on such a cross-cultural scale? Before
Hollywood, before TV, before *Playboy*, before football, how else could
human males have learned how to embody male supremacy en masse? Surely
not at their mothers' breast. Perhaps it was no deity that "created them male
and female" but rather some ancient cult of patriarchal monotheism, which

literally invented the constructs "man" and "woman." Perhaps that was monotheism's original purpose: to generate a mythology of absolutist social gender, and lock it into place as one guy god's will.

Today radical feminism's exposé of sexual violence—including rape, battery, prostitution, pornography—unravels whole skeins of scriptural lies. Today radical feminism explains, as humans have never before comprehended, the function of gendering violence in the social creation of manhood. Today men's violence has been revealed as that which human males are acculturated to transact—with one another and against female flesh—in order to prove their manhood, in order to be real men. The jig is pretty much up. Manhood is a myth, a chimera, a delusional state of subjectivity that feels real only episodically in interactions that are unjust and/or injurious.

Religious fundamentalism has historically found its cohesion by denouncing those outside the tribe—for the ancient believers in Yahweh it was Baal worshipers and Canaanites; for Christians it has been Jews, more recently homosexuals; for Muslims it has been Jews and women, sometimes Christians. This is how all true believers know who they are: by demarcating who they are *not*. This dynamic, reiterated throughout recorded history ad infinitum, originates in the fact that a bold brotherhood of male supremacists can thrive only in contradistinction to a common gender enemy. Their manhood does not exist otherwise. Penised people who believe passionately in manhood are incapable of making common cause without at least subtly deriding *someone*, usually females. Men's sense of public gender definition cannot feel real unless some third party to a male bond is treated as inferior, as the demonized other. If penised people did not mutually target those who they are not, they could not be men. Worse yet, they would end up treating one another as the requisite gender enemy and destroy one another.

In sports arenas, secular shrines to manhood, Promise Keepers has created safe public space for males to feel like real men but without incessant anxiety about other men's judgment on their sexual performance, orientation, and identity. The Promise Keepers gender message is simple: Men are from God. This obviates the sorts of gender-defender dramas that would-be real men are prone to—contests and put-downs to prove who's got real manhood and whose is greater. *God's* manhood is greater, enough said. That tenet—combined with the physical absence of women from the premises—seems to put these men on equal footing (all benched sinners, all accountable to the same Coach). This in turn reduces peer-pressured urgency for put-downs of women in order to mark off "who are the real men here and am I among them?" Promise Keepers has transformed genderizing peer pressure away from the relativistic world's to that of an absolutist religion (or, as they might put it, away from "Sodom and Gomorrah" to "Bible-based Christian values"). This predictably safe social cohesion is based on each man's promise (to his God and to his brethren) to be strictly nonsexual with one another and to have sex solely with his own wife in private.

The men of Promise Keepers have discovered that "sexual purity" is a better basis for male bonding than the "sexual revolution" could ever be. The men of Promise Keepers have discovered that unless males are reliably in league as men, male supremacy can no longer claim credible authority over females one-on-one. And Promise Keepers has figured out how to put perhaps the most beneficent face possible on patriarchal authority. Certainly no other men's movement, nor any other moral revivalist crusade in U.S. history, has sought such thoroughgoing improvement in men's interpersonal conduct.

Today, especially in the United States, evangelical Christianity has become a last bastion for those who do acknowledge the sins of individual men against individual women (unlike sexual liberals and leftists) but who do not want to parse those sins too literally (or politically, as radical feminists do). Far more reassuring to view these gender crimes euphemistically, idiosyncratically. Let us admit of our generic responsibility for our sins, these men seem to say, but let us not allow the political premise of our very gender to be indicted. Surely let us shield from women's eyes our cumulative sins as a class; let us whisper our sins one by one, in prayer; let each man report to other men in his accountability circle; let our sins be also known unto God, Who forgives us completely; but let women not infer from our injuries against them a gender-class pattern; and let our manhood be honed in our hearts and honored in our homes. Let us be saved both from the wages of our sin and from radical feminists' structural analysis of how those systemic injustices constitute the very gender identity to which we aspire.

What Promise Keepers promises is a stopgap plan to clean up patriarchy's act, to expunge the most egregious manhood-affirming behaviors toward women—everyday acts of betrayal, promise-breaking, deceit—yet keep delineated the social constructs "men" and "women" as monotheism intends and as monotheism requires. In this sense the Promise Keepers movement represents an unprecedented social experiment: Can males embody male sexual identity *simply* by believing they're real men in God's sight and by being head of the household at home? Can males dependably embody a kinder, gentler male supremacy and thereby *merit* being gladly accepted as their wives' personal lord and spiritual leader? Promise Keepers' answer is an unqualified yes—but with a handy fallback position: God, who makes real men to begin with, also absolves. Promise Keepers' inspired solution to the crisis of male sexual identity is not to let men off the hook for their misdeeds (that's too big a job for anyone but the Redeemer) and not to put the blame for their misbehavior on women (as secular men's movements are wont to do) but rather—within what is essentially an ethical-rehab movement for conservative Christians—to model only the most respectful and trustworthy standards of interpersonal behavior: not cockfighting among men, not sexual exploitation of women, simply monogamous heterosexual marriage in which the man is final authority and his wife is not.

Through its emphasis on worship and forgiveness, Promise Keepers has created a shimmering, airy sanctuary where a man, as if hovering in free fall, can expose his human soul far away from women and without homosexual panic—because he knows that he and his brethren are working with a net of polar and hierarchical gender. The possibility of being perceived as a real man and at the same time not feeling so damned ashamed for what he has done to become one—that's the real high in this inner sanctum; that's the promise that's a keeper. Fixed social gender remains the ground of their being, but release from its intrinsic sins is their emotional antigravity.

The Promise Keepers phenomenon was flawed in a way that mere bashing of the political right could not possibly discern or illuminate, because Promise Keepers—exactly like the liberal left—was premised on belief in manhood. But the Promise Keepers phenomenon was also onto something that the liberal left had completely ignored: men's "sins," which (freely translated into the language of radical feminism) can best be understood as a generic code word for all the sexual secrets, the backlog of betrayals, the unconscionable cruelty that characterize most men's biographies and that, if ever acknowledged with complete honesty, would (and should) plunge most men into a morass of remorse. Feminists' perhaps most rash act of faith was to presume that something like that process had to be going on in some men *somewhere*—call it their conscience, maybe?—some residual shred of humanity that could still feel another person's pain and could occasionally feel *bad* if that pain resulted from something that they *did*. But as most women learned, whether feminist or not, getting a man to be accountable for his interpersonal actions is pretty much like pulling teeth. Then suddenly, as if out of nowhere, Promise Keepers produced what were in effect mass confessionals, and men came in droves, in city after city, because somewhere inside each of them they needed to come clean.

I would like to believe that such a moral reckoning does not require a belief system that posits a patriarchal deity. I would also like to believe that such a turning of the heart does not require a heterosexual hierarchy of social gender. I would like to believe that neither conceptual crutch would be needed by people born with penises in order to repudiate an ethic of manhood-proving and to live instead by an ethic of selfhood-affirming. I would like to believe that the self, or the conscience, or the soul, or the personhood of the human male—one who has been taught from birth to love the myth of manhood—can turn, can change, can choose to love justice more. I recognize that living out of one's selfhood, loving justice more than manhood, one would still make mistakes that hurt people, and (heaven knows) one would still need to be forgiven (surely on earth, maybe also from on high). But I would like to believe that one would no longer be driven to subordinate anyone in order to feel gendered or in order to feel God.

9

Patriarchy's Second Coming
as Masculine Renewal

Michael S. Kimmel

It was Shea Stadium in late September, after all, so a crowd of 35,000 men chanting, whooping, hollering, and high-fiving each other wasn't all that unusual. But the Mets attract barely half that number late in their woeful season. And there are no women in the stands. That is unusual. And besides, the Mets are on the road.

On this day Shea is the setting for the latest rally by Promise Keepers, a Christian organization that seeks to revitalize men through a mass-based evangelical ministry. The dramatic growth and continuing appeal of Promise Keepers indicate that the movement of masculine fundamentalism has struck a nerve among American men with its messages of personal responsibility and racial reconciliation: Promise Keepers is arguably the largest "men's movement" in the nation. Its calls to men to be more domestically responsible, socially conscious and responsive friends, fathers, and husbands make Promise Keepers seem innocuous at worst, and potentially a force for masculine reform. But its ominous ties with fanatic right-wing organizations and their views on women, homosexuals, and non-Christians, however, suggest that the rest of us had better start paying attention.

Who Are Promise Keepers?

Promise Keepers hasn't been around very long to have caused such a monumental stir. The group was founded in 1990 by former University of Colorado football coach Bill McCartney who had brought a national title to his school that year. A devout Catholic, McCartney had become, he admits, a workaholic absentee husband who demanded that family life be

This chapter, with the exception of the endnotes, is reprinted from March/April 1997 issue of *Tikkun* magazine, a bi-monthly Jewish critique of politics, culture, and society. Information and subscriptions are available from *Tikkun*, 26 Fell Street, San Francisco, CA 94102.

subordinated to his professional ambitions. In 1989, his unwed teenage daughter Kristyn had given birth to a child fathered by one of McCartney's players. The following summer, after a religious epiphany, he left the Catholic church for the more evangelical Protestant Vineyard Christian Fellowship and heeded the call to expand his mission from athletes to men in general.

The move wasn't that uncharacteristic. McCartney had always been pulled towards the charismatic and evangelical. While an assistant coach at Michigan in the 1970s, he had become involved with the right-wing Catholic "Word of God" movement, with its emphasis on Biblical literalism. The Vineyard Fellowship's cultish theology uses faith healing, miracles, and other "signs and wonders."

With a diagnosis of the nation's moral and spiritual crisis gleaned partly from his family's sexual scandals and partly from the Vineyard Fellowship's ultra-right political agenda, McCartney put out a call to men to come to a rally for masculine Christian renewal. Just over 4,000 men turned up in July, 1991, at the Colorado basketball arena.

From that modest beginning, the organization's growth has been almost exponential. Twenty-two thousand half-filled the Colorado football stadium in 1992, and 50,000 filled it the next year. In 1994, 278,600 men attended several stadium events, 700,000 came in 1995, and an estimated 1.2 million met this year at 22 sites. Now, the organization's promising their own two-million man march in Washington for 1997.[1] (One assumes they'll keep their promise.)

The organizational infrastructure has kept pace, growing from 22 full-time staff with a budget of $4 million in 1993 to more than 400 full-time employees, and a budget of more than $100 million today.[2] They publish a slick magazine, New Man,[3] which places devotional stories and prayers alongside political debates on questions like home schooling (they're for it), more practical tips like "how to save bucks on your home mortgage" (standard fare like comparing rates, paying more than the monthly premium, and refinancing the home), and advertisements for various Christian consumables.

McCartney himself now works for the organization full time, having resigned from his more secular coaching duties—followers still call him "coach"—in 1994, after Kristyn had given birth to yet another illegitimate child fathered by another of his players, and his wife had threatened to divorce him if he did not pay more attention to his home life.

Although data on the rank-and-file Promise Keepers are scarce, the National Center for Fathering in Shawnee, Kansas, found that, as of 1995, 88% of rally attendees were married, 21% had been divorced, and about 20% had parents who were divorced. Median age was 38, and 84% were white. Over one-fourth reported becoming Christian after age 24, and one-third had attended Baptist or Southern Baptist churches. Half reported that their own fathers were absent while they were growing up.

Unlike the Fellowship for Christian Athletes, which organizes prayer meetings among athletes in virtually every sport, including those little devotional moments at midfield for religious gridders from both teams, Promise Keepers wants more than just jocks. They want all men.

Sports seems to be the way they intend to get them, at least metaphorically. At their stadium rallies, the parade of speakers, dressed in vertically striped polo shirts, khakis and sneakers, look more like a lineup of sales clerks at Foot Locker than of evangelical stump preachers. Coach McCartney, and the other speakers—who include Ed Cole, organizer of the Christian Men's Network, who had the guys high-fiving for Jesus, and Charles Colson, convicted Watergate conspirator who found God in prison and now runs the Prison Fellowship Ministries—exhort their "worshipping warriors" with manly homilies like "go the distance," snatched from that masculine weepy, *Field of Dreams*, and "break down the walls," the rally's theme, which sounds like a cross between *Home Improvement* and a karate exhibition. The massive tent set up in the parking lot is a virtual messianic mini-mall, hawking books, T-shirts, and souvenirs; but the best-selling items by far are the ubiquitous baseball caps.

Non-Muscular Christianity?

Such a move to bring men back into the church by muscling up is not new in American history. And, after all, athletes are used by advertisers to sell everything from shoes to cologne and flashlight batteries, so why not God? At the turn of the century, the fleet-footed former Chicago Cub right fielder Billy Sunday quit professional baseball and remorphed into a Bible-Belt evangelist, preaching "Muscular Christianity" to throngs of men, and bringing, in the words of one journalist, "bleacher-crazed, frenzied aggression to religion." To Sunday, Protestantism had turned Christ into a henpecked wimp, whose angelic countenance smiled down even on his enemies from the national pulpit. Inveighing against this "dainty, sissified, lily-livered piety" to massive men-only crowds in tents throughout the Midwest and the South—the same states where Promise Keepers today find the majority of their audience—Sunday offered his minions a "hard muscled, pick-axed religion, a religion from the gut, tough and resilient." Jesus himself was no "dough-faced lick-spittle proposition," he roared, but "the greatest scrapper who ever lived."

Some Promise Keepers echo Sunday's critique of feminized masculinity. "The demise of our community and culture is the fault of sissified men who have been overly influenced by women," writes Tony Evans, a black

Dallas-based evangelist, who is among the Promise Keepers' most popular rally speakers. Men, he admonishes, must "reclaim" their manhood, saying, "I want to be a man again."

But in the bright September sun at Shea Stadium one would search in vain for such hypermasculine bravado. Gone also are the virulent misogyny, the homophobia, and the specter of theocracy that has brought most of the criticism of the organization. Instead, one is struck by the immense sincerity of the guys in attendance, the earnestness of their searching, the heartfelt expressions of remorse. Were it not for the exclusion of women and the end-less, tacky sports stuff, this could have been any Billy Graham Crusade. And were it not for the Christian fundamentalism, this might have been a mythopoetic men's meeting with Robert Bly and Sam Keen.

While Muscular Christians railed against a feminized Christianity grown soft and indolent, drawing on inspiring oratory about religious combat and righteous rage, most Promise Keepers are virtual SNAGs, "sensitive new age guys" celebrating Christian sweetness and kindness. They are less Christian soldiers "marching as to war," and more friends, confidants, therapists and partners, promising to listen carefully to their wives and children, sharing with their friends, healing their wounds and their worlds.

A Kinder, Gentler Patriarchy

The message has certainly resonated for large numbers of American men, who feel their lives are less deeply fulfilling, less meaningful, less animated by higher purpose than the one to which they believed they were entitled. Without community, a sense of purpose and connection, masculinity can feel hollow; we become ectomorphs—hard-shelled workaholics who are afraid there is nothing of any substance inside, and who deny that fear with drugs, alcohol, or strings of meaningless affairs. The marketplace is a perilous place to seek to prove one's manhood, what with plant closings, corporate layoffs, and downward mobility. Better to seek affirmation of manhood someplace safe, like as a father, husband, and an ethical man among men.

Promise Keepers ministers brilliantly to men's anxieties and needs, while promoting that masculine sense of entitlement that we believe is our birthright. The key words in their message are relationships and reconcilia-tion. The organization's founding document proclaims the group's dedication "to uniting men through vital relationships to become godly influences in their world." Men have abdicated responsibility; at home, husbands are "not giving their wives the support they need," and are absent in the lives of their children or their friends. Among the "Seven Promises of a Promise Keeper" (also the title of their chief doctrinal book) are building strong marriages, families, and friendships, and working in the church.

Promise Keepers promotes a kind of soft patriarchy, male domination as obligation, surrender and service—sort of "Every Man's Burden." There's lots of rhetoric about men becoming servants of Christ at home, administering to their families as he did to his church. "A real man is one who accepts responsibilities and doesn't run away from them. He raises his family and takes a leadership role," says one rally-goer. Men are entitled to lead, expected to do it, soberly and responsibly. Masculine malaise, the search for meaning and community, is resolved by the reassertion of a kinder, gentler patriarchal control.

At one rally, Bill Bright, head of the Campus Crusade for Christ, opined that while men should respect women, the man "is the head of the household and women are responders." At Shea, Rev. Ed Cole reminded the audience that "God's revelation comes through man," not woman, and so the two genders can never be equal, and self-anointed "Bishop" Wellington Boone noted that "how you handle your wife" would reveal how you "handle the world." Boone relies on Biblical inversion of biology—"woman came from man, not man from woman"—and describes his own conversion from absentee landlord to dutiful dad and husband. It's a form of competition, "spiritual warfare," a test of masculine strength to do more at home than his wife does. "I'm never gonna let no woman outserve me," he shouts to thunderous applause.

In his essay in *Seven Promises of a Promise Keeper*, the organization's best-selling text, Tony Brown advises men to "sit down with your wife and say":

> "Honey I've made a terrible mistake. I've given you my role. I gave up leading this family, and I forced you to take my place. Now I must reclaim that role." Don't misunderstand what I am saying here. I'm not suggesting that you ask for your role back, I'm urging you to *take it back*. . . . There can be no compromise here. If you're going to lead, you must lead.

(For their part, women are urged to give it back, "for the sake of your family and the survival of our culture.")

To some women, this traditional patriarchal bargain sounds a whole lot better than the deals they'd already cut. After all, the organization lists among its primary goals deepening "the commitment of men to respect and honor women." In return for submission, or being "responders," women are promised the respect and honor that went with the traditional patriarchal pedestal—and they get in return husbands and fathers who forswear drinking, drugs, smoking, and gambling, who lovingly support their families by steady work, and who even choose to go shopping with them as a form of Christian service. Not bad, perhaps—even if it does require that women remain absolutely obedient and subordinate to men. It's unclear to me whether having a job or even going to college fits into that picture. Some members want their wives home at all times; others say they still need the money. Perhaps we'll know soon enough: Promise Keepers has announced a women's organization, "Suitable Helpers," sort of its Ladies' Auxiliary, where, according to the Christian Coalition, women can "learn what it means to be a godly support and partner to man."

To some listeners, though, this message sounds like male supremacy with a beatific smile. "Promise Keepers are about the return of patriarchy in its Sunday best: spiffed up, polite, and earnest but always, and ultimately, in charge," noted Unitarian minister Rev. David Blanchard of Syracuse. The resolution of the crisis of masculinity cannot come at the expense of women. Though the Promise Keepers hear men's anguish, they offer a traditional patriarchal salve on a wound that can only be closed by gender equality.

The Racism of Racial Reconciliation

Promise Keepers' message of racial reconciliation is as compelling as it is troubling. On the one hand, reconciliation means that white people must take responsibility for racism and take the initiative in seeking fellowship with men of color. Noting that eleven o'clock on Sunday morning is the most racially divided hour of the week, Promise Keepers seeks to heal racial divisiveness by bringing black and white men together under the canopy of patriarchy.

At Shea Stadium, it falls to McCartney—grandfather to two interracial children (both of Kristyn's lovers were men of color)—to sound the call for racial reconciliation. Racism is a white problem, he argues. A "spirit of white racial superiority" maintains "an insensitivity to the pain of people of color." Like harmony between women and men, which can be won only when men return to the home, racial harmony relies on white people's initiative. It is the privileged who must act.

Racial reconciliation is the organization's boldest move into the political arena, and it makes Promise Keepers one of the few virtually all-white groups in the nation willing to confront white racism. At Shea Stadium, that message energized the mostly white (I estimated about 80%) crowd. Rich, who is 39 and white, is a single parent from New Jersey, who brought his two sons. He feels that the racial component is important. "In Christ we're all the same," he says. Daniel, a white 27 year old, from a working-class neighborhood in Queens, came with another man from his Baptist Church, Joseph, a 35 year old black man originally from Ghana. "As a white person, you kind of take race for granted, you don't see it," Daniel says. "I'm not the one being hurt, but my people have done some terrible things to blacks. As a white person, it's important to take responsibility."

So, what's wrong with this picture of white people taking responsibility for racism, of men becoming more loving, devoted and caring fathers, friends, and husbands? It's a nagging question that emerges once you begin to examine what lies outside the framing of each carefully orchestrated PK photo-op.

For one thing, there's the message of reconciliation itself. Theirs is not a call to support those programs that would uplift the race and set the nation on a course toward racial equality. This is not about anti-discrimination legislation or Affirmative Action—heck, it's not even about integration. It's about being kinder and more civil. It's about hearing their pain, not supporting its alleviation. It's choosing to be nicer, but not about policies that force us to be fairer. In the PK world view, racial reconciliation is an individual posture, but not a collective struggle. Being less racist in one's personal life may be laudatory, but without a program of institutional remedies, it leaves untouched the chief forces that keep that inequality in place.

Which is why it doesn't seem so strange to see who else is eagerly lining up to slap some high-fives on the Promise Keeper rank and file. Although McCartney and the Promise Keepers elite maintain a publicly apolitical position, there are increasingly ominous signs of connections between Promise Keepers and far right religious organizations like Focus on the Family, Christian Coalition and the Campus Crusade for Christ. James Dobson, founder of Focus on the Family, appears regularly at Promise Keeper functions, as does Bill Bright, whose Campus Crusade lent 85 full-time staffers to the Promise Keeper headquarters, and whose most recent book (sold at all Promise Keepers rallies) raves against the "homosexual explosion," the teaching of evolution, and abortion, as well as the laws against school prayer.

In addition to McCartney's well-publicized right-wing ties, other Promise Keepers maintain a "warm fellowship" with the far right. Mark DeMoss, the organization's national spokesman, worked for Jerry Falwell before serving on the advisory committee for Pat Buchanan's presidential campaign. In a sense DeMoss neatly encapsulates the three successive waves of the religious right in America—from Falwell's Moral Majority to Reed's Christian Coalition, to a sanitized theocracy designed to appeal to Generation X. Promise Keepers is only the most recent example of a well-established and well-financed theocratic movement.

This movement promises that "America will be a Christian nation by the year 2000"—not a cheery prospect for Jews, Moslems, atheists, agnostics, and others. Urging his followers to "take this nation for Jesus," McCartney has made clear the political agenda:

What you are about to hear is God's word to the men of this nation. We are going to war as of tonight. We have divine power; that is our weapon. We will not compromise. Wherever truth is at risk, in the schools or legislature, we are going to contend for it. We will win.

So much for the avowed apolitical stance of the organization. Theocracies are not known for their tolerance of difference, and their use of these earnest young minions is reminiscent of some New Left organizations, which were propelled from below by youthful idealism but steered from above by apparatchiks who were not especially taken with the idea of participatory democracy.

But the radical religious right is currently jumping on the racial reconciliation bandwagon, in part because it allows them to sound supportive of people of color, without actually having to support any of the political and social policies that would benefit people of color. Even Ralph Reed, Promise Keeper supporter and head of the Christian Coalition, protested the burning of black churches this past summer [1996], only to be more than a little embarrassed when his organization floated overtly racist mock-election guides to potential voters.

Such racial tokenism extends also to the black clergy who are part of the Promise Keepers team. Wellington Boone and other black speakers like E. V. Hill, from Los Angeles, and Pittsburgh's Joseph Garlington are also on the Steering Committee of the Coalition on Revival (COR), an extreme right-wing religious group that espouses Biblical literalism and promotes "Christian reconstructionism." Boone himself was a consultant to Pat Robertson's presidential bid.

Though the Shea Stadium rally was endorsed by several prominent local black clergy, other prominent religious leaders, like Rev. Calvin Butts of the Abysynnian Baptist Church in Harlem or the ubiquitous Rev. Al Sharpton, were conspicuously absent from the mutual love fest.

Nationally, too, some black clergy are skeptical, to say the least. "It doesn't translate into how you bring black and white together," noted the Rev. Christopher Hamlin, pastor of the 16th Street Baptist Church in Birmingham, Alabama. "The barriers that are broken down in the stadiums are still there when people come home to their communities. I think most black pastors see it as being rhetoric, which is something most of the black community has heard for a long time."

Eventually, those black pastors who have innocently supported Promise Keepers' masculinist ministry will have to face the seamier political underside of their messages of hope. Though Promise Keepers were among the only white organizations to raise money for burned black churches this past summer (they raised over $1 million), the traditional liberalism of the black religious constituency, which favors welfare, civil rights, and women's right to choose will sit uneasily with a right-wing theocratic evangelism. Though both sides agree that racism is a white problem, about the only policy issue they agree on is home schooling.

What is more, the inclusion of men of color comes at an exorbitant multicultural price—lopping off several bands of the rainbow through continued exclusion.

Gays and lesbians, for example, don't even get near the pearly gates. Echoing familiar "love the sinner, hate the sin" rhetoric, McCartney and Dr. Raleigh Washington sidestep the question at the rally's press conference. "It's like lying," says Washington. "God doesn't like lying but he loves liars." Perhaps, but would God support a Constitutional Amendment banning marriages between liars? Would God sanction discrimination against confessed liars?

Though rallygoers barely heard a word about it, homosexuality is a hot topic among both rank and file and for PK leaders. It's the hottest topic on Promise Keepers' web site. Since the Bible never uses the term, or clearly defines homosexuality, these Biblical literalists are forced to struggle with interpretations. The leaders see no ambiguity nor any need for equivocation. When he pronounced homosexuality "an abomination against Almighty God," McCartney was a board member of Colorado for Family Values, the statewide coalition of right-wing religious groups that sponsored Amendment 2, the unconstitutional Colorado initiative that would have permitted discrimination against gays and lesbians. Later, McCartney called homosexuals "a group of people who don't reproduce yet want to be compared to people who do." (One pities the Doles and the Buchanans, as well as other non-breeders.) He's also addressed Operation Rescue rallies, calling abortion "a second Civil War."

Given such obviously political positions, it would appear that Promise Keepers' notion of gender reconciliation is also an individual outpouring of concern, however heartfelt, for individual women, while ignoring collective efforts at building a new society together. Good, kind, decent men (and white people) can indeed develop better, more emotionally resonant and caring relationships with women and people of color, and then support precisely those policies that perpetuate their pain.

Male Supremacy as Racial Healing

Perhaps what we are witnessing in this strange alliance of right-wing evangelists and liberal black clergy is that the reassertion of male supremacy can serve as the foundation for both to sit down at the table of brotherhood. "What happened here is that the boys' club has expanded to include people of color," writes Chip Berlet, who is researching right-wing populism in America. "When push comes to shove, what's more important, race or gender?"

Here, then, is a concept that both black and white clergy can unite behind. The resurrection of responsible manhood is really the Second Coming of patriarchy. Gender and racial healing is a more unified masculine entitlement. Such allies could even reach out to Louis Farrakhan, the Black Muslim leader of his Million Men, and invite him to the party, since he also excludes women and gay men and lesbians from the table of humanity.

Of course, like the Million Man March, the earnestness and sincerity of the movement adherents—and a genuine alliance with a wide range of black clergy—might in time outstrip Promise Keepers' right-wing political agenda. More likely, and more ominous, however, is the possibility that the repressive and censorious voices of theocratic authoritarianism will continue to whisper in the ears of the movement leaders, long after the shouts of the men themselves have died down.

10

Godly Masculinities Require Gender and Power

John P. Bartkowski

Leading Promise Keepers' desire to rejuvenate "godly manhood" has attracted nationwide attention and has stimulated intense political debate within the past several years. Yet what exactly do PK luminaries understand to be "godly manhood"? I sought to address this vexing question by analyzing the gender discourse contained in popular advice manuals written by two leading PK authors—Ed Cole and Gary Oliver. My analysis of these advice manuals reveals that no single definition of masculinity is advanced by PK advice authors. Rather, leading PK authors promulgate a diversity of masculinities.

Some PK authors, such as Ed Cole, champion a highly instrumentalist view of masculinity that privileges radical notions of gender difference, advocates a patriarchal family structure, and is explicitly antifeminist. Gary Oliver and other PK advice authors advocate a more expressive vision of manhood that defends androgynous gender conceptualizations and marital egalitarianism. This discourse of expressive masculinity also offers a somewhat more conciliatory appraisal of feminist politics.

While these competing discourses of masculinity offer remarkably divergent portrayals of godly manhood, each of these discursive regimes is rent with internal contradictions. Despite their respective points of divergence, such internal contradictions make these discourses appear to be overlapping and complementary viewpoints rather than overtly discrepant ideologies. In this way, PK is likely to attract the support of progressive evangelical men without sacrificing the allegiance of their more traditional counterparts.

Vive la Différence: PK's Discourse of Instrumental Masculinity

How do leading spokesmen for PK define masculinity and address the hot-button issues of gender difference and family power that have taken center stage within contemporary U.S. debates over gender and family relations? A careful reading of men's advice manuals produced by Promise Keeper luminaries[1] highlights several points of discursive divergence concerning these issues.

It would be difficult to find a more enthusiastic purveyor of instrumental definitions of masculinity than Edwin Louis Cole, a popular PK author and speaker. Cole's *Maximized Manhood: A Guide to Family Survival*[2] is in its eighteenth printing and boasts 800,000 copies in print; it is sometimes credited with having helped launch the modern Christian men's movement. The instrumental gender discourse invoked by Cole is radically essentialist (i.e., predicated on notions of essential gender difference), as well as patriarchal and antifeminist.

The discourse of masculinity invoked by Cole begins with the assumption that men and women are innately, categorically, and immutably different from each other (hereafter described as radical essentialism). Purveyors of this radical essentialist discourse[3] hold that manhood is characterized by strength and rationality as well as a focus on long-range vision and instrumental achievement. Men, according to many purveyors of this discourse, are "initiators." By contrast, in this radical essentialist discourse, womanhood is characterized by fragility, intuition, emotional attunement, and relational attachment. Women are portrayed by many radical essentialist authors as "responders."

Clearly beholden to these radical essentialist presuppositions, Cole places a premium on this apparent chasm of gender difference: "It is possible to get spirituality from women, but strength always comes from men. A church, a family, a nation is only as strong as its men. Men you are accountable. There is no sleek escape chute. God requires manhood of all men."[4] Consequently, totalizing statements about masculine-feminine difference are shot through Cole's writings: "Men and women are different. Really different. For example—Men are head-liners, women are fine-print people."[5] Men's ostensible penchant for long-range vision, then, is contrasted with women's apparent attunement to nuance and detail. Cole is unrelenting in his essentialist rhetoric: "Every woman needs to be unique in her own eyes. . . . Every woman craves the intimacy of some man. She was made that way. When she is denied that intimacy with her husband, her nature is to seek out an alternative source. . . . Every woman needs to know she is unique to her man."[6] References to women's "intuition" are common and are used to draw in male readers who share such sexist sensibilities. After discussing his own wife's apparent reliance on her inborn intuition, Cole tellingly concludes: "You know how women are."[7]

Such categorical claims are not simply cast about as innocuous rhetoric by the likes of Cole and other radical essentialist PK authors. The clear implication of this rhetoric is the belief that men's and women's divergent, divinely ordained natures predispose them to occupy different social roles. For example, women's "fine-print" nature makes them apparently more capable caregivers for young children. Cole adroitly conveys this point via a narrative recollection of a visit he and his wife paid to their new granddaughter:

> I flew across the continent and then drove for hours to see my brand-new granddaughter in the hospital. When I saw her, I checked her out thoroughly. There she was—arms, legs, eyes, nose, mouth—all the parts were there, everything was okay. That was sufficient for me. I was ready to leave. Not my wife and daughter. Half an hour later, they were still examining the length of the eyelashes, the shape of the fingernails, the texture of the skin, as if the nursery window were a magnifying glass. Fine print, fine print.[8]

Cole's vision of instrumental masculinity also leads him to defend a patriarchal family structure in which the husband is the undisputed leader of the family who acts as the "priest" or "head" of the house. He believes that married women actually desire male leadership within the home.[9] In case readers question the veracity of such claims, Cole quotes 1 Peter 3:1–2, a portion of which reads, "You married women, be submissive to your husbands—and adapt yourselves to them . . . [show] reverence for your husband . . . which includes, respect, deference, honor, esteem, admiration, praise, devotion, deep love, and enjoyment" (Amplified Bible).

According to Cole's tautological reasoning, household authority could not legitimately be allocated in any other fashion. He argues that one of the essential characteristics of manhood is courage and then concludes, "Courage has always been a requirement of leadership. . . . God has planned for someone to take charge. Men—it is you."[10] In a similar fashion, he reasons: *The Kingdom of God is based on truth, not human sentiment.* Decisions must be made the same way. Decision-making is one of the marks of a man. Every man I know that is a success is decisive."[11]

Masculine initiation and feminine submission would seem to be endemic to virtually all aspects of male-female relationships, including sexual relations. Mixing metaphors of biological sex, sexual intercourse, and submission, Cole even goes so far as to characterize sexual intercourse as an encounter in which an emotionally tender woman "submits" herself to the sexual needs of her aggressive male lover. He argues: "Even women who are promiscuous feel a measure of guilt in having sexual relations without any love. So, prior to submitting to a man's love-making, they ask the age-old question, 'Do you love me?'"[12]

Underlying this radically essentialist view of gender is a belief in the God-ordained appropriateness of heterosexuality, as well as a revulsion for homosexuality and any attempts at perceived "gender blending" (e.g., feminism and gay rights advocacy). Cole's advice manual even draws connections between sin, apocalyptic imagery, and perceived gender blending. He describes the end times as a period when "the 'problem person' plunges into a Christless eternity . . . and homosexual 'problems' will be no more." Shifting deftly from such macabre and heterosexist apocalyptic imagery to a more salvific football metaphor, Cole immediately reminds his readership that "sins" and "perversion[s]" such as homosexuality can be eradicated in this lifetime if males "begin to tackle sin like men."[13] The alternative to God's plan for patriarchal leadership—what Cole calls the emerging "matriarchal society"—is a development he finds most disturbing.

Why all of the concern about homosexuality, feminism, matriarchy, and gender blending? Many purveyors of this radical essentialist discourse are clearly anxious about what they perceive to be a cultural devaluation of masculinity within contemporary U.S. culture and even within some evangelical churches. Such authors are especially troubled by the willingness of "feminized" contemporary men to relinquish leadership to women. Again mixing sexual metaphors with gender rhetoric, Cole argues: "I like real men. . . . I don't like the pussyfooting pipsqueaks who tippy toe through the tulips. . . . I like men to be men."[14]

In the foreword to Cole's manual, Ben Kinchlow (cohost of *The 700 Club*) is similarly critical of the subversion of male authority wrought by feminism and is baffled by the complicity of U.S. men in this seemingly sinful enterprise: "Today's man may wear jewelry—bracelets, necklaces, and perhaps, an earring. He has long hair, usually styled by a unisex hairstylist; he wears unisex pants and soft, silky shirts opened to display 'cleavage.' . . . In any case, man is 'liberated.' Or, so he's been told by the feminist principles which are designed to undercut his position as a male."[15] In short, the discourse of instrumental masculinity promulgated by leading PK authors such as Ed Cole is founded upon a notion of radical gender difference, a commitment to a patriarchal family structure, and sharp criticism for those who would deign to mix "the masculine" and "the feminine."

Caveats and Contradictions within Instrumentalist Discourse

Despite Cole's strong advocacy of instrumental masculinity, he offers various warnings in the form of contradictory caveats to discourage men from indulging in the perceived excesses of the very manliness he champions. Cole seems more than a little worried that some male readers will misinterpret his call for men to "maximize their manhood" as a license to engage in promiscuous sex—what he calls the "playboy problem." To circumvent such a misinterpretation of his position, Cole argues that the "playboy" is not genuinely manly (i.e., "tough") because such sexually undisciplined men are enslaved to their own prurient appetites: "Affections, desires, appetites, all must be dealt with in discipline. Even love must be disciplined, or what we love will kill us. Discipline requires toughness."[16]

The self-contradictory Cole also seems periodically concerned that his advocacy of a patriarchal family structure may be misinterpreted by men who wish to act in a callous, cavalier, or abusive fashion toward the family members that Cole himself charges them to lead. Thus, while Cole unabashedly crowns the husband/father as "leader," "priest," and undisputed patriarch of the family, he is expressly critical of patriarchs who would use their authority in a heavy-handed fashion. He decries such abuses of power as "dictatorial authoritarianism" and even goes so far as to insinuate that such patriarchal leadership does not rule out "equality" with one's wife, who is scripturally described as the husband's "joint heir" (1 Peter 3:7) within the home.[17] Cole does not elaborate on this latter contradiction. His readership is thus left to sort through a rhetorical paradox commonly deployed by such evangelical authors—an advocacy of radical essentialism and domestic patriarchy set alongside contradictory claims about the purported "equality" of husband and wife in God's eyes.

Instrumentalist Contradictions Explained

What is the source of such contradictions within Cole's rhetorical construction of godly masculinity? It would seem that Cole is caught in a discursive paradox not restricted to his own contradictory definition of masculinity. On the one hand, Cole is trying to convey a bold—some might even say prophetic—message to contemporary men in the United States: do not sacrifice your essential (i.e., strong, ruthless, [hetero]sexualized) masculinity to a feminized contemporary evangelical and American culture. Yet on the other hand, this masculinist "call to arms" is in danger of being radically misunderstood as a tacit endorsement of the very forms of masculinity Cole decries (e.g., male-perpetrated violence against women, unbridled masculine hypersexuality).

To adopt for a moment the sports metaphors that are so common in tracts popular with, or written for, Promise Keepers: Cole is just one "player" who is "competing" for attention in an "arena" of discursively constituted, historically situated masculinities. Who, then, are Cole's "rivals" in this discursive "contest" over the meaning of manhood? On the one hand, Cole positions himself against feminists, gay rights activists, and purveyors of progressive gender relations in the United States. Cole spares neither ink nor paper in deriding these advocates of gender progressivism. On the other hand, Cole does not wish wholeheartedly to embrace discourses of traditionalist masculinity that have linked "real" manhood with the despotic use of physical or sexual force. But of course, in painting men as inherently strong, ruthless, and hypersexualized creatures, Cole comes dangerously close to advocating the very forms of masculinity he reviles. So, what's a Promise Keeper or, for that matter, any other Christian man with such ambivalently traditionalist sensibilities to do?

In the face of this vexing problem, Cole engages in a time-worn rhetorical strategy. He seeks to portray his position as the "sensible center" juxtaposed to various discursive "extremes." Particularly prominent within the middle of his advice manual, Cole attempts to cast his advocacy of "masculine toughness" as a reasonable middle path to some men's use of excessive force (decried as "roughness") on the one hand, and to other men's capitulation to a feminized contemporary American culture (derided as "softness") on the other.[18] Consequently, in apparent contradiction to his definition of manhood as "ruthless courage" not prone to "sentimentalizing," Cole peppers such assertions with periodic admonitions that men must balance "tenderness" with "toughness."[19]

Yet Cole is unable to sustain his rhetorical commitment to a middle path charted between the "tough" and the "tender," leading one to wonder if rank-and-file Promise Keepers can accomplish such a daunting task in their lived relationships. Ultimately, Cole prefers to err on the side of the "tough" man rather than his "tender" counterpart: "Perhaps years ago, as a general rule, parents, educators, and political leaders may have erred on the side of toughness—but today it is the softness that is killing us. We must learn to be ruthless with ourselves at times."[20]

If this rhetoric fails to carry force with his male readership, Cole points to the person he considers the paragon of toughness, albeit balanced with a minimal amount of tenderness—Jesus Christ: "Jesus was a perfect balance of the tender and tough." Still, Cole betrays his preference for toughness over tenderness by relegating Jesus' alleged tenderness to one concise sentence in his manual: "[Jesus] revealed His tenderness in His messages of love, His actions of healing and comforting, His death on the cross."[21] Immediately after conceding this point, however, and in considerably more detail, Cole waxes poetic over Jesus' apparent toughness. In exhortations reminiscent of Muscular Christianity texts of the late nineteenth and early twentieth centuries,[22] Cole warns his readers against feminizing Jesus:

> But—the same Jesus who swept little children up into His arms gripped that scourge of cords and drove the money-changers out of the temple. Some "sissified" paintings of Jesus come nowhere near showing the real character of Him who was both Son of Man and Son of God. Jesus was a fearless leader, defeating Satan, casting out demons, commanding nature, rebuking hypocrites. He had a nobility of character and a full complement of virtues which can be reproduced

in us today—by the same Holy Spirit that dwelt in Him. God wants to reproduce this manhood in all men. What kind of manhood? *Christlikeness! Christlikeness and manhood are synonymous.* . . . Since to be like Jesus—Christlike—requires a certain ruthlessness, manhood does also.[23]

Androgyny as the Discourse of Expressive Masculinity

The discourse of instrumental masculinity outlined above is only one of several different definitions of "godly manhood" promulgated by authors popular with Promise Keepers. Another prominent Promise Keeper who promotes a more expressive discourse of masculinity is Gary Oliver. Oliver's *Real Men Have Feelings Too*[24] was not written with Promise Keepers in mind but is one of many manuals sold through PK and is heartily endorsed by PK founder Bill McCartney. And like Ed Cole, Oliver is a frequent contributor to PK anthologies comprising works by an array of the organization's leading spokesmen.

Sensitized Masculinity:
Emotional Expression and Marital Egalitarianism

In *Real Men Have Feelings Too*, Gary Oliver positions himself within a discourse based largely upon androgynous conceptualizations of gender. In stark contrast to the radical essentialist discourse of instrumental masculinity articulated above, Oliver argues that traits commonly associated with being male (e.g., bravery, strength, stoicism, an insatiable sex drive, a preoccupation with achievement) are not really "masculine" at all.[25] In addition, he contends that characteristics typically associated with being a woman (e.g., gentleness, compassion, tenderness, meekness, sensitivity) are not really the property of an essential "feminine" temperament.[26]

And in stark contrast to Ed Cole's criticism of "sissified" depictions of Jesus Christ, Oliver contends that traits often linked with womanliness are actually "human" traits clearly exemplified by Jesus Christ:

> Here's what for many is the shocker. All of those words [e.g., "compassion," "tenderness," "sensitivity"] are descriptors of our Lord Jesus Christ. *And that's the problem!* Those words don't describe a woman. They aren't feminine, they're human! They describe emotions and actions of healthy males and females. But sin has so damaged and distorted our culture that what God designed to characterize healthy people now characterizes only women. That's tragic![27]

Oliver's men's advice manual, then, has a very different agenda from what informs Cole's treatise. Rather than have men "maximize" the instrumental aspects of their manhood, Oliver argues for a more sensitized masculinity—one that enables men to learn "how to be human, how to feel, how to love, how to be better husbands, fathers, and friends."[28] While he does not single out evangelical essentialists by name for criticism, Oliver is quite critical of radical views of gender difference. He says that such "myths of masculinity" have "produced a generation of men who define themselves by the negative. Whatever women are, whatever strengths or attributes they have, whatever characteristics they possess, positive or negative, men aren't. And if women are emotional, then real men aren't. And any attempt to say they could be or should be is an attempt to 'feminize' men."[29]

Therefore, throughout his advice manual, Oliver encourages men to explore, trust, and express their emotions rather than place the "mind over emotions"; to recognize that the free expression of emotions is supported by a careful reading of the Bible; and to acknowledge the apparent benefits of this expressive masculinity (e.g., the physical, psychological, and relational benefits of open emotional expression). In articulating this discourse of expressive masculinity, Oliver pays sustained attention to the emotional issues with which he thinks most men wrestle, due to human sinfulness and its pernicious counterpart, gender stereotyping. Oliver provides chapter-length discussions detailing the steps by which his male readers can learn to process a wide range of otherwise unwieldy emotions, including fear (chap. 4), anger (chaps. 5–7), loneliness (chap. 8), love (chap. 9), worry and depression (chaps. 10–11), grief (chap. 13), and—for the somber, overly serious Christian man—joy (chap. 14).

Particularly noteworthy is Oliver's treatment of conflict resolution (chap. 12). Whereas the discourse of instrumental masculinity is often predicated upon the concept of husband-headship and wifely submission (see above), many traditional Christian purveyors of expressive manhood (especially Promise Keepers) articulate support for marital egalitarianism through "mutual submission."[30] To make his case for marital egalitarianism, Oliver's treatment of effective conflict resolution mixes popular psychological rhetoric with biblical references. Using a married couple as an example of this process, Oliver outlines five different "conflict styles" that couples often employ; assesses each conflict style with regard to meeting one's "personal needs" and the couple's "relationship needs"; and then provides seven steps to follow so that couples may achieve "resolution"—the conflict style that he recommends above all others.

Rather than advocate a patriarchal chain of command for familial decision making, Oliver argues that achieving "resolution" entails discussing and deciding "on a mutually acceptable solution." So, whereas Cole is dismayed by men's relinquishing of family leadership, Oliver laments that men are often reluctant to find a mutually acceptable solution to family problems:

Deciding on a mutually acceptable solution can sound easy. Over time it can become easy, but in the early stages of changing your conflict patterns it may be difficult. Be sure to set aside ample time for discussion and prayer. . . . Remember that you are choosing to bargain some of your personal needs for some of your relationship needs. Read 1 Corinthians 13 out loud. [First Corinthians 13 contains the oft-quoted biblical passages describing love as "patient," "kind," "not proud," "not self-seeking," etc.] . . . At this point in workshops men have raised their hands and asked, "But what if we can't agree on a mutually acceptable solution?" After a brief pause I usually smile and respond by saying, "Well, if you can't agree on a solution, reach into your pocket, pull out a coin, ask the other person if they want heads or tails, and flip it." This usually brings a lot of laughter. "I'm serious," I quickly add. "If you can't decide, it's better to try something that might work than something that is a proven failure."[31]

The "Sensible Center" Revisited

The seemingly progressivist discourse of expressive masculinity articulated by Oliver is not without its own internal contradictions. Two interrelated contradictions are particularly noteworthy: (1) the strategic insertion of gender difference rhetoric into a broader commitment to androgyny, and (2) a corresponding ambivalence toward feminism. Again, the bulk of Oliver's book is dedicated to debunking the six "myths of masculinity"—including "Myth 6: Men Are the Opposite of Women." Yet woven into Oliver's strong dismissal of radical gender difference is a strategic strand of suspicion for what he calls "radical" feminist discourses of gender sameness. In a scant four pages of a nearly three-hundred-page tome on expressive masculinity, Oliver blasts the "lunacy" and "ridiculous assumption[s]" of those who have "jumped on the gender-same bandwagon."[32] Paradoxically, even this four-page nod toward gender difference is laden with doublespeak that, in the end, echoes Oliver's overarching argument against gender stereotyping: "It's true that men and women differ in the physiology of their brains. They are different. However, there is an unfortunate tendency to attribute many differences in individuals to sex/gender rather than numerous other factors that contribute to and shape our development [e.g., ungendered personality characteristics such as mathematical acumen]."[33]

Like Cole, then, Oliver is interested in portraying his position as a sensible middle course between two discursive "extremes"—in this case, radical essentialism and radical feminism: "The feminist movement has been correct in emphasizing that men and women are of equal value and equal worth. Unfortunately, some of the more radical feminists have failed to emphasize important ways in which men and women are different. They have interpreted equal to mean same. The two are *not* synonymous."[34] Like the discourse of instrumental masculinity, PK manuals that defend an expressive definition of godly manhood are replete with discursive contradictions that mix and meld apparently competing gender ideologies. In the end, these seemingly disparate discourses of instrumentalism and expressivism "hang together" via points of overlap provided by such contradictory rhetoric.

Conclusion

This chapter has illustrated that leading texts among Promise Keepers are the purveyors of several distinctive, yet overlapping discourses of masculinity. I have contrasted the discourse of instrumental masculinity (predicated primarily upon radical notions of gender difference and a patriarchal family structure) with the discourse of expressive masculinity (founded largely upon androgynous gender conceptualizations and marital egalitarianism). I have also outlined the contradictions endemic to each of these discourses that provide them with the appearance of overlap and complementarity. Such discursive heterogeneity may provide one key to PK's rapid membership growth. Indeed, the organization may be able to attract evangelical men with traditionalist leanings, progressivist sensibilities, or genuinely ambivalent feelings about contemporary gender and family relations.

Despite the ideological diversity outlined herein, some definitions of masculinity would seem to be overwhelmingly rejected by virtually all leading PK authors. Almost without exception, gender discourses promulgated by PK are heterosexist (if not explicitly antihomosexual), ambivalent toward feminism (if not explicitly antifeminist), and generally founded upon a rather narrow definition of the family (e.g., a legally married versus a cohabiting couple) that may seem anachronistic to a growing number of contemporary Americans. Consequently, rhetorical "limits" are placed around the discursive "invention" illustrated here.

How might these discourses impact gender relations among rank-and-file Promise Keepers and their relationships with significant others (e.g., family members, primary friendships)? Interviews and ethnographic research may clarify the points of (dis)connection between the various gender discourses advanced by Promise Keeper luminaries and the actual gender practices in which this organization's members engage. Because gender is constituted not only through rhetoric, but is (re)constructed through quotidian social practices, future research should examine how the advice within these manuals is accepted, rejected, and amended by the rank-and-file Promise Keepers participants at whom these media are targeted.[35]

part 3

women as (more than)
suitable helpers?

11

Promise Keepers Welcomed Home by Wives

Clella Iles Jaffe

In the last half of the twentieth century, women's gender role transformations have been facilitated by all-female support groups and retreats, consciousness-raising activities, women's studies departments in universities, and the like. Men, in contrast, have had fewer supports to guide them into new gender role paradigms. However, in the 1990s, several movements emerged to help men reexamine masculine dynamics within a group of other men.[1] One of them, the evangelical Christian Promise Keepers (PK) organization, has as its stated goal reconciliation between men and their God, their families, their churches, their brothers of other races and denominations, and their world at large.[2] In October 1997, a huge crowd of men met on the Mall in Washington, D.C., for a Stand in the Gap rally;[3] there they read a covenant with God that contained the following promise: "to love and serve our wives and children . . . to give them first priority in our prayers and schedules. . . . Where we have used our masculinity against others, we now commit to honor all women . . . through our words and in our actions."[4]

The group naturally attracts critics. Prominent among them is Patricia Ireland, leader of the National Organization for Women (NOW), who portrays PK participants as men who "come to their rally and check their wives and daughters at the door like coats."[5] She further labels the movement "the greatest danger to women's rights."[6] Detractors typically focus on such PK terminology as "men assuming their God-given role as head of the family" or "submission." They frequently cite African American pastor Tony Evans's injunction: "Sit down with your wife and say something like this: 'Honey, I've made a terrible mistake. I've given you my role. I gave up leading this family, and I forced you to take my place. Now, I must reclaim that role.' . . . I'm not suggesting you *ask* for your role back, I'm urging you to *take* it back."[7]

However, not all avowed feminists denounce PK. Joan Ryan, a "huge supporter of NOW," argues that NOW rejects wholesale a movement that benefits thousands of women because it fails to frame equality issues in ways

rhetorically congruent with NOW's upper-middle-class, independent, educated standards. She believes many women see PK as a true godsend, for PK
embraces values that feminist groups champion: nonviolence, fidelity, and
responsibility. Ryan concludes that, for each man who finds "new life" at a
PK rally, a woman's life similarly changes, because "the men's movement, if
that's what it is, is not just about men, any more than the women's movement has been just about women."[8]

But how do PK wives respond? After all, they would arguably suffer most
should their husbands negatively enact the rhetoric of "taking back" their
rightful leadership roles. Rather than indignantly protest their subjection,
PK wives generally support the movement. For example, Dr. LaRae Kemp
characterizes herself as "equally yoked together" (2 Cor. 6:14) with her husband—with "both in the yoke." She claims to be "not submissive at all,"
although in some cases her husband may make "the final decision." Kemp's
household is a "sanctuary" in which she can "spread [her] wings." Without
her husband's help with child care and housework, this physician and mother
of seven "cannot fulfill [her] womanly role and desires."[9] Kemp's appraisal
may be fairly representative; PK surveys indicate that among the top three
reasons men give for attending rallies is their wives' prodding.[10]

This chapter argues that the contrast between PK protesters' and supporters' perspectives highlights the difference between the concept of social status
and that of rhetorical status identified by Cal Logue and Eugene Miller;[11] these
two concepts will first be defined and contrasted. A discussion of evangelical
beliefs that offer alternative ways to reframe power issues follows. Finally, the
chapter concludes by arguing that a man's participation in PK may increase,
rather than decrease, his wife's rhetorical status within the home.

Data for this study come from printed reports and videotaped interviews
with PK adherents and their wives, from testimonials sent to the PK Internet
Web site, and from analysis of print media coverage of the movement.
Additional data derive from structured telephone interviews with twenty-
four PK wives: nineteen small-town Anglo women and five urban African
Americans.[12] All were associated in some way with the Free Methodist
Church, a denomination that ordains women. Additional information was
elicited through further interviews and e-mail follow-up questions.

Social Status and Rhetorical Status

Logue and Miller contrast two theoretical constructs: social status and
rhetorical status. Although both address the notion of relative standing
or position, social status indicates a generalized position within a social
system—a position not specifically tied to communication or to concrete
interactions. Those who apply the power perspective to gender relations are

struggling to free women from inferior or subjected positions within patriarchal or "phallo-centric" societies. Women are victims of inequitable institutions that reward men's activities and cooperate to keep females oppressed and dominated.[13] Consequently, "head of the household" connotes a negative hierarchical relationship in which a relatively powerless wife submits, willingly or not, to her husband's leadership. The PK movement becomes just another way to empower men and once again put women at a disadvantage, whether with benign intent or with malice.[14] Put simply, critics who hold this power perspective believe that the PK movement reinforces men's social status as "head" of the home, positionally "over" their wives in power. As such, PK goals are subversive: these men, associated with the Christian Right, aim to turn back the clock on decades of women's progress and return women to oppressed social statuses.

Jennifer Coburn exemplifies this view. In contrast to NOW, made up of both men and women, whose goal is "social and economic equity for women," she argues that PK participants see happy homes as sites wherein wives submit to their husbands' authority. Rather than *share* power—a value essential to NOW supporters—PK men, Coburn is convinced, want to *hoard* it.[15] Lee Cokorinos, editor of *Promise Keepers Watch*, shares Coburn's concern. Cokorinos commends NOW for raising alarms about this "well-financed organization" consisting of "angry white males" who promise to behave themselves when women submit to their demands.[16]

Not everyone defines power so hierarchically, however. Logue and Miller see rhetorical power or influence as an element of *ethos* or source credibility that interactants can negotiate and renegotiate within specific communicative contexts. Rhetorical status, in short, is a mediating phenomenon that links communicators, contexts, and outcomes in such a way that individual speakers *gain or lose efficacy in particular situations*. The concept involves a cognitive dimension—the communicator's beliefs regarding "how I stand" within a specific context, and how those beliefs empower or place her or him at a disadvantage within that context. That is, in different instances interactants position and reposition themselves relative to each other in light of salient qualities of self and others. Statuses may be congruent or incongruent, meaning that someone with higher rhetorical status or persuasiveness in one situation may rank lower in another.

To some extent one's social status does affect her or his rhetorical status. However, social status does not entirely shape rhetorical status, which is influenced by other factors, such as the topic or the goals of the communication. To illustrate, PK wives may actually have greater influence or "say" regarding decisions in some situations; correspondingly, the husband's opinion may weigh more heavily in others, depending on each individual's interest, expertise, knowledge, and the like.

Interpretation of ways in which PK couples negotiate power relationships may be enhanced by understanding a number of variables: the concept of power in the evangelical Christian context, notions of a Christian home, and definitions of the contested term, "submission." We now explore these concepts in turn.

Power in the Evangelical Christian Context

Evangelical Christians take the Bible as an authoritative source for issues of faith and practice.[17] Christianity's founder, Jesus of Nazareth, held standards for leaders that contrasted sharply with his contemporaries' views of power relationships. For instance, in response to his disciples' question, "Who is the greatest?" Jesus answered, "If any one would be first, he must be last of all and servant of all" (Mark 9:35). Shortly afterward, two disciples asked for seats of honor in Jesus' realm. Again, Jesus subverted his contemporaries' notions of power:

> You know that those who are supposed to rule over the Gentiles lord it over them, and their great men exercise authority over them. But it shall not be so among you; but whoever would be great among you must be your servant, and whoever would be first among you must be slave of all. For the Son of man also came not to be served but to serve, and to give his life as a ransom for many. (Mark 10:42–45)

Finally, when the disciples at the Last Supper quarreled over who would perform the lowliest servant's task of foot washing, Jesus took a towel and basin and performed the menial job, exemplifying the humility his followers should enact (John 13:1–17).

Within this broader context, PK wives in the study do not feel squelched, and they do not express the need to wrest power from tyrannical husbands. In fact, Holly Phillips argues that the potentially threatening term "submit" is not frightening, although it might be if a man were on a power trip; however, she concludes, "That's not what I get; that's not what Promise Keepers teaches."[18] Bill McCartney, appearing on *Larry King Live*, frames the issue in this way: "We're not talking about lording authority. We're talking about servanthood. There's a big difference there."[19]

Some outside observers of the movement agree. For example, Peggy Ruppe, a former NOW chapter board member, believes that "misguided" critics have misread PK's social goals. She argues, "In the Jesus model, you give up power; you're a servant-leader. It's a certain sacrificial form of leadership, but it's different from the worldview that power is a zero-sum game."[20]

In a seminar on servant-leadership, Dan Riemenschneider identifies a servant-leader as one who empowers others (Mark 9:35), shares power, position, and decision making (Mark 10:42–45), listens to others (Prov. 19:20), and puts their needs before her or his own (Phil. 2:3–8). This person leads through teamwork (Luke 9:10), a participatory problem-solving approach (Prov. 11:14), and listening to and learning from others (Prov. 13:10; Matt. 8:10). In short, the ideal servant-leader exercises power from an egalitarian position.[21]

Further, Tony Evans, who implored men to "take back" their rightful roles in the home, fleshes out his concept of a Christian husband in a thought-for-the-day calendar with the following entries:

January 10. A husband's giving of himself to his wife needs to take place every day in small as well as large ways, not just in rare heroic moments.

June 1. Men, you have authority in your home—no question about it. But your authority is limited to what you're supposed to do, not to whatever you want to do.

June 11. A Christian marriage partner has a frame of reference totally different from the world's values. Instead of saying, "This is what you should do for me," a Christian mate says, "Honey, what do you need?"[22]

"Leadership," consequently, is a contested term, and wives' definitions must be taken into account. In structured interviews, PK wives typically define the term "leader" within a context of respect and mutual influence, supporting the notion of rhetorical status that is negotiated contextually. For instance, some wives describe a leader as "a strong presence" who is "able to see weaknesses" and "step in" or "fill in." However, leaders "direct," "steer," and "motivate by example"—"without being overpowering." Moreover, leaders are "team players" who are "aware" of those they lead and "take their feelings into consideration." A few wives mentioned that leaders have "the final say"; yet they must "bear the responsibility" for their decisions.

Many wives give a more generalized definition of "leader" rather than link leadership to power within family relationships. They define a leader as one who "knows how to make a plan" and can determine "purposes and goals and the way they're achieved." Leaders decide "for the good of the whole group," which they assess by being "good listener[s]." Leaders "follow through" and complete necessary actions "without backing down." Leadership involves "more emphasis on the process" than on the leader's knowledge.

In short, the Christian Scriptures consistently support the notion of mutual caring and service within respectful relationships. For example, the Bible encourages husbands to be considerate fathers (Eph. 6:4) and to love their wives as Christ loved the church, giving his very life for it (Eph. 5:25–33). Evangelical feminists have been actively pointing out these concepts since the 1970s. Their reinterpretations of dominant readings of contested terms such as "submission" and "head" provide oppositional interpretive codes that allow Bible-believing women to define scriptural truths "within the intersections between female experience and scriptural texts."[23] Many PK wives seem to do just that.

The Context of a Christian Home

Ask an evangelical woman what she considers a "Christian" home, and she may respond with the metaphor of a triangle; the marriage relationship consists of a husband, a wife, and a third participant—God, who is over both partners. In a variation on the triangle metaphor, Phillips identifies God as her family's founder, her husband as chief executive officer, and her function as chief operating officer.[24] In addition, one woman defines the "head of the household" as "Christ," and the metaphor "head" is consistent with the biblical analogy of the church as Christ's body in which Jesus is the head who controls interdependent organs. Paul wrote,

> For just as the body is one and has many members, and all the members of the body, though many, are one body, so it is with Christ. . . . God arranged the organs in the body, each one of them, as he chose. If all were a single organ, where would the body be? . . . But God has so composed the body . . . that there may be no discord . . . but that the members may have the same care for one another. (1 Cor. 12:12–31)

In yet another metaphor, former coach Bill McCartney often uses a team analogy to describe family relationships.[25] Many PK wives similarly identify themselves as part of a team with the husband as coach of the family or with God as head coach and husband and wife as assistant coaches with approximately equal roles. No wife in the interview sample offered the hierarchical metaphor "chain of command" that a well-known seminar leader, Bill Gothard, commonly promoted during the early 1970s.

Although press accounts as well as Web site testimonials highlight dramatic turnaround accounts of families whose lives were transformed by the movement, data from interviewees reveal that most wives classified their pre-PK marriages as "very good," "satisfying," "secure," "solid," "compatible," or "spiritual."[26] Some mentioned "normal stresses." A few mates were poor husbands, fathers, or responsibility sharers. But while one respondent mentioned financial problems, only two marriages in the sample were about to break up.

Despite a majority of women who reported satisfactory pre-rally marriages, participation in a mass gathering had immediate behavioral consequences for PK men, most of whom were initially excited by their experiences. In the short term, husbands wanted to talk; in general, they were more attentive and thoughtful, more open and in tune to their marriages and to their children. Several were humbled, more considerate, and less impulsive. A few became better listeners. The experience of being with other men left many renewed, encouraged, optimistic, and challenged. One husband quit drinking and swearing; another vowed to deal with the family's financial problems. A third, who was at the point of leaving his family, expressed sorrow and vowed to change his behaviors. One committed his life to Christ for the first time. Three wives reported no immediate, dramatic change.

Wives also attributed initial attitudinal changes to PK involvement. Husbands came home with better attitudes: men were more positive, happier, nicer, more confident, forgiving, or compassionate. Several became more accountable to other men and to the church. One-fourth of the interviewees said they believed their husbands were more attuned to their wives' views, more helpful, more open, more equal. One husband expressed remorse at the pain he had caused his family.

Long-term effects were less dramatic. Women commonly mentioned increased involvement with others—especially with other men—which wives saw as positive. Indeed, PK participants often became more involved in church and spiritual matters, and half the wives interviewed noted long-term spiritual growth. Women also characterized their husbands overall as less selfish and more understanding; many became better husbands who were more helpful in the home and more serious about fathering roles. Character traits changed for the positive, and men became more disciplined or more humble as a result of their participation. However, three interviewees indicated no change—two because their marriages were already highly satisfactory. In short, when asked to assess the overall effect of PK, more than half of the interviewees used the word "positive" or a synonym. Two marriages were saved; one man became a PK leader.

The Context of Submission

Many objections to PK are situated in the term "submission." According to the *American Heritage Dictionary*, relevant denotative meanings of the term include "(a) the act of submitting to the power of another, (b) the state of having submitted, (c) the state of being submissive or compliant; meekness." The root term "submit" is defined as "(a) to yield or surrender (oneself) to the will or authority of another, (b) to commit (something) to the consideration or judgment of another, (c) to offer as a proposition or contention, (d) to give in to the authority, power, or desires of another, (e) to allow oneself to be subjected to something."[27] A thesaurus provides the following connotative associations: "surrender," "give up," "capitulate," "yield," "waive," "subordinate," "comply," "meekness," "subject to control," "dependent." While the denotative meaning of the word provides rhetorical space for a wife to argue or negotiate in favor of a proposition, most connotative meanings support the power relationship model inherent in the notion of social status.

The real issue, however, lies in the term's meaning in PK households. In short, if the wife must always submit, the husband has, by definition, higher social or positional status within the home. But if decisions are negotiable, depending on the topic and situation, rhetorical status contextually shifts from husband to wife, wife to husband.

PK wives answered the question, "How do you define submission?" in a variety of ways. Some used a spiritual definition such as "obedience to Christ and the spirit of God" or "letting God take control"; one saw submission as "a version of obedience to God." Others defined the term more neutrally. Those who submit are "following the leadership," "agreeing with another," "letting go," or "surrendering" their will—"but not being subordinant [sic] or a doormat." Such a one is flexible and "able and willing to meet other's needs without compromising" personal standards. One wife identified submission as "having an unconditional love for someone and sticking with them [sic] no matter what."

Many interviewees defined the term in a way congruent with an argumentation context. Their responses illustrate the notion of mutual influence and decision-making power; that is, although wives sometimes yield, so do husbands, and both have a "say" in decision making. To these women, a submissive person "respects authority figures" but "voices opinions and is heard"; one who submits is "willing to listen to the other's views and viewpoint." Respect is vital, especially during disagreements. Then, the couple should "work through" the issue, and in case of an impasse, "the husband should have the decision; however, a man should listen to his wife's point of view" and take "into consideration the wife's needs" in a spirit of "respect and love for [her]." One woman said, "It's OK with not always getting your way if you are open to discussion."

Several women felt that submission is "really more of a partnership" or "a teamwork thing" that must be "learned by both husband and wife" as they make "joint decisions" wherein "a husband can give authority to his wife as well." And God can become involved; one wife, "after weighing things together with her husband, immediately asks the Lord to direct." Another couple sometimes have a "debate or spiritual conference" in order to make decisions.

Finally, some women's definitions comprised mainly words that supported the negative connotation of the term "submission." Those who submit are "willing to let go of what they want." These individuals "submit negative behavior," yield to another's authority, relinquish "individual control over to someone else," give way, and "sacrifice things." To submit is "to lay aside one's own power or will for the sake of another's will or decision." It involves a willingness to follow and to "give in on other views to make harmony in the relationship." Submission is "the other half of the 'head of the household' equation" in which one is "under the authority of someone else."

These answers indicate the dialectical tension between legitimate denotative meanings for the word "submit" that include both giving in and arguing one's own position. Most interviewees recognized that submit means to yield, but a majority also stressed the importance of voicing opinions, and many emphatically disavowed the doormat metaphor. In many ways, Griffith argues that evangelical women subvert the notion of submission: "Once I began to understand what they meant by 'submission' and how they went about subverting that doctrine, I began to see they're not just passively accepting. They really find ways to get their husbands to do what they want."[28] The notion of joint decisions, of husbands who yield as well as wives, supports Logue and Miller's concept of a rhetorical status that varies situationally; this demonstrates that, at least in some PK households, couples negotiate power contextually.[29]

Discussion

The movement known as Promise Keepers arouses controversy about power relationships within Promise Keeper households. Those who should suffer most from the determination of males to retake the authority in their homes are the wives. But no wife in this study identified her returning husband's behaviors as oppressive and abusive, even though Cokorinos's *Promise Keepers Watch* organization claims to have spoken with thousands of people from various regions, including PK wives, who are "terribly concerned about this dangerous movement."[30] In contrast, all but two interviewees said they would encourage their husbands to attend another rally. (One said, "If he wanted to," and another said, "I don't know.") Overall, the majority of women involved viewed the movement positively. A number credited PK with saving their marriages, but more commonly, good marriages were strengthened as husbands focused on their responsibilities as husbands and fathers.

Logue and Miller's concept of *rhetorical status* offers a theory for interpreting the power relationships negotiated within PK households.[31] That is, when a husband returns from a rally determined to listen to his wife and serve her and other family members, a PK adherent may, in fact, strengthen his wife's rhetorical status within the context of her home and her marriage. True, within the evangelical Christian context of servant leadership, many wives yield power—but often to men who have listened to their concerns and considered the needs of the family within a specific situation. Further, submission is not *necessarily* one-sided, and husbands' and wives' rhetorical status varies contextually; sometimes the woman's opinions and ideas prevail; at other times the husband "wins" the argument. In addition, the concept of a Christian marriage commonly includes God as a third partner. And God participates in decision making; for instance, one wife called a "spiritual conference" as a way to resolve an impasse; another weighed matters with her husband, then asked God to direct the couple's deliberations. Apparently, God does not automatically side with men.

The contested terms "submission" and "leadership" continued to create questions about the movement's overall motives, and tension was present in a number of wives' definitions. However, issues of power relations were found to be more complex than Cokorinos's view of the angry white male, willing to trade good behavior for domination within his home. Logue and Miller's concept of rhetorical status provides a more satisfying means of acknowledging the complexity of power relations. If power is not a zero-sum game, interactants in an ongoing relationship can negotiate and renegotiate winning and losing contextually, a scenario that appeared to work itself out in many PK households.

Further research is needed to identify power distribution within Promise Keepers' homes. This chapter relied on data from print media accounts, from PK materials, and from structured interviews with PK wives. Additional research is necessary to determine how Promise Keepers and their wives enact contested rhetorical terms such as "leadership" and "submission" in specific contexts within their homes.

12

Wives, Daughters, Mothers, and Sisters as Kept Women

Lauren F. Winner

arah Peterson[1] met with a lawyer about filing for divorce. She has not decided if she will take this final drastic step. "Divorce, you know, is not supposed to be an option for Christians," she says ruefully.[2] Since she was a small girl, Sarah believed marriage was the path to a "fulfilled and fulfilling" life. This belief has helped her keep the marriage vows she exchanged with Steve for almost twenty years, through times of financial hardship, moments when she thought they were no longer in love with each other, the move that took her a thousand miles away from her parents and sister so that Steve could accept a new job. But she does not see how they will get through the change that has occurred in the marriage in the past year or so, since Steve first attended a Promise Keepers (PK) rally.

It is not that Sarah minds Steve's growing commitment to Christianity. On the contrary, she welcomes it. Sarah has always been a churchgoer, and she is thankful that she no longer has to "sit alone in the pew" on Sunday mornings. What she cannot countenance, however, is Steve's new assertiveness in the family. Sarah has never considered herself a feminist. In fact, she thinks most feminists are strident, bitter women who have placed their careers above all else. But you do not have to be a feminist, Sarah huffily declares, to want to have "some say-so in what happens in your own house." The first time Steve wanted to plan the meals for the week—which Sarah does a month in advance, posting a laminated menu-for-the-week on the refrigerator door—Sarah was amused and happy to have one less chore. But now she does not think Jesus intended for husbands to have final authority on all matters in the home, from menus and car pools to vacations and the household budget. Sarah wonders if this is really how PK leaders intended their message to come across; she thinks Steve might have "taken the whole thing to an extreme."[3]

An article about PK in *Time* magazine declared that the wives of PK participants are a happy bunch, thrilled to a woman with their husbands' participation in the all-male evangelical group. According to the article, the wives credit PK with making their husbands more responsible in all areas of life—they are better fathers for their participation in PK, more willing to do the laundry, more willing to act as spiritual heads of their families.[4] Disclosures about the travails of Lyndi McCartney—wife of PK founder Bill McCartney—seem not to have tarnished the commonly held view that the wives of PK participants are a satisfied lot. Mrs. McCartney's months of depression and eating disorders and her claim that, all his lip service to the contrary, her husband did not make his own family a priority but sacrificed it to the movement, have not encouraged reporters or scholars to delve further into the lives and feelings of the wives or daughters of PK adherents.[5]

A number of oral history interviews with "PK women"—the wives, daughters, mothers, and sisters of PK participants—reveal a different story: many of the female relatives of PK men are extremely dissatisfied with their husbands', fathers', sons', and brothers' participation in the group. Spanning the spectrum from evangelical wives, who are devotees of parallel Christian groups such as Praise Keepers, to teenage daughters who are dipping their toes into feminist theory and activism for the first time, many women are at best ambivalent about how their husbands' and fathers' involvement in PK is changing their families. That PK is having an impact on at least some of the men who attend PK rallies is clear; what impact PK is having on the women in these men's lives is an equally important subject. When we listen to the voices of the women themselves, it becomes clear that, contrary to the picture presented in the media, many "Promise Keeper women" see their marriages, families, and lives as being worse for their men's involvement in PK.

PK, of course, bills itself as a movement that is good for families. In addition to Tony Evans's much ballyhooed directive that men "take back" their roles as heads of their families from their wives, PK offers men plenty of advice about how better to serve their families.[6] John Yutes advises his readers to pray every night before going to sleep with their wives.[7] McCartney's children offer readers testimonials that are models of unwavering filial devotion.[8] The McCartneys "appeal" to their readers to "consider your wife as your teammate, not just someone to protect, direct, and lead, but also as someone who can help you."[9]

The McCartneys' instructions that a man consider his wife both as a "teammate" and as a person to "protect, direct, and lead" appear somewhat contradictory. While many men may have embraced the teammate metaphor, a number of husbands, fathers, sons, and brothers have focused instead on the injunction to direct and lead. A text may appear to say one thing, but different readers will understand that one text in wildly different ways. Readers, after all, are engaged in an active process, and their interpretation of a given book or passage may differ radically from what another reader might assume is the author's intended message. What is important, therefore, is not what McCartney intends his audience to take away from his preaching, but what his audience in fact takes away. If the McCartneys hope for marriages in which husband and wife work together as a team, they may be disappointed because many wives of PK participants attest that the reality in their homes is far from that ideal.

If PK writings are geared toward men, many women read them nonetheless, if for no other reason than to gain some familiarity with the organization that has suddenly become so important to the men in their lives. Not surprisingly, women often have a different take from that of men on PK literature. One twenty-year-old student at Princeton University, whose father had recently become a Promise Keeper, read *Seven Promises of a Promise Keeper*[10] and was particularly struck by Evans's insistence that men "take back" their role in the family. "Of course, there's no way he realized the irony," said June. "He's probably completely in the dark that those words 'take back' have been some of the most powerful, resonant words for young feminists in the past decade." June was referring to the Take Back the Night marches and speak-outs, held annually on college campuses throughout the country, where women are encouraged to reclaim the night as a time when women should feel safe to walk outside without male protection, and where survivors of sexual assault and other violence tell their stories publicly. "I pointed it out to my dad, you know, that his daughter had been organizing a very different type of taking back during her two years at college, a type of taking back that is clearly at odds with the type of taking back Promise Keepers is trying to bring about."[11]

II.

Candyce Wentford haunts used bookstores in her North Carolina hometown. She has gradually traded in all of her Sweet Valley High romances, which she claims to have read only through sixth grade, and acquired a bookcase full of books that any college women's studies major would envy: Shulamith Firestone, Naomi Wolf, Alice Walker, Alix Kates Shulman, Betty Friedan, Mary Daly, Audre Lorde, Adrienne Rich, Simone de Beauvoir. No, she hasn't read them all yet, she confessed. "But," she added defensively, "as Walter Benjamin wrote when someone asked him if he had read all the books he owned, he replied, 'No, but do you eat off your Limoges china every day?'" She is precocious for a fifteen-year-old, even if she did mispronounce Benjamin and Limoges. Friedan was "what really got to" Candyce. "There were all these women who'd had these great educations and then they just gave them up to go take care of babies." She was particularly struck by Friedan's account of the junior at a southern university who was passionate about her bacteriology studies during her first two years of college, but then switched her major to home economics because she realized she "shouldn't be that serious. I'll go home and work in a department store until I get married."[12] That passage "just really got to me," explained Candyce. "I just thought that is outrageous."

Enter Candyce's father, who had always supported her doing "basically whatever I wanted—sports, dance, [church] youth group, school. Both my parents always insisted that my sister and brother and I keep a B average, but as long as our activities didn't interfere with that or church, they were happy for us to do whatever we wanted." Candyce had planned to attend an academic summer camp for gifted students the summer before tenth grade. "We had picked out the course and everything. I was going to take a course on Thoreau." Shortly after her father became a Promise Keeper, however, he decided that Candyce could not go. "I was, like, what do you mean I can't go? My parents are pretty easygoing people. They've never, like, not let me do something before, really." The screaming and door-slamming in Candyce's house after her father decided she could not go to camp lasted for weeks, Candyce screaming that she hated him and that he was being unfair, her father insisting that this was the decision he had made and "that was that. How dare I speak back to him? Didn't I know it was one of the Ten Commandments to honor thy father? That sort of thing."

Candyce believed that her father would never have forbidden her to go to camp if he had not gone to a PK meeting. He returned from the meeting, Candyce said, "all fired up about spending more time with us—that was good, because he does work a lot. Although, now, it's like, I don't think I want to spend time with this person." Spending more time with the family was not the only bee in her father's bonnet. Shortly after returning from the meeting, he suggested to Candyce's mother that she could quit working if she wanted to. "We had enough money," said Candyce's mother, Rena. "And Joe really seemed to think that the kids needed us home more, both of us. To me it seemed a little like closing the barn door after the horse was already well out, since they're all in high school, practically grown. If we were suddenly going to effect a major change in terms of being home after school, it would have made more sense to do it ten years ago, when they were home after school, instead of slumming with their friends at tennis practice. Plus, I like working. Joe knows that. But he seems to have forgotten," added Rena, who is not alone in managing the demands of children with a full-time job: at least half of U.S. women with children under age three work outside the home for pay, and more than two-thirds of those with children under age eighteen.[13]

Why did her father insist that Candyce could not attend the summer camp of her choice? "The camp runs all sorts of research at the same time as it's a camp," Candyce explained to me. "And one of the things they're really interested in is girls' education and self-confidence," she said, breezily waving in the direction of the Carol Gilligan books on her shelf. "They are really interested in finding out how to increase girls' self-confidence about learning, speaking up in class, doing math, all that sort of stuff." Nothing terribly revolutionary, said Candyce, but the research into girls' confidence and learning patterns disturbed her father. "He said he thought I had just about enough self-confidence for any girl, and he wasn't going to pay good money to send me to a camp that was going to turn me into some sort of bossy, assertive girl who wouldn't be able to attract any men to date or marry and then, if I did, I wouldn't know how to be a good wife to them because I'd be too busy being self-confident and working algebra problems."[14]

If Candyce's father can cite Scripture, so can Raphael Morgan's mother, Anne. She, too, draws on Exodus 20:12. Rafe had attended a Christian college and then went on to become a certified actuary. He had always been a "church-going family man," and he attended a PK rally more out of curiosity than because he thought he had much to learn. "I knew they preached about responsibility," Rafe told me, "and I figured I already lived a pretty responsible life—held a steady job with a good income, loved my family, never cheated on my wife, had dinner with my mother once a week, the whole nine yards." But what Rafe heard at the PK rally he attended in Texas made him realize he had not been quite so responsible after all. "I'd been letting things slip," he drawled. "I'd especially been letting things slip with Mama. I hadn't taken over after Daddy died like I needed to, like she needed me to. I left her alone too much, expected she could pick up all the pieces, not only emotionally, but also that she could handle things that Daddy always handled, like the money." It was with the money that Rafe began, first urging his mother to let him look over her bookkeeping, and then talking to his cousin, an attorney, about "getting everything signed over to me, so that I could manage it. It just wasn't something Mama should have to handle."[15]

But Rafe's initial assumption—that his father had taken care of all the money and that his mother now saw it as a burden—was incorrect. For the last twenty years of the elder Morgans' marriage, Anne had handled all the investments, paid all the bills, and kept track of all the money. "Of course, I consulted Bill, but I always enjoyed taking care of accounts. It was a challenge, and it gave me something to do once the kids were in school. Kind of like these women who start new jobs when their kids are grown, except, in my case, instead of waking up in the morning and being excited to hop in the car and go to the office, I couldn't wait to read over the *Wall Street Journal* during breakfast." Anne resented her son's assuming he could—and should—take over her affairs for her. "There's an irony there, you know. I never would have thought of Rafe as inattentive, not until he pointed out that he was—but I didn't think he was inattentive because he was failing to manage my money. I thought he was inattentive because in almost two and a half decades he apparently never noticed that I was handling them just fine, and quite happily, on my own." Frankly, she added, if anyone should be managing anyone else's financial affairs, it should be Anne looking after her son, not the other way around. "I reckon I've made twice as much money on the stock market this year as Rafe. He's a little too conservative with his investments."[16]

The commandment to honor thy father and mother is not the only biblical verse that Christians with whom I have spoken have noted in articulating their feelings about male relatives who have become involved in PK. One woman, whose brother rededicated his life to Christ at a PK rally, opened our conversation by talking about 2 Samuel 13:1–22. She and her brother had barely spoken since he became involved in PK. "He was here for dinner a few nights after the rally. Naturally, I was overjoyed at first," Marie said. She had been praying for years that her brother would come into a fuller relationship with Christ. "And he said very touchingly how he felt called not only to be more involved with his wife and kids, but also with me, especially since I'm not married. I thought that was touching." Then Marie's brother said something to her that she thought was not moving, but outlandish. "He began talking about how in the absence of a father or husband, I should really rely on him as I would a husband, that he could guide me in the same ways as our [deceased] father would have until I got remarried." The Bible, Marie's brother explained, was full of examples about how sisters needed to listen to their brothers. Miriam, he said, would never have been stricken with leprosy if she had refrained from gossiping about Moses. "Then he said that Tamar would not have had to suffer the humility of being raped if she had just submitted to Amnon's wishes. I couldn't believe he said that. I asked him if he was serious, and he said, 'Well, absolutely, of course I'm serious. It's right there in Scripture,' and I told him that was nowhere in any Bible I'd ever read and asked him to leave the table."[17]

III.

"I just had to laugh," Sheryl Kelley, an African American Charlestonian, said to me, "when all that stuff about Bill McCartney's wife came out. I mean, I know I shouldn't laugh, and I don't wish bulimia on anybody, but really, here's the man who's preaching to all these men to be better fathers and better husbands and he didn't notice that his own wife had been throwing up everything she ate for a year? I mean, really."[18] Sheryl does not like to see anyone suffer a misfortune like Lyndi McCartney's eating disorder. But "part of me in fact is a little glad it happened," Sheryl went on, "because when all that came out, that was when Bob took a step back and said, 'Wait a minute, maybe I should be thinking about this all a little more critically.'" Sheryl's husband, Bob, had attended his first PK rally in Colorado when he was there visiting friends and taking in some of the great outdoors, and he was hooked.[19]

Lyndi McCartney is not the only female relative of a Promise Keeper to develop an eating disorder. Geraldine Bransen, the daughter of a PK adherent in the Boston area, was recently released from a clinic that specializes in treating anorexia nervosa. Anorexia, as experts have long known, is about control. It is perhaps then no surprise that a young woman who felt herself suddenly deprived of what little control she had exerted over her own life would begin to starve herself. "Sometimes I wonder how much of this is true and how much just got fed to me by my doctors—no pun intended," Geraldine joked as she swished her long corn-silk blonde hair. "But, you know, when Dad came back from those [Promise Keeper] meetings and started insinuating himself into every arena of my life—look, I know I'm a teenager, and this is what teenagers do, they think their parents are everywhere when they should be nowhere, but this was just out of hand. He really started trying to make every decision for everyone in our house. He made me get up for a newly instituted family prayer at 6:30 every morning. Saying that now, it doesn't sound like much, but it sure felt like a lot at the time," Geraldine said ruefully. Her father also imposed a stricter curfew on Geraldine, and told her she could no longer car-date or go to movies unless he had seen them first. "But he couldn't make me eat. He could make me do the dishes, but he couldn't make me eat." Like Bill McCartney, Geraldine's father had little idea that his daughter was slowly wasting away. Her mother finally took her to the doctor.[20]

It is perhaps not surprising that many secular women are dismayed at their husbands' and fathers' newfound religious commitments. But not a few Christian women are dismayed by their husbands' involvement in PK. Evangelical women have not embraced PK uncritically. One telling letter to the editor of *Christianity Today*, the nation's largest and most influential evangelical magazine, expressed the feelings of one woman:

> I read *Seven Promises of a Promise Keeper*. I told myself I would remember it was a man's book and that I would be objective. I prayed I would have an open mind. I hadn't gone 20 pages until I thought, these men are being led to believe they are "saviors," and by 50 pages I was convinced. I am not a radical feminist or a member of NOW. I am a retired military wife, and we worshiped in an army chapel. We always treasured our worship there. When Promise Keepers came in we couldn't accept their theology, felt uncomfortable, and left. If the

church we now worship in is invaded by Promise Keepers, we will again depart.[21]

"I feel like it is dangerously close to reversing many hard-won gains, although not that I am a feminist," said one woman, who considers herself an evangelical Episcopalian, and whose brother is involved in PK.[22] She is hesitant to pass judgment because "of course, I haven't been to one of the meetings. So I know that I am relying, yes, on what my brother says, but also on the caricatures of a secular media." Nonetheless, this woman is concerned because of the subtle changes she has noticed in her brother over the last year. "And there undeniably are changes. If there were no changes, the movement would be a failure." In particular, she is worried about her brother's new emphasis on socializing with men, "and with men only. You know, I lived in England when I was younger for a year, and it very much reminds me of England, very homosocial, if you know what I mean, men always hanging out with men and women with women. I'm about expecting my brother to insist that after a family dinner, the women retire with cordials to the drawing room while the men drink whiskey and smoke cigars."[23]

A Christian Rhode Island woman, whose son and husband attended their first PK rally together, is equally concerned. "I don't see that what they're doing comes from Scripture. On the other hand, it is hard for me to see that so many people could be coming to Christ if God's hand wasn't in it. But Bill McCartney isn't talking about the things Jesus talked about. Jesus didn't talk about any of this stuff. I don't see that they're talking about love."[24] Josie Marsh, finally frustrated with her husband's insistence that she "accept her role," screamed, "Did you miss Mary and Martha? Jesus told her to get out of the kitchen, and come sanctify herself at his feet. He told her Mary had made the better choice. Tell me where that is in these sermons you're hearing."[25]

Evangelicals have never lacked templates for reading the Bible. The day when the Ryrie and Scofield Bibles were the only glosses available to evangelicals is long past. Today, study Bibles proliferate; the Bible shopper could likely locate a study Bible geared toward almost any set of concerns. There are several Bibles with commentaries specifically aimed at women, and the commentaries offered by these Bibles often have a profound effect on how women interpret Scripture, especially in regard to the highly contentious passages written by Paul that discuss male "headship" and wifely submission. Among the women I spoke to, not a few had been influenced by these biblical commentaries, so much so that the commentaries often formed the basis for their critiques of PK. Liz Abbot, who pulled her *Study Bible for Women* off her desk and flipped through it as we spoke, said, "You know, there's a lot of truth in that old saying 'The devil can quote scripture.' That means, we know that you could take a piece of scripture out of context and find something to support almost any position you wanted to make. And that, of course, is what a lot of people do with these passages in Paul about male headship." But the *Study Bible for Women* includes the essay "Men and Women in Relationship," which explains that

> often some aspects of a biblical perspective have been stressed . . . whilst others have been ignored. Or writers have engaged in a "renaming" process, whereby words are used but not in a biblical way. One clear instance of this is the way that the word "complementarity" has often been misused. Rather than meaning the mutual acceptance and endorsement of woman and man, it has been used to evoke the idea of male dominance and female submission. Similarly, the terms "equal but different" have often been twisted to mean "unequal and hierarchical."[26]

Said Liz, "It just strikes me as dishonest—deceptive—for Promise Keepers to ignore interpretations like this, to pretend they don't exist. I mean, this book is published by Baker, for goodness sakes! It's not exactly radical feminist!"[27]

African American Christian women with whom I have spoken often feel uncomfortable with their husbands' participation in PK for a different reason. Despite PK's vocal denunciation of racism, these women, members of historically black denominations, believe that their husbands and brothers have betrayed the African American community by devoting so much energy to PK. "If anyone needs to be told to take his responsibilities seriously," Lisa Marcus told me, "it is the black man. There is no question of that. But if they are doing all that responsibility taking outside the community, then it's only going to help that one man; it's not going to help the community."[28] Another woman cautioned, "I hardly wish my husband had participated in the Million Man March instead of Stand in the Gap; I just wish he had participated in neither. All this time he's devoting to Promise Keepers, he ought to be devoting it to our home church." Rebecca Wright, whose brother is an avid PK participant, put it bluntly: "These white folks don't understand what it means for a black man to take responsibility. Part of a black man taking responsibility is not going and getting indoctrinated by a bunch of white preachers. [African Methodist Episcopal Church founder] Richard Allen is rolling in his grave."[29]

Many black women are suspicious of what they see as mere pretenses to eradicating racism in the PK ranks. "Of course, they always . . . feature a black speaker at their meetings," said one Carolina woman to me, "but obviously they have to do that. I'm wary of it. Which wasn't helped any by that letter in CT." The letter in question, written by a professor at Trinity

Graduate School, California,[30] was in response to *Christianity Today's* November 17, 1997, story on PK, "Will the Walls Fall Down?" "Although I support Promise Keepers and its mission," declared the professor, "I am unclear what the group means when its leaders call for repentance for racism." If by this, McCartney and others merely mean that individual PK members who "have harbored racist thoughts or engaged in racist behavior ought to repent," the letter went on, "that seems right. However, if they are calling for all members of PK to repent for racism, as if the guilt of some were imputed to all, that cannot be right, since clearly not all men (including both whites and blacks) who attend PK Rallies are racists . . . PK should not be PC." To my interlocutor, this PK supporter had plainly missed the point, and PK may have missed the point as well: "If all they're talking about is an individual man having a racist thought, then their call for racial reconciliation doesn't really mean very much, does it? Who would disagree with that? I mean, that is hardly some great challenge." Bill McCartney's recent impassioned pledges that "racism within the church will have been eradicated" by the year 2000 have not impressed her.[31] "What is needed is, of course, a call to alter the structure of society in a way befitting the message of Jesus—Jesus, who, as the Bible reminds us, was no respecter of persons. But, somehow," this woman said caustically, "I don't think we should hold our breath waiting for such a challenge to come from the ranks of Promise Keepers."[32]

IV.

There are, to be sure, many wives, daughters, sisters, and mothers of PK adherents who believe that their family life has improved noticeably since their husbands, fathers, brothers, and sons dedicated or rededicated their lives to Christ at the urgings of Bill McCartney. These satisfied women include those whose husbands have heard a radically different message from that of Joe Wentford and Steve Peterson. Kimberly, for example, says her husband has become notably less authoritarian since pledging himself to PK. "I believe he has a new respect for me," Kimberly says, "and not an I-respect-you-when-you-stay-in-your-place kind of respect either. We had been battling for months over whether I could go back to school." Kimberly, who had dropped out of college after two years to get married, had always intended to return to school to finish her B.A., but in the last five years, once her youngest child had entered pre-school, she began investigating her educational options seriously—collecting the catalogues of the local community college and the nearest branch of the state university, locating and talking to other women who had made the same choice in their thirties. "But my husband really felt it wasn't feasible. He wasn't really willing to explore the options with me, though—he just said it wasn't feasible and then dropped the subject." After he attended a PK rally and began attending church, he "became really supportive of the idea. He said that he believed he'd been failing in his duties as a husband, that one of his duties was to help his wife grow and develop as a person, and that he hadn't really been supporting that." At the time I interviewed her, Kimberly was in her second year of full-time college study; she expected to receive her B.A. in anthropology from the University of Wisconsin in the spring of 1998.[33]

Lynn Stuart, whose husband had been coercing her to have sex with him when she did not want to, says she gives thanks to God for PK every day; her husband, Mike, came home from a Promise Keeper rally and burst into tears. "I realize I had only been reading half the verse," he told his wife. "I hadn't been reading the whole verse." Mike was referring to 1 Corinthians 7:4 (NRSV): "For the wife does not have authority over her own body, but the husband does; likewise the husband does not have authority over his own body, but the wife does."[34]

But many wives do not share Kimberly's and Lynn's positive experiences. When pressed, women critical of PK differ as to what exactly they think is wrong with the organization: some, sounding like the NOW declaration about PK that proclaimed the organization to be the "greatest danger to women's rights," believe that PK is, in the words of one woman whose brother is a Promise Keeper, "rotten to the core."[35] The very idea of PK is, as Candyce claimed in the somewhat purple prose of a teenager, "to reassert the patriarchy. They just clothe it in all this language about happy families to make women buy it." Other women think the exact opposite is true: the essence of PK is a valuable good. The movement seeks to make men more responsible, and women, especially poor women who see a stable marriage as their bedrock of economic security, think that anything that does that deserves plaudits.[36] "But they're going about it in such an old-fashioned— such a misguided, wrong way," said one exasperated New York woman, whose husband is a Promise Keepers devotee. She explained, "If the movement made men come home and do the dishes or take their kids off their wives' hands one night a week so she could go out with some friends or something, then that would be something altogether different."[37]

13

A Womanist/Feminist Lives
with a Promise Keeper and Likes It

Valerie Bridgeman Davis

O n the morning of October 3, 1997, I sat in my car in the church parking lot as we loaded the luggage into the trunk for men who would
join my husband-pastor for Promise Keepers' Stand in the Gap meeting in Washington, D.C. A man who had come to Austin from Houston to
fly out with them said to me, "Well, you know, if he's a Promise Keeper, then
you're a promise reaper." "I know," I said and smiled. What he had said was
true. In the years since my husband attended his first PK stadium event in
Dallas, he has become more sensitive, more proactive as a father and husband, even more supportive of my goals and needs than he had already been,
and more of a feminist. I love it.

As a professor of religion and an avowed and long-standing womanist/
feminist, I have some of the same suspicions and concerns that most feminists
would have toward Promise Keepers, given the rhetoric of the movement.
But at a critical time in our nineteen-year marriage, PK was there, teaching
my husband to look at his passivity in the relationship and his own culpa-
bility in its problems, and to share his emotions and concerns from his heart,
historically a very unmanly thing to do, especially for an African American
man. In this chapter, I explore in an autobiographical and critical way the
questions and concerns, and the gifts and surprises, that the Promise Keepers
movement has brought into our lives.

My husband, Don, and I met at a church musical in 1978. By June of
1979 we were married and on our way to a rocky first half of married life. It
was clear that my husband, who grew up in a large family of ten siblings, six
of whom were boys, and both parents, had some definite ideas about what
a woman should be. They did not mesh with those I brought into the
relationship, with my strong background of woman-identified living, a semi-
single mom (my father was out of the home until I was much older), three
sisters, a grandmother next door, and a "big mama" in Miss Essie up the hill.
Miss Essie was my grandmother's best friend and a surrogate grandmother to

us. I lived in female culture and absorbed their strength and values without even realizing it.

My mother taught us from a very early age not to depend on a man for anything. She drummed into us that we were to be independent, to take care of ourselves financially, and to have a wide array of interests and emotional support systems. We were never to find ourselves subservient to a man or his needs. All our male–female relationships were to be mutual, equal, and strictly voluntary. One of my most vivid memories of exchanges between my parents was a retort from my mother when my father quoted a biblical text from 1 Peter 3:5–6 (NIV): "For this is the way the holy women of the past who put their hope in God used to make themselves beautiful. They were submissive to their own husbands, like Sarah, who obeyed Abraham and called him her master." My mother said in a low and steady, but emphatic tone, "Well, you're not Abraham, I'm not Sarah, and these are not Abraham's times." My mother ended the debate about submission for me long before I knew what a feminist was.

So, when I married in 1979, I rejected rhetoric about submission even though I had no clue what a feminist or womanist was. And my husband, either intuitively or from his own background, never used such language with me. Still, he is an evangelical, and so am I. So biblical wording and visions of family and relationship were and are important to us.

We got married during my freshman year of college at Alabama State University, and my husband was in the air force at the time, stationed at Gunter Air Field in Montgomery. During that year, I got pregnant with my first child and was told by the counselor at Planned Parenthood that I could have an abortion without my husband's knowledge, but I rejected that option. My pregnancy meant that I had to sit out from classes for the summer quarter. In the meantime, the air force moved my husband to Texas, which meant, if I was to go with him, I would have to delay my education longer. There seemed no question in my husband's mind about what I would do. Of course I would follow my husband and "submit" to his career goals. At the time, I did not realize how much I resented that expectation from everyone, including myself. But I did go with him to Texas, and it took me three years to get back to my education. It had been my mother's greatest fear when I got married, and subsequently became pregnant, that I would not finish my education, and that I would be stuck in the shadow of a man, needy and without skills.

In January 1984, I returned to my education at Trinity University in San Antonio, and I discovered professor Paula Cooey and feminist thought. That semester I read *The Color Purple*, *Woman Warrior*, *The Bluest Eye*, and several articles by Mary Daly, Elisabeth Schüssler Fiorenza, Audre Lorde, Alice Walker, and many, many more feminists. Reading the work of powerful women who owned their power and named the pain and violence against women resonated within me. Each writer gave me a different piece, but the largest piece was a "Yeah!" feeling that connected the dots of my feeling alienated through the years of being a tomboy with a big, deep voice. I began to think about how often my mother had said, "You should have been a boy," mainly because I hated to "girly" up my hair, or because I wanted to wear slacks all the time in order to be ready for the pick-up flag football game with the boys. Those writings reminded me that I often bought into the cultural norms for a woman, what a woman should "naturally" like, such as cooking, even though those were things I "naturally" disliked. They reminded me that I often hid my gifts, talents, and powerful presence to avoid intimidating men. I was confronted with how often my life was a lie simply because I was not being me. It was not one thing that any of the writers said, but a gathering body of belonging that made me really think about the world in which I lived, including my internal self. I felt as if the world opened up and suddenly someone was putting into words what I had always known. Dr. Cooey called it conscientization. I called it coming home to myself. My husband called it drifting from God.

As an evangelical, I had never examined the Christian tradition to which I was and am wed, nor had I ever looked at the sacred texts of Christianity with anything but pure acceptance. The feminist/womanist call to a hermeneutic of suspicion—the feminist insistence that I see misogyny at worst and neglect at best in the way the dominant (read, male) culture experiences women—had never been within the range of my thinking. Although I have always been inquisitive, I had never questioned Scripture or the God of the Bible. As an evangelical, I had come to believe that there was something called an objective reality that all people could know at the same time. The more I put my experience of Scripture up against my husband's or other men's, or even other women's, I began to understand the power of one's personal history, and the truth that we can see only from the vantage point at which we stand. The more I became an evangelical womanist, the more willing I was to challenge the conventional, and to trust my own intuition. Prior to owning up to being a womanist, I had taken the dominant interpretation of my history and of the texts uncritically, something feminism and womanism expressly warn against. During the final years in college, however, I became a ruthless questioner of every culture in which I lived, including and especially the church and Christian culture.

My questioning led me to many crises of faith. I began to identify myself as a feminist. When I began to call myself a "woman-identified" woman, that is, seeing the world and issues first and foremost from how they affect women and their lives, my evangelical status became suspect. I found myself between two worlds—not radical enough to be accepted by many of the feminists I knew, too far gone to be considered evangelical or even Christian by some of my colleagues. But I was struggling to find the ground on which I could stand, a ground made solid by a belief in a God of justice who defends widows and orphans and who accepts gladly back from all God's creation the gifts so graciously bestowed.

By 1990 I had switched from identifying myself as a feminist to identifying as a womanist so that I could be identified as a woman of color who seeks survival and quality of life for all people, but especially for the groups that have historically been marginalized, especially women and children. The term "womanist" became popular and the accepted coinage for women of color (womanist is to feminist as purple is to lavender). The term had been adopted from Alice Walker, and her definition in her collection of essays, *In Search of Our Mothers' Gardens*, became the standard by which people judged themselves a womanist. Alice Walker and her work became a conversation partner for me. I began to ask some of her questions of myself. How could I continue to hold allegiance to a God who sanctioned the murder of women and children (a theme that plays several times in the Hebrew Scriptures)? How could I continue to be a member in an institution such as the church where misogyny and racism threatened to annihilate my womanself? How could I continue to proclaim the gospel of Jesus Christ? I had been a lay preacher since 1977 before I married my husband. I was a member of the Church of God movement; my call was not a problem since that tradition of Christianity has always had women preachers. But since I found myself examining my faith so rigorously, I did not know whether I could in good faith keep preaching. A friend once said he alternated between being a passionate Christian and a profound atheist or pagan. I understand that statement because in the years that formed me into a womanist, I experienced those extremes in my being, even as I continued to try to function as a "good little Christian."

I do not want to suggest that feminism and womanism had only negative consequences for my faith. Indeed, I felt closer to the God of all creation, and to the rising womanspirit, the spirit that is unashamed of loving, appreciating, delighting in, and affirming other women. I began to have more healthy views of relationships, seeing mutuality and voluntary response as primary ways in which to interact within relationships. My inner life, full of turmoil, became paradoxically full and centered as my prayer life became more honest and rigorous. My Bible study became intense and determinative. I refused to go with "standard" interpretations of texts and stories. I often played "so what" and "what if" games when searching the Scriptures for meaning and hope. Sometimes, I walked away from the search angry with God and angry with myself that I felt compelled to return to the text and to its God. At the same time, I discovered new images of God and found the Eagle, the Rock, the Suckling Mother, the Water, all ways to imagine God more and more comforting. I found myself praying the Scriptures and railing against texts that spoke of death. I found myself asking "why" more than ever. I discovered a God who likes inquisitive children. And because of that discovery, I knew I could keep preaching the good news of my elder brother, Jesus. It meant that I had to stay true to my call to be a prophetic voice, a preacher within the church.

My discoveries, though, were straining my marital relationship. The man who had always been very supportive of whatever I wanted for myself suddenly believed that the very foundation of our relationship was being threatened by foreign, unbiblical content. "I don't know you," he said to me whenever we got into a deep discussion about God or women or male-female relationships. "You don't believe the Bible anymore," he accused. I took back my birth name, the one I had rejected out of anger toward my father. But I realized I wanted that verbal connection to my beginnings; no one asked my husband to give up his birth name when he married me. We remained married, held together by a tenuous commitment to God more than to each other.

I do not mean to mislead. Our relationship was not continuously contentious. We just knew that there were taboo subjects and waters never to be tread between us. We coexisted with an armistice instead of a partnership. What we did together we did well: rearing our sons, working in the church, and being physically intimate. But I believed that I was making some concession as a womanist to be with him and let Don be himself, even as he let me be me. By year twelve of our marriage our tenuous relationship, hindered by surface dwelling instead of deep, intimate relationship, began to unravel. It was not enough. Still we stayed. Don withdrew further into his shell, becoming less and less emotionally available. And I found myself looking well beyond the borders of my marriage for friendships and comfort, from women and men.

By the time Promise Keepers came along, both of us were ready to quit. The intermittent good years could not, did not, assuage the really bad ones. When Don left for Dallas, I viewed his trip as a time when I could relax without him at hand; a time for him to rest. I did not expect what I got: a changed, responsive man. The only words that really fit his attitude when he returned to Austin were "repentant" and "renewed." He was genuinely expressing sorrow for the pain he had caused between us, asking for my forgiveness, and never once blaming me for any of it (though I am really clear about my contribution to the pain bank of our lives). He was looking for ways to bless me, to be more communicative, and to really listen to me.

I knew we had stumbled onto a life-saver and a marriage-saver when early one morning about one o'clock he asked me to explain what I really believed: about God, about men, about marriage, about the Bible. We talked and laughed and cried and listened with and to each other into the dawn. Several times he interrupted me: "I believe that, too," or "That makes sense now that I hear you," or "We're not as far apart as I always thought." I felt as if I had come up from under water after having held my breath forever. Our relationship was re-created in those early Promise Keepers days. We talked about submission, a subject that had come up for us probably only two or three times in our marriage. In the rhetoric of the Bible, Don said, "I believe in submission, but as us submitting to each other," quoting from Ephesians 5. I had heard him say those words before, always followed with the qualifier that the final authority rests with the man. This time he said the final authority rests with God. We talked about what mutuality looks like, whether we could keep the rhetoric of submission with our own redefinition, whether submission need ever be mentioned between us again. We decided it did not.

I was very much aware that the "pep rally" in Dallas fueled this newfound openness between us. As I have said, before the trip both of us were ready to quit. But one of the things that Don brought from the PK meeting was the determination of commitment to the marriage and to relationship with me and with his sons, a commitment that would make him "sacrifice" his ego and dreams in order to be a loving husband and loving father. What we both found in his commitment was that the "sacrifice" turned out to be a gift of mutuality. His willingness to take responsibility for his part of the relationship fueled my desire to be with him. We learned anew that we liked each other and enjoyed stimulating conversation with each other. Doing kind acts for each other was a joy. That gift came from Promise Keepers.

I am not naive. I read the PK literature, and it is conservative and sometimes restrictive. But my mother taught us another lesson growing up. We loved fish, but the freshwater fish of Alabama were brim and bass, both bony fish. My mother said, "Don't stop eating fish. Just eat the fish and leave the bones." That was the approach we took with Promise Keepers. My husband has never taken anything verbatim. He certainly did not start with Promise Keepers. He and I read the literature with a critical eye and accept what works for him and us. Some may say that such picking and choosing is not true to the movement. That statement may be true, but it is true to us. We talk about the movement's racial reconciliation plans. Since we have been actively trying to build a genuine multiracial community, that goal of the movement is nothing new to us. We do not judge the movement's sincerity. We simply take the information into our lives as we need it; we discard what we do not. As for the need of men to have authentic relationship with other men, I agreed wholeheartedly. I have a cadre of sister-friends who challenge, support, and nurture me. I have always wanted for my husband to find the same support in some brother relationships, and PK urges such relationships and helps men figure out how. I am not intimidated that men are getting together with other men: women get together all the time with conferences and retreats—and rightfully so. There are some things that men need to say to each other. I am learning that I do not have to overhear the conversation to say "amen." My husband's new relationship with me is proof enough.

I know that every trip Don makes to these all-male conferences brings him back to me more loving, more supportive, and more responsive, and always with a gift in hand and an "I love you" and kiss on his lips. When I get in the company of women who reject the movement out of hand, I always ask whether they actually *know* a Promise Keeper. Inevitably the answer is no. "Well, I sleep with one," I say, "and I'm a happily married womanist."

14

Dale Came Home a
Different Husband and Father

Jeanne Parrott

I attended several women's conferences and always came home pumped—ready to soar with the eagles. I had been convicted by the Holy Spirit of how far I had strayed from God's plan for my life. I came home determined to make the necessary changes. I increased the amount of time spent with God in prayer and meditation, and a more gentle spirit began developing in me. God was developing my spiritual gifts. I started concentrating on *knowing* God's character so I could trust God completely as God works in my life. Each conference speaker and others whom God placed along my path taught me additional lessons that God had for me to learn.

Returning from the mountaintop has one drawback—you were there alone. The response from my husband, Dale, had always been rather *ho-hum* because it is very hard to bring home a mountaintop experience and pass it on. But in 1994, Dale was going to attend his first Promise Keepers event in Boulder, Colorado. We were living in Raymore, Missouri, and he was to go with a group of men from our church. I was so excited that he was going to experience the mountaintop for himself. I prayed that God would open the floodgates and that Dale would come home touched by the Spirit in a new way.

My prayers were answered! Dale came home so excited about what he had seen God do in the lives of so many men and in his own heart. New love emerged for God, for me, and for our family. Against the platform of a fading sunset behind the Rockies' purple mountains, God had visited that stadium and touched deep into the lives of God's men. Dale recounted the Friday night altar call—many, many men made their way to the front to proclaim a brand-new relationship with God. God used the speakers to challenge (and reassure) men to return to the role God has especially created for them and to become the godly men who will in turn lead their families. They were charged to return to their jobs and communities as men of ethics and moral convictions. They were exhorted to uplift and support their pastors and to become committed to their local churches. Most impressive to Dale was Saturday evening's last service, when pastors in the stadium were called to the front and resounding applause affirmed all of the spiritual shepherds. I saw the shadow of the Spirit move across Dale's face as he told of all the stadium lights being lowered and then one by one the men lit candles to demonstrate how the Light of the Word can be spread by the men of this country.

Dale came home a very different husband and father. Although our children were grown and on their own, they gained a dad with new insight and a new spirit of love. God had definitely moved into his life, and that weekend's light still glows. Dale expresses a new tenderness that he had never shown before. Dale is a very quiet, reserved, gentle man. But after his first experience with PK, he exhibited an uninhibited excitement for this ministry and its vision for men. He absolutely could not keep silent about what he experienced in Boulder, and he shared it with anyone who would sit and listen. Our marriage received many benefits: more peace, more gentleness in our conversation, a deeper respect from him, and a sincere interest in my needs. Our marriage was not on a bad track before PK influenced Dale's life, but it was on a much better track afterward.

Both our daughter and our son had married, living in Texas and nearby, respectively. Since neither of them lived at home, changes they observed in their dad probably had more to do with the way he dealt with and responded to me. Each of them did have a time with their dad when he was able to share and explain what God had taught him at the PK event. They will tell you they saw changes in him. Dale developed an openness in sharing that had never been there before—an excitement for what God was doing in his life. They saw their dad resolved to follow God's leading in his life.

And when all of the men in the stadium stood to their feet and the applause thundered in affirmation for the pastors present, God touched Dale's heart with a new love and appreciation for our pastor and for the entire church family. Dale brought this message from God home to me, and loving our pastor and affirming him became a priority in our lives. We quickly became the couple who would champion for the pastor and influenced others to support and affirm him.

Dale has attended a PK event each year since 1994, and the highlight was the 1995 Dallas event when he took our son and son-in-law with him. It was a great moment to see his son go forward and recommit his life and to know of the heart changes in both young men who are so special in our hearts.

Dale still supports PK with prayers and financial support and believes strongly in its mission and focus. He realizes the changes that need to happen in the lives of the men of this country. He believes that for the present, PK is still calling men to return to what God has called them to be and to the special role God has for them in their homes, churches, and communities.

As I listened to Dale share his experience with PK and after I observed the changes in him, God started drawing me to a deeper walk with the Divine Self. One morning as I was sitting on my porch swing praying, God whispered to me, calling me to become a prayer warrior, working with the women in the lives of PK men. I immediately started seeking out a ministry that would fulfill this leading in my life. From a call to Focus on the Family, I learned of Cheri Bright and her ministry of Suitable Helpers.

When I first attended a Suitable Helpers conference in 1995, I was confronted with an attitude that had developed in my marriage: I was in total control and leading when I should have been helping, completing. At that time in our lives, we were dealing with our daughter marrying and leaving our home, and our son was running from our value system and from God. I did not deal with the empty nest or Brett's being a prodigal in the manner God would have had for me. I had taken control and authority away from Dale and God in their lives. Through conference speakers, God led me to leave both situations with God and to trust Dale as the head of our home.

Dale and I have been called to serve on the board of the Suitable Helpers ministry, and I also serve on the working staff. This ministry stands on God's Word by using Genesis 2:18 as the standard by which we measure our God-created role for marriage. God created woman from a very special place inside man—and we were created to complete the man in our lives. Suitable Helpers is a teaching ministry committed to teaching women how to receive the change God is calling the men in their lives to make. Unconditional love is taught, and the result is a new knowledge of God's love and the ability to stand in the gap as mighty prayer warriors for our men. It is imperative that the women be prepared for the changes that God is calling their men to make. It is a sad day when God reaches deep into a man's heart and the wife is holding so many hurts and such resentment that she turns him off. Suitable Helpers strives to prepare women by teaching them how to give those hurts to God and that God loves them with an agape love. In turn God wants them to receive their men with the same unconditional love.

Dale's attendance at a PK event started God's real work in our lives. We both started seeking God's will and were more in tune to divine leading. God burdened me with the knowledge that women need to be more supportive of men in their lives and gave me a vision of each man standing in front of God with at least one woman (wife, mother, daughter) standing beside him. That makes a mighty army for God! In 1997, God started leading us out of our comfort zones. We are serving God in Colorado Springs on the staff of Focus on the Family and the National Day of Prayer. Had it not been for PK and Suitable Helpers, I am not sure if Dale and I would have been open to God's leading—or if we would have been available to send. We thank God for raising up ministries that teach the basics of returning to God and God's teaching—only then can we be open to God's leadership in our lives.

15

Promise Keepers Has Not Changed Our Family

Anonymous

lthough thousands of men across the nation have had the same experience, some men, for some reason, have times in which they are not open to this movement. (For reasons that will become clear, I prefer that my name and our family name remain anonymous.) After I attended my first Suitable Helpers conference in 1994, my attitude toward my husband and life in general drastically changed.

On our way across the Midwest to Denver for Suitable Helpers, a friend and I encountered buses full of men on their way to a PK event in Boulder. Buses were coming from many states, and the men appeared to be having a great time. Weekend events such as PK and Suitable Helpers are hard to leave when it is time to head home. As we headed home on Sunday after our conference, we stopped at a rest stop to have lunch. While we were there, some of the buses full of PK men pulled in and unloaded. We watched as the men literally jumped out of the buses and ran to the nearest phone to call their loved ones at home. As we passed by the phones on our way back to our car, we overheard some of the conversations. Overjoyed by what they had learned over that weekend, some men were apologizing for past actions at home. Some were anxious to get home and put into effect what they had been challenged to change in their marriage and family. Some wept. Some laughed. As other men were waiting for their turn at the phone, they huddled in small groups hugging each other, praying with each other, and encouraging each other.

I wondered to myself, Is this what heaven will be like? People in harmony with their spirits united for the good of others? It was an awesome experience and one that I will never forget. Needless to say, I arrived home with a longing in my heart for my husband and adult son to have this same experience. I wanted them to share in what God was doing in the lives of other men. I wanted our family to experience a moving of God. What I failed to remember is that all men are different in their personalities and how they perceive what they experience.

PK soon was coming to our Midwest city, and my husband and son planned to attend. Because of my son's recent injury, they had to enter through the gate for disabled persons, and they became isolated from other men they knew. They felt very alone in that big arena. They experienced differences in worship styles, praise styles, and prayer styles. Although my husband was understanding of the differences, my son was unnerved by them.

Speakers shared their specific messages with the men, and my son walked away that night lifted up and ready to attend again. However, his father would attend only the next day to drive his injured son. He had no desire of his own to return.

What was the difference between what my men and the ones I had seen at the rest stop experienced? I did not see that same joy and unity in my men. PK has not changed our family in the way I hear other people talk about. However, as a result of this movement, Suitable Helpers became a vision that God implemented. The biblical teaching I received from this ministry has changed my life. I now know the role that God created for me within my family, and I strive to be the completer, the helper of my mate. I am trusting that the exposure that my husband and son had at their only PK event will have planted a seed that will be watered and harvested in their lives at some point in the future.

Taking an active role in the Suitable Helpers ministry for three years enabled me to not only learn but also teach how to get back to the basics of a God-filled attitude and life. That in turn helped me to be the supportive wife and mother that God would have me to be.

Recently, our family experienced a crisis when our son was not following the biblical teaching that our home and PK have offered him. He has willingly turned away from Jesus and his young family to satisfy his own selfish desires. As a Christian mother and grandmother, I have had to remind myself that God's will comes first—not that of my son. I tell you this only to remind you that all who walk the aisle of a church or PK conference and make a profession of faith are not always secure in that faith.

The one concern I see many years later is that some people appear to be worshiping the organization as a "fix-all" to all types of social issues. More emphasis needs to be made on the biblical teaching than on the event or speakers. We all possess the ability to assess the Word, and all teaching should be tested against the Scripture. We need to be prudent in our individual walks and search the Scripture for ourselves and verify that what we are being taught is of God.

16

Fulfilling God's Role for the
Woman Is the Most Rewarding Feeling

Marilyn Kenaga

About five years ago my husband, Dave, went to his first Promise Keepers (PK) meeting. He was so excited to go and hear the Word of God. As a child of God, he wanted to please God. I was excited for Dave. We had both heard how God moved in lives through PK the previous year, and we had our hearts open to God. We desired to serve God in an honoring and pleasing way.

When Dave came home, I could see he was not the same man. Dave felt a renewed hope in his spirit after seeing more than 50,000 men pumped with excitement to follow Christ, and to make decisions and commit to finding another brother or brothers to hold them accountable. There is a willingness to be transparent; who you see is who he is. Each man works to be a man of integrity each new day—determined not to give up after all the excitement settles down. Dave and the men in his Bible study are still holding one another accountable today, several years after their first PK conference in 1994. I also see these men reaping the joy of serving Jesus. To see Dave and the men in his Bible study following through, holding one another accountable for the decisions that were made at PK, thrills me.

At the PK event men committed to be the husbands God has called them to be, and they committed to break down the walls of racism. God clearly states in the Word that men are to be the head of their homes and to love their wives as Christ loves the church and gave his life for it (Eph. 5:25). As Dave was sharing how the Holy Spirit moved through this event, my heart turned toward the wives. I then shared with Dave that the wives need to be excited and to come up beside their husbands and share their excitement with them. In doing that, they support what God is doing and become an encouragement to their men. I felt that God's plan could not come together in God's timing if we as wives were interfering by not sharing in our husbands' joy and not supporting the decisions they had made before God. We must pray for our husbands and encourage them to follow God and God's will for their lives and for the lives of their families.

After I attended my first Suitable Helpers conference and listened to the speakers, I knew in my heart that God was calling God's daughters to come alongside their husbands and pray, pray, pray for them. God is calling all of God's children to come together in unity in the Divine, giving assignments to both women and men. Men are to work and provide for their families and bathe them in the Word of God. Women are to help the husbands by taking care of what God has given them. It is called teamwork! Women today often feel that they have to compete with men. That is a lie from Satan! God made woman to complement man, come alongside him, and work together with him for the glory of God.

The following year I was able to volunteer at a PK event where it was awesome to hear men in person praise their God. That year, I also attended another Suitable Helpers conference, after which God called me to the Suitable Helpers staff, a role I fulfilled until 1998.

It is an honor to be called a Suitable Helper. I do not feel any less of a person just because I am not working outside our home nor do I feel like a doormat for my husband to wipe his feet on. Fulfilling God's role for the woman in my marriage and family is the most rewarding feeling—God blesses when we are obedient to divine teachings.

Promise Keepers and Suitable Helpers have encouraged me to work at being all I can be—one day at a time. My husband and I start each day committing to do God's will in our lives, and we put on the full armor of God (Eph. 6:10–18). Being obedient is the beginning of God's opening your eyes to the beauty of marriage.

notes

Preface

1. Richard Hofstadter, *Anti-Intellectualism in American Life* (New York: Knopf, 1963), and Donald N. Wood, *Post-Intellectualism and the Decline of Democracy* (Westport, Conn.: Praeger, 1996).

1. *Standing on the Promises* and the Broader Conversation

1. Donald W. Dayton and Robert K. Johnston, eds., *The Variety of American Evangelicalism* (Knoxville: University of Tennessee Press, 1991), chap. 13.

2. Dayton suggests that the category "evangelical" is an "essentially contested concept," while Johnston regards "evangelicalism" as "an extended family" that includes those who believe the gospel is to be experienced personally, defined biblically, and communicated passionately (ibid., chaps. 14 and 15). For the purposes of this chapter, I have cast my lot with Johnston and thus continue to use the term "evangelical," while acknowledging the validity of much of what Dayton argues concerning how the term is equivocal and can obscure fundamental differences.

3. Allan Richardson and John S. Bowden, eds., "Evangelical, Evangelicalism," in *The Westminster Dictionary of Christian Theology* (Philadelphia: Westminster Press, 1983), 191.

4. I owe this insight to my colleague, James S. Dalton, professor of religious studies at Siena College, Loudonville, New York.

5. Martin E. Marty, "Tensions within Contemporary Evangelicalism: A Critical Appraisal," in *The Evangelicals: What They Believe, Who They Are, Where They Are Changing*, rev. ed., ed. David F. Wells and John D. Woodbridge (Grand Rapids, Mich.: Baker, 1971), 193.

6. Dayton and Johnston, *The Variety of American Evangelicalism*, 268.

7. Government officials stopped trying to give any official estimate of numbers for such gatherings, following a huge controversy that erupted when they gave a much lower figure than the organizers of the Million Man March said were present at that earlier event in 1995.

8. Promise Keepers, "Promise Keepers Reaches More Than 450,000 Men: Thousands Receive Christ at Free Conferences in 1998," Promise Keepers Web site, 1998, <http://www.promisekeepers.org/pkpress/98conf-final-pub.html>.

9. Edward E. Plowman, "What Went Wrong?" *World*, March 21, 1998, 15.

10. Promise Keepers, "'99 Men's Conference Theme: Choose This Day," Promise Keepers Web site, 1999, <http://www.promisekeepers.org/pkpress/99conf-sched-pub.html>.

11. In a recent provocative—and in many respects antifeminist—book *The Church Impotent: The Feminization of Christianity* (Dallas: Spence Publishing, 1999), Leon J. Podles argues that Western churches have become "women's clubs," and that Christianity has been emasculated in a way that is dangerous not only for the church but also for society. After documenting the highly feminized state of Western Christianity, Podles argues that a masculine presence can and must be restored.

12. Robert Bly, *Iron John: A Book about Men* (Reading, Mass.: Addison-Wesley, 1990).

13. Michael Meade, *Men and the Water of Life: Initiation and the Tempering of Men* (San Francisco: Harper San Francisco, 1993).

14. Kenneth Clatterbaugh, *Contemporary Perspectives on Masculinity: Men, Women, and Politics in Modern Society*, 2d ed. (Boulder, Colo.: Westview Press, 1997).

15. Gil Rugh, *Promise Keepers and the Rising Tide of Ecumenism* (Lincoln, Nebr.: Indian Hills Community Church, 1994).

16. Christians whom I would designate as the "hard Religious Right" are quick to point out that McCartney is a member of a charismatic megachurch, that the Promise Keepers board includes some charismatics, and that the movement's rank and file includes many Spirit-filled worshipers. These points, from their perspective, leave the movement wide open to the introduction of countless errors and heretical teachings.

17. Laurie Coene Dashnau, "Rhetorics of Gender: Christian Traditionalists, Biblical Feminists, and Promise Keepers" (Ph.D. diss., Miami University of Ohio, 1996).

18. L. Dean Allen II, "Amen Brother Ben!: An Outsider/Insider's Reflections on the Promise Keepers" (paper delivered to Men's Studies in Religion Group, Annual Meeting of American Academy of Religion, New Orleans, November 25, 1996); and "Beyond Brotherhood: The Rise of Promise Keepers in Baptist Churches," *Baptists Today* 15, no. 1 (January 9, 1997): 2.

19. L. Dean Allen II, "Break Down the Wall?: An Insider Look at the Promise Keepers," *Church and State* 50, no. 1 (January 1997): 10–13.

20. David Wade, "Keeping the Promise," *Sojourners*, July–August 1995, 11–12; Duane Shank, "Danger or Opportunity? Promise Keepers Draws Mixed Response," *Sojourners*, September–October 1997, 11–12.

21. Promise Keepers, "Do Promise Keepers Have Plans to Hold Events in Countries Other Than the United States?" Promise Keepers Web site, 1999. The Web address is <http://www.promisekeepers.org/2d0e.htm>.

22. Ken Abraham, *Who Are the Promise Keepers? Understanding the Christian Men's Movement* (New York: Doubleday, 1997), chap. 1.

23. Promise Keepers, "Do Promise Keepers Have Plans to Hold Events in Countries Other than the United States?"

24. Garth Kasimu Baker-Fletcher, ed., *Black Religion after the Million Man March: Voices on the Future* (Maryknoll, N.Y.: Orbis Books, 1998).

25. Patricia Ireland, letter to the editor, *New York Times*, July 13, 1997, 16.

26. Joe Conason, Alfred Ross, and Lee Cokorinos, "The Promise Keepers Are Coming: The Third Wave of the Religious Right," *Nation*, October 7, 1996, 11–12, 14, 16, 18–19.

27. Sterling Research Associates, *Promise Keepers: The Third Wave of the Religious Right* (New York: Sterling Research Associates, 1996).

28. Conason et al., "The Promise Keepers Are Coming," 14.

29. Ibid., 19.

30. Ibid.

31. Donna Minkowitz, "In the Name of the Father," *Ms.*, November–December 1995, 70.

32. Suzanne Pharr, "A Match Made in Heaven: Lesbian Leftie Chats with a Promise Keeper," *Progressive* 60, no. 8 (August 1996): 28–29.

33. Suzanne Pharr, "Our Search for Liberation in the Time of the Right" (keynote address delivered to the 22nd National Men and Masculinity Conference ["Spirituality, Community & Social Change"], sponsored by the National Organization of Men Against Sexism, St. John's University, Collegeville, Minn., July 19, 1997).

34. Jeff Wagenheim, "Among the Promise Keepers: An Inside Look at the Evangelical Men's Movement," *New Age Journal*, March–April 1995, reprinted in *Utne Reader*, January–February 1996.

35. Dane S. Claussen, personal communication to Merle Longwood, August 1998.

2. What the Media Missed about the Promise Keepers

1. Bill McCartney, *From Ashes to Glory*, 2d ed. (Nashville: Thomas Nelson, 1995), 286.

2. Bill McCartney, *Sold Out: Becoming Man Enough to Make a Difference* (Dallas: Word, 1997), 180–81.

3. Mary Stewart van Leeuwen, "Mixed Messages on the Mall," *Christian Century* 114 (1997): 932–34.

4. Steve Rabey, "Where Is the Christian Men's Movement Headed?: Burgeoning Promise Keepers Inspires Lookalikes," *Christianity Today*, April 29, 1996, 46–49, 60.

5. Gustav Niebuhr, "Men Crowd Stadiums to Fulfill Their Souls," *New York Times*, August 6, 1995.

6. David Halbrook, "Is This Revival? How Does the Promise Keepers Movement Compare with the World's Historical Revivals?" *New Man*, November–December 1995, 20.

7. Rabey, "Where Is the Christian Men's Movement Headed?"

8. Gary Scott Smith, "Men and Religion Forward Movement of 1911–1912: New Perspectives on Evangelical Social Concern and the Relationship between Christianity and Progressivism," *Westminster Theological Journal* 49 (1987): 109.

9. Robert D. Linder, personal communication to Dane S. Claussen, 1996.

10. William G. McLoughlin, *Revivals, Awakenings, and Reform: An Essay on Religion and Social Change in America, 1607–1977* (Chicago: University of Chicago Press, 1978), 143.

11. William G. McLoughlin, *Modern Revivalism: Charles Grandison Finney to Billy Graham* (New York: Ronald Press, 1959), 173.

12. William Warren Sweet, *Revivalism in America: Its Origin, Growth and Decline* (New York: Charles Scribner's Sons, 1944), 169–70.

13. McLoughlin, *Revivals, Awakenings, and Reform*, 144.

14. Ibid., 143.

15. McLoughlin, *Modern Revivalism*, 278.

16. Michael S. Kimmel, *Manhood in America: A Cultural History* (New York: Free Press, 1996), 177.

17. Norman Vance, *The Sinews of the Spirit: The Ideal of Christian Manliness in Victorian Literature and Religious Thought* (Cambridge: Cambridge University Press, 1985), 1–2.

18. Ann Douglas, *The Feminization of American Culture* (New York: Knopf, 1977); Vance, *The Sinews of the Spirit*; Ted Ownby, *Subduing Satan: Religion, Recreation, and Manhood in the Rural South: 1865–1920* (Chapel Hill: University of North Carolina Press, 1990); Gail Bederman, "'Civilization,' the Decline of Middle-class Manliness, and Ida B. Wells's Antilynching Campaign (1892–94)," *Radical History Review* 52 (1992): 5–30; Kimmel, *Manhood in America*.

19. Vance, *The Sinews of the Spirit*, v.

20. Ownby, *Subduing Satan*.

21. Thomas Hughes, *The Manliness of Christ* (Boston: Houghton Mifflin, 1880); Robert W. Conant, *The Manly Christ: A New View* (Chicago: Robert W. Conant, 1904); C. D. Case, *The Masculine in Religion* (Philadelphia: American Baptist Publication Society, 1906); Harry E. Fosdick, *The Manhood of the Master* (New York: Association Press, 1911); Jason Noble Pierce, *The Masculine Power of Christ, or Christ Measured as a Man* (Boston: The Pilgrim Press, 1912); Kenneth Henroian Wayne, *Building the Young Man* (Chicago: A. C. McClurg & Co., 1912); Fred B. Smith, *A Man's Religion* (New York: Association Press, 1913); Bouck White, *The Call of the Carpenter* (Garden City, N.Y.: Doubleday, Page & Co., 1913); and Bruce Barton, *The Man Nobody Knows: A Discovery of the Real Jesus* (Indianapolis: n.p., 1924).

22. Kimmel, *Manhood in America*, 179.

23. Theodore Thomas Frankenberg, *Spectacular Career of Rev. Billy Sunday: Famous Baseball Evangelist* (Columbus, Ohio: McClelland & Company, 1913).

24. McLoughlin, *Modern Revivalism*, 399.

25. Sweet, *Revivalism in America*, 170–71.

26. William G. McLoughlin, *Billy Sunday Was His Real Name* (Chicago: University of Chicago Press, 1955), vii.

27. Roger A. Bruns, *Preacher: Billy Sunday and Big Time American Evangelism* (New York: Norton, 1992), 15.

28. Kimmel, *Manhood in America*, 180.

29. McLoughlin, *Billy Sunday Was His Real Name*, 226.

30. Gail Bederman, "'The Women Have Had Charge of the Church Work Long Enough': The Men and Religion Forward Movement of 1911–1912 and the Masculinization of Middle-class Protestantism," *American Quarterly* 41 (1989): 432–65; Kimmel, *Manhood in America*; Mary Stewart van Leeuwen, "Weeping Warriors: What's New about Promise Keepers' Effort to Reclaim Men for the Church?" *Books & Culture*, November–December 1997, 9–11; and others.

31. Smith, "Men and Religion Forward Movement," 107.

32. *The Message and the Program* (New York: YMCA, 1911); Clarence Barbour, *Making Religion Efficient* (New York: Association Press, 1912); *Men and Religion Messages* (New York: Association Press and Funk and Wagnalls, 1912).

33. Smith, "Men and Religion Forward Movement," 102, 104.

34. Bederman, "'The Women Have Had Charge of the Church Work Long Enough,'" 452.

35. Smith, "Men and Religion Forward Movement," 108, 109.

36. Ibid., 110.

37. Ibid., 116.

38. Ibid., 118.

39. A. E. Gross, R. Smith, and B. S. Wallston, "The Men's Movement: Personal Versus Political," in *Social Movements of the Sixties and Seventies*, ed. Jo Freeman (New York: Longman, 1983).

40. John S. Guarnaschelli, "Men's Support Groups and the Men's Movement: Their Role for Men and for Women," *Group* 18 (1994): 197–211.

41. Michael A. Messner, *Politics of Masculinities: Men in Movements* (Thousand Oaks, Calif.: Sage, 1997).

42. Bliss cited in Michael S. Kimmel, *The Politics of Manhood: Profeminist Men Respond to the Mythopoetic Men's Movement (and the Mythopoetic Leaders Answer)* (Philadelphia: Temple University Press, 1995).

43. Richard K. Gilbert, "Revisiting the Psychology of Men: Robert Bly and the Mythopoetic Movement," *Journal of Humanistic Psychology* 32, no. 2 (1992): 41–42.

44. Ted Solotaroff, "Captain Bly," *Nation* 253, no. 7 (1991): 270.

45. George Myers Jr., "'Iron John': An Interview with Robert Bly," *Literary Review* 35 (1992): 408–14; and Guarnaschelli, "Men's Support Groups and the Men's Movement."

46. Dwight Fee, "Masculinities, Identity and the Politics of Essentialism: A Social Constructionist Critique of the Men's Movement," *Feminism and Psychology* 2 (1992): 171–76.

47. Chris Harding, ed., *Wingspan: Inside the Men's Movement* (New York: St. Martin's Press, 1992).

48. Sam Keen, *Fire in the Belly: On Being a Man* (New York: Bantam Books, 1991).

49. William V. Davis, *Robert Bly: The Poet and His Critics* (Columbia, S.C.: Camden House, 1994), 79–80.

50. Shewey in Kimmel, *The Politics of Manhood*, 338.

51. Bly, *Iron John: A Book about Men*, 5.

52. Robert Bly, *The Sibling Society* (Reading, Mass.: Addison-Wesley, 1996), 177–78.

53. Ibid., 179.

54. Cited in Kimmel, *The Politics of Manhood*, 293.

55. Rabey, "Where Is the Christian Men's Movement Headed?"

56. Ibid.

57. Michael J. Chrasta, "The Religious Roots of the Promise Keepers," in *The Promise Keepers: Essays on Masculinity and Christianity,* ed. Dane S. Claussen (Jefferson, N.C.: McFarland & Company, 1999).

58. Lynne Marie Isaacson, "Delicate Balances: Rearticulating Gender Ideology and Rules for Sexuality in a Jesus People Communal Movement" (Ph.D. diss., University of Oregon, 1996).

59. John Dart, "Promise Keepers, A Message to L.A. Men Conference: Gathering at the Coliseum Includes 15 Hours of Events Designed to Spread the Group's Belief in Traditional Father-Husband Duties; about 70,000 Are Expected to Attend," *Los Angeles Times*, May 6, 1995.

60. Rabey, "Where Is the Christian Men's Movement Headed?"

61. Ibid., 49.

62. Ibid., 60.

63. Ibid., 47.

64. G. Garrison, "Leader Sets National Baptists' Agenda," *Plain Dealer* (Cleveland, Ohio), September 9, 1995, 13A.

65. A. Dager, "Promise Keepers: Is What You See What You Get? Media Spotlight," 1994, <www.demon.co.uk/cross/pk/WYSWYG.html>; L. Leslie and S. Leslie, "Promise Keepers and the Men's Movement: Resurrecting Pagan Rites—Part 1: The Men's Movement," *Christian Conscience,* 1995, <www.demon.co.uk/cross/pk/PK_MM1.html>; J. Stephens, "The Seven False Promises of Promise Keepers," *Ohio Bible Fellowship Visitor,* 1995, <www.demon.co.uk/cross/pk/PK3.html>; and others.

66. James D. Spinnati, *Promise Keepers Exposed Through Denominational Eyes* (Connersville, Ind.: TNT Ministries, 1997); Phil Arms, *Promise Keepers: Another Trojan Horse* (Houston: Shiloh Publishers, 1997); David G. Hagopian and Douglas J. Wilson, *Beyond Promises: A Biblical Challenge to the Promise Keepers* (Moscow, Idaho: Canon Press, 1996); and others.

67. Dane S. Claussen, "United States Print Mass Media Coverage of Two Men's Movements: Robert Bly, Iron John, and the Mythopoets, and Bill McCartney and the Promise Keepers" (master's thesis, Kansas State University, Manhattan, 1996); and Dane S.

Claussen, "U.S. Print Mass Media Coverage of the Promise Keepers: The First Five Years" (paper presented to the Mass Communication and Society Division, Association for Education in Journalism and Mass Communication convention, Baltimore, 1998).

68. John D. Spalding, "Bonding in the Bleachers: A Visit to the Promise Keepers," *Christian Century* (March 6, 1996): 260–65.

69. S. Raab, "Triumph of His Will," GQ, January 1996, 110–17.

70. Claussen, "United States Print Mass Media Coverage of Two Men's Movements," Claussen, "U.S. Print Mass Media Coverage of the Promise Keepers: The First Five Years," Dane S. Claussen, "'So Far, News Coverage of Promise Keepers Has Been More Like Advertising': The Strange Case of Christian Men and the Print Mass Media," in *The Promise Keepers: Essays on Masculinity and Christianity*; George L. Daniels, "Praying Portrayals: How Newspapers Covered the Promise Keepers 'Stand in the Gap' Rally" (paper presented to the Newspaper Division, Association for Education in Journalism and Mass Communication Southeast Colloquium, New Orleans, April 1998).

71. Minkowitz, "In the Name of the Father."

72. Terry Eastland, "Promise Keepers and the Press," *Weekly Standard*, October 20, 1997, 17; Neil Swanson, "A Report from the Promise Keepers' Washington Gathering," *Flagpole*, October 15, 1997, 6–7; and Kathleen Adams et al., "Winners and Losers," *Time*, October 13, 1997.

73. Nancy Novosod, "God Squad," *Progressive*, August 1996, 25.

74. Claussen, "'So Far, News Coverage of Promise Keepers Has Been More Like Advertising': The Strange Case of Christian Men and the Print Mass Media."

75. Claussen, "United States Print Mass Media Coverage of Two Men's Movements."

76. L. Dean Allen II, "They Just Don't Get It!: Promise Keepers' Responses to Media Coverage," in *The Promise Keepers: Essays on Masculinity and Christianity*.

77. Hillary Warren, "Promise Keepers and TV News Coverage of the Stand in the Gap Rally: Conservative Protestants as an Audience and Public" (paper presented to the Radio-Television Division of the Association for Education in Journalism and Mass Communication convention, Baltimore, 1998).

78. See the article by Keeler, Fraser, and Brown, "How Promise Keepers See Themselves as Men Behaving Goodly," in this volume, or McCartney's discussion of PK's racial reconciliation efforts in *Sold Out*.

3. A Reaction to Declining Market and Religious Influence

1. Harvey Cox, "Into the Age of Miracles: Culture, Religion, and the Market Revolution," *World Policy Journal* 14, no. 1 (spring 1997): 87–95; Harvey Cox, *Fire from Heaven: The Rise of Pentecostal Spirituality and the Reshaping of Religion in the Twenty-first Century* (Reading, Mass.: Addison-Wesley, 1995); and Scott Thomas, "The Global Resurgence of Religion and the Study of World Politics," *Millennium* 24, no. 2 (summer 1995): 289–99.

2. Cox, "Into the Age of Miracles"; Elizabeth Brusco, "The Reformation of Machismo: Asceticism and Masculinity among Colombian Evangelicals," in *Rethinking Protestantism in Latin America*, ed. Virginia Garrard-Burnett and David Stoll (Philadelphia: Temple University Press, 1993); Bronislaw Misztal and Anson Shupe, eds., "Making Sense of the Global Revival of Fundamentalism," in *Religion and Politics in Comparative Perspective: Revival of Religious Fundamentalism in East and West* (Westport, Conn.: Praeger, 1992); Hans A. Baer and Merrill Singer, *African-American Religion in the Twentieth Century: Varieties of Protest and Accommodation* (Knoxville: University of Tennessee Press, 1992); Martin E. Marty and R. Scott Appleby, "Conclusion: Remaking the State—The Limits of the Fundamentalist Imagination,"

in *Fundamentalisms and the State*, ed. Martin E. Marty and R. Scott Appleby (Chicago: University of Chicago Press, 1993); and Steve Brouwer, Paul Gifford, and Susan D. Rose, *Exporting the American Gospel: Global Christian Fundamentalism* (New York: Routledge, 1996).

3. Brouwer et al., *Exporting the American Gospel.*

4. Ibid., 250.

5. Cox, *Fire from Heaven*; Mark Hulsether, "Evangelical Popular Religion as a Source for North American Liberation Theology? Insights from Postmodern Popular Culture Theory," *American Studies* 33, no. 1 (spring 1992): 63–81; Thomas, "The Global Resurgence of Religion and the Study of World Politics"; Jorge E. Maldonado, "Building 'Fundamentalism' from the Family in Latin America," in *Fundamentalisms and Society*, ed. Martin E. Marty and R. Scott Appleby (Chicago: University of Chicago Press, 1993); Virginia Garrard-Burnett, "Conclusion: Is This Latin America's Reformation?" in *Rethinking Protestantism in Latin America*, 199–208; and Brusco, "The Reformation of Machismo."

6. Maldonado, "Building 'Fundamentalism' from the Family in Latin America"; Garrard-Burnett, "Conclusion: Is This Latin America's Reformation?"; and Brusco, "The Reformation of Machismo."

7. Sara Diamond, *Facing the Wrath: Confronting the Right in Dangerous Times* (Monroe, Maine: Common Courage Press, 1996), *Roads to Dominion: Right-Wing Movements and Political Power in the United States* (New York: Guilford Press, 1995), and *Spiritual Welfare: The Politics of the Christian Right* (Boston: South End Press, 1989); Alister McGrath, "Why Evangelicalism Is the Future of Protestantism," *Christianity Today*, June 19, 1995, 18–23; Robert Wuthnow and Matthew P. Lawdon, "Sources of Christian Fundamentalism in the United States," in *Accounting for Fundamentalisms: The Dynamic Character of Movements*, ed. Martin E. Marty and R. Scott Appleby (Chicago: University of Chicago Press, 1994); Hulsether, "Evangelical Popular Religion as a Source for North American Liberation Theology? Insights from Postmodern Popular Culture Theory"; and Thomas Robbins, *Cults, Converts, and Charisma: The Sociology of New Religious Movements* (London: Sage Publications, 1988).

8. Judith L. Newton, "The Politics of Feeling: Men, Masculinity, and Mourning on the Capitol Mall," in *The Bounds of Feeling*, ed. Millette Shamir and Jennifer Travis, forthcoming.

9. Brouwer et al., *Exporting the American Gospel*, 250.

10. David Blankenhorn, *Fatherless America: Confronting Our Most Urgent Social Problem* (New York: Basic Books, 1995).

11. Brouwer et al., *Exporting the American Gospel.*

12. Lisa Lowe, *Immigrant Acts: On Asian American Cultural Politics* (Durham, N.C.: Duke University Press, 1996).

13. Mattias Gardell, *In the Name of Elijah Muhammed: Louis Farrakhan and the Nation of Islam* (Durham, N.C.: Duke University Press, 1996); Na'im Akbar, *Visions for Black Men* (Tallahassee, Fla.: Mind Productions, 1991); Haki Madhubuti, *Black Men: Obsolete, Single, and Dangerous? Afrikan American Families in Transition: Essays in Discovery, Solution, and Hope* (Chicago: Third World Press, 1990); Molefi Kete Asante, *Afrocentricity* (Trenton, N.J.: Africa World Press, 1988), and *The Afrocentric Idea* (Philadelphia: Temple University Press, 1987).

14. Kimmel, *Manhood in America.*

15. John Dart, "Southern Baptists Vote to Issue Apology for Past Racism," *Los Angeles Times*, June 21, 1995, A28; and Helen Lee, "Racial Reconciliation Tops NAEs Agenda," *Christianity Today*, April 3, 1995, 97.

16. Gary David Comstock, *Unrepentant, Self-Affirming, Practicing: Lesbian/Bisexual/Gay People within Organized Religion* (New York: Continuum, 1996); and John Gallagher and

Chris Bull, *Perfect Enemies: The Religious Right, the Gay Movement, and the Politics of the 1990s* (New York: Crown, 1996).

17. Jim Wallis, "All Together Now! From the Strength of Our Church Traditions Has Come a New Ecumenical Spirit for the 21st Century," *Sojourners*, May–June 1997 [cited July 8, 1998], <http://sojourners.com/soj9705/soj9705.html>; and Gordon Aeschliman, "Outside the Gate: Will Progressive Evangelicals Please Stand Up and Be Counted?" *Sojourners*, May–June 1995 [cited July 8, 1998], 2, <http://sojourners.com/soj9505/950521.html>.

18. See comments by Ken Abraham in Art Moore, "More PK Downsizing: McCartney Admits Staff Morale Problem," *Christian Century* (October 5, 1998): 20.

4. Race and Religion at the Million Man March and the Promise Keepers' Stand in the Gap

1. Christopher Hitchens, "Another March, Another Prick in the Wall," *Nation*, October 27, 1997.

2. Michael Janofsky, "Marches Indicate Personal Strivings: Rallies Today Are Different from Previous Gatherings," *Chattanooga Times*, October 26, 1997, A1; Eric Utne, "Masses of Men," *Utne Reader*, January–February 1996, 3; and Scott Bowles, "The March Becomes the Thing: Mass Gatherings Are Becoming the Way to Get Message Across," *USA Today*, October 27, 1997.

3. Laurie Goodstein, "For Christian Men's Group, Racial Harmony Starts at the Local Level," *New York Times*, September 29, 1997, A12.

4. George L. Daniels, "Praying Portrayals: How Newspapers Covered the Promise Keepers 'Stand in the Gap' Rally."

5. Ellen Goodman, "A Subtext Emerges in Men's Rhetoric," *Boston Globe*, October 29, 1995, A21.

6. Emile Durkheim, *The Elementary Forms of Religious Life*, trans. Joseph Ward Swain (New York: Free Press, 1915).

7. Randall Collins, *Conflict Sociology: Toward an Explanatory Science* (New York: Academic Press, 1975).

8. Nancy Whittier, "Political Generations, Micro-Cohorts, and the Transformation of Social Movements," *American Sociological Review* 62 (October 1997): 761.

9. Christian Smith, "Introduction: Correcting a Curious Neglect, or Bringing Religion Back In," in *Disruptive Religion: The Force of Faith in Social Movement Activism*, ed. Christian Smith (New York: Routledge, 1996), 17.

10. Kenneth Gergen, *The Saturated Self* (New York: Basic Books, 1991).

11. Kim Martin Sadler, ed., *Atonement* (Cleveland: The Pilgrim Press, 1996), 69.

12. Ibid., 131.

13. Haki Madhubiti and Maulana Karenga, *Million Man March/Day of Absence* (Chicago: Third World Press, 1996), 150.

14. Jeremiah Wright, *When Black Men Stand Up for God* (Chicago: African American Images, 1996), 14–15.

15. Sadler, *Atonement*, 42.

16. Melinda Beck, "Beyond the Moment, What Can One Day Do?" *Newsweek*, October 30, 1995, 38–39.

17. Ivory L. Lyons, "God's Message, God's Call," in *Black Religion after the Million Man March: Voices on the Future*, ed. Garth Kasimu Baker-Fletcher (New York: Orbis Press, 1998), 126.

18. Sadler, *Atonement*, 49.

19. Wright, *When Black Men Stand Up for God*, 17.

20. Madhubiti and Karenga, *Million Man March/Day of Absence*, 20.

21. Sadler, *Atonement*, 56.

22. Howard Fineman and Vernon Smith, "An Angry Charmer," *Newsweek*, October 30, 1995, 32.

23. William H. Lockhart, "'We Are One Life,' but Not of One Ideology" (paper presented at the annual meeting of the American Sociological Association, San Francisco, August 1998).

24. Bill McCartney, "Letter to Potential Stand in the Gap Participants," 1997, <http://www.promisekeepers.org>.

25. Bill McCartney, speech at Break Down the Walls (Promise Keepers conference, Pittsburgh, 1996).

26. Clark McPhail, quoted in "Metro in Brief," *Washington Post*, October 15, 1997, B03.

27. Richard Morin and Scott Wilson, "Men Torn by Social Change, United by Faith, Poll Shows," *Washington Post*, October 5, 1997, A1.

28. 1990 U.S. Census, cited by R. Famighetti, ed., *World Almanac* (Mayhaw: Funk and Wagnalls, 1996).

29. Lockhart, "'We Are One Life,' But Not of One Ideology."

30. John Maracle, "Past, Present, Future" (speech at Stand in the Gap, Washington, D.C., October 4, 1997).

31. Lockhart, "'We Are One Life,' But Not of One Ideology."

32. Andras Tapia and Rodolfo Carrasco, "The High Stakes in Promise Keepers Bid to Reconcile Races," *Prism* 5, no. 2 (January–February 1998): 28–29. Reprinted from "The Racial Promise: Could the Promise Keepers Be the New Beacon of Civil Rights?" (Pacific News Service).

33. Bill McCartney, "An Extraordinary Hope" (speech at Stand in the Gap, Washington, D.C., October 4, 1997).

34. Messner, *Politics of Masculinities*, 91.

35. William H. Lockhart, "Defining the New Christian Man" (paper presented at the annual meeting of the Association for the Sociology of Religion, New York City, August 1996), and "'We Are One Life,' but Not of One Ideology."

36. Mary Stewart van Leeuwen, "Weeping Warriors"; and Lockhart, "'We Are One Life,' but Not of One Ideology."

37. Maranatha! Promise Band, *Promise Keepers: Stand in the Gap* [recording album] (Laguna Hills, Calif.: Maranatha! [Music # 38597-1112-4], 1997).

38. Steve Nock, *Marriage in Men's Lives* (New York: Oxford University Press, 1998).

39. Stephen Hart, "The Cultural Dimensions of Social Movements: A Theoretical Reassessment and Literature Review," *Sociology of Religion* 57 (1996): 87–100.

40. The authors contributed equally to this chapter.

5. Biblical Interpretations That Influence Promise Keepers

1. Alister McGrath, *Modern Christian Thought* (Cambridge, Mass.: Blackwell, 1993), 231.

2. Marian Hetherly, "PK Publicity and Production: Between the Lines and Behind the Scenes," *Humanist* (September–October 1997): 14–18.

3. Hetherly, "PK Publicity and Production: Between the Lines and Behind the Scenes," 15.

4. Ibid.

5. Martin Luther, "Lecture on Genesis," in vol. 1 of *Luther's Works*, ed. Jeroslav Pelikan (St. Louis, Mo.: Concordia Press, 1958), 203.

6. Spalding, "Bonding in the Bleachers: A Visit to the Promise Keepers," 262.

7. John Higgins, "A Humanist among the Faithful," *Humanist* (September–October 1997): 19–24.

8. Ibid.

6. The Need to Develop Male Friendship

1. Gilbert Meilaender, *Friendship: A Study in Theological Ethics* (London: University of Notre Dame Press, 1985), 1.

2. Francis Schaeffer, *Genesis in Space and Time* (Downers Grove, Ill.: InterVarsity Press, 1972), 17.

3. John M. Reisman, *Anatomy of Friendship* (New York: Irvinton Publishing, 1979), 93.

4. Robert N. Bellah, Richard Madsen, William M. Sullivan, Ann Swidler, and Steven M. Tipton, *Habits of the Heart: Individualism and Commitment in American Life* (New York: Harper & Row, 1985), 115.

5. Bly, *Iron John*, 19.

6. Jack Balswick, *The Inexpressive Male* (Lexington, Mass.: Lexington Books, 1992), 197.

7. Ibid., 36.

8. Meilaender, *Friendship: A Study in Theological Ethics*, 96.

9. Roger Rickets, "Single-Mindedness: Firms Become Willing—or Eager—to Hire Divorced Executives," *Wall Street Journal*, May 18, 1978.

10. Robert Hicks, *Uneasy Manhood* (Nashville: Thomas Nelson, 1991), 66.

11. Don Williams, *The Bond That Breaks: Will Homosexuality Split the Church?* (Los Angeles: Regal Books, 1978), 53.

12. Ibid.

13. Ibid., 139.

14. Greg Lewis, *The Power of a Promise Kept* (Colorado Springs: Focus on the Family, 1995).

15. James B. Nelson, "Sources of Body Theology: Homosexuality as a Test Case," in *Homosexuality in the Church: Both Sides of the Debate*, ed. J. S. Siker (Louisville, Ky.: Westminster/John Knox Press, 1994), 86.

16. Jack Balswick, *Men at the Crossroads* (Downers Grove, Ill.: InterVarsity Press, 1992), 16.

17. Beverly W. Harrison, "Misogyny and Homophobia: The Unexplored Connections," *Church and Society* 73, no. 2 (1982): 20–33.

18. Williams, *The Bond That Breaks*, chap. 1.

19. Archibald Hart, *The Sexual Man* (Dallas: Word, 1994), 3.

20. Ibid., 37.

21. Ibid., 56.

22. Bruce J. Melina, "Let Him Deny Himself (Mark 8:34 & par): A Social Psychological Model of Self Denial," *Biblical Theory Bulletin* 24 (fall 1994): 109.

23. Reisman, *Anatomy of Friendship*, 164.

24. George Edgar Sears, "Men's Search for Male Friendship" (D.Min. diss., Fuller Theological Seminary, Pasadena, Calif.).

7. How Promise Keepers See Themselves as Men Behaving Goodly

1. Blankenhorn, *Fatherless America*, quoted in Joseph P. Shapiro, "Heavenly Promises," *U.S. News & World Report*, October 2, 1995, 68–70.

2. Joe Maxwell, "Will the Walls Fall Down?" *Christianity Today*, November 17, 1997, 62–65.

3. David W. Bohon, "A Look at the Promise Keepers," *New American*, November 25, 1996, 37.

4. It is recognized, and must be noted, that survey respondents tended to be those who seem to be seriously involved with PK; this was evident both from their participation in the study itself and in their responses to the questions.

5. Patricia Ireland, Kim Gandy, Karen Johnson, and Elizabeth Toledo, "Open Letter to Activists," National Organization for Women Web site, August 15, 1997 [cited July 8, 1998], <http://www.now.org/issues/right/promise/letter.html>.

6. Armstrong Williams, "Promise Keepers: Being a Man," *New York Amsterdam News*, October 2, 1997, 8.

7. Katherine Keratin, "Male Models," *American Enterprise*, November–December 1997, 16–17.

8. Marci McDonald, "My Wife Told Me to Go," *U.S. News & World Report*, October 6, 1997, 28–29.

9. David Van Biema, "Full of Promise," *Time*, November 6, 1995, 62–63.

10. Karen Grasse, quoted in Frederic L. Rice, "The Promise Keeper Cult: It Can Happen Here," *Skeptic Tank*, January 1998.

11. Patricia Ireland, "A Look at . . . Promise Keepers," *Washington Post*, September 7, 1997.

12. James Davison Hunter, *Culture Wars: The Struggle to Define America* (New York: Basic Books, 1991).

13. Ralph Reed, *Politically Incorrect* (Dallas: Word, 1994).

14. Stephen W. Littlejohn and W. Barnett Pearce, *Moral Conflict: When Social Worlds Collide* (Thousand Oaks, Calif.: Sage, 1997).

15. John Swomley, "Storm Troopers in the Culture War," *Humanist*, September–October 1997, 11.

16. Becky Beal, "The Promise Keepers' Use of Sport in Defining 'Christlike' Masculinity," *Journal of Sport & Social Issues*, August 1997, 274–85; and Kenneth L. Woodward, "The Gospel of Guyhood," *Newsweek*, August 29, 1994, 60–61.

17. The idea of Promise Keepers as the "third wave of the Religious Right" was forwarded by Alfred Ross and Lee Cokorinos of the Center for Democracy Studies. Center for Democracy Studies, "The Promise Keepers Are Coming: The Third Wave of the Religious Right" [cited April 10, 1998], <http://www.cdresearch.org>.

18. James Hannaham, "God and Man at Shea," *Village Voice*, October 1, 1996, 31.

19. Pharr, "A Match Made in Heaven."

20. Jesse L. Jackson Jr., "Promise Keepers—Watch as Well as Pray," National Organization for Women Web site, 1997 [cited July 8, 1998], <http://www.now.org/issues/right/promise/jackson.html>.

21. John Leo, "Men Behaving Well," *U.S. News & World Report*, November 3, 1997, 16.

22. David Wagner, "Blessed Are the Promise Keepers," *Insight*, September 1997, 10–13.

23. Maxwell, "Will the Walls Fall Down?"

24. Arms, *Promise Keepers: Another Trojan Horse.*

25. Promise Keepers, "Fact Sheet," Promise Keepers Web site [updated February 24, 1998; cited April 10, 1998], <http://www.promisekeepers.org>.

26. Ibid., "Statement of Faith."

27. Richard Wolf, "Men at Work—On the Power of Prayer: Growing Movement Shows Husbands, Fathers New Way," *USA Today*, August 8, 1995.

28. Taken from the results of a variety of surveys conducted by Promise Keepers through its national Internet Web site in fall 1996 and throughout 1997.

29. On the other hand, McCartney, though professing optimism about race relations overall, noted: "Of the 1996 conference participants who had a complaint, nearly 40 percent reacted negatively to the reconciliation theme. I personally believe it was a major factor in the significant fall-off in P.K.'s 1997 attendance—it is simply a hard teaching for many. But many in Jesus' day also turned back from His 'hard teaching' and followed Him no more (John 6:66). In all actuality, I suspect that much of the criticism leveled at Promise Keepers from within the Christian community—typically cloaked in assorted, usually untested claims that we're an ecumenical movement, or that we preach a gospel palatable to Mormons or fringe cults—has as its true root a deep-seated cultural resistance to the message on reconciliation. It simply tells me we're on the right track" (*Sold Out*, 180–81).

30. Bill McCartney, "Promise Makers," *Policy Review* 85 (1997): 14–19.

31. Quoted in A. D. Banks, "Bill McCartney Bares His Soul in New Book," *Raleigh News and Observer*, November 28, 1997, E3.

32. M. Cimons and K. Zeuthen, "Participants, Doubters Ponder Premise of Promise Keepers Movement; As Huge Gathering Nears, Leaders of Christian Group Consider Ways to Broaden Impact. Critics Fear a Return to Restrictive Roles for Women," *Los Angeles Times*, September 30, 1997, A5.

8. Christianity, Feminism, and the Manhood Crisis

1. John Stoltenberg, "Male Virgins, Blood Covenants, and Family Values," *On the Issues* 4, no. 2 (spring 1995): 25–29, 51–53. Available on-line at <www.igc.apc.org/onissues/male.htm>.

2. E. Glenn Wagner, interview by author, Irving, Texas, 29 October 1994.

3. Promise Keepers, "Reconciliation Statement," information sheet for the news media distributed at Texas Stadium, Irving, 28 October 1994.

4. Galatians 3:27–28: "For as many of you were baptized into Christ have put on Christ. There is neither Jew nor Greek, there is neither slave nor free, there is neither male nor female; for you are all one in Christ Jesus" (Revised Standard Version, the translation I read growing up). "All baptized in Christ, you have all clothed yourselves in Christ, and there are no more distinctions between Jew and Greek, slave and free, male and female, but all of you are one in Christ Jesus" (The Jerusalem Bible, the translation I prefer).

5. Wagner with Dietrich Gruen, *Strategies for a Successful Marriage: A Study Guide for Men* (Colorado Springs: NavPress, 1994), 4.

6. John Stoltenberg, *Refusing to Be a Man: Essays on Sex and Justice*, revised ed. (London and New York: UCL Press, 2000), 4.

7. John Stoltenberg, *The End of Manhood: Parables on Sex and Justice*, revised ed. (London and New York: UCL Press, 2000), 304.

8. Ibid.

9. Quoted in Catharine A. MacKinnon and Andrea Dworkin, eds., *In Harm's Way: The Pornography Civil Rights Hearings* (Cambridge: Harvard University Press, 1998), 346n.

10. Ibid., 13n.

11. National Organization for Women (NOW), "Resolution by the National Conference for Its Promise Keepers Mobilization Project," 1997, <www.now.org>.

12. Promise Keepers, "Homosexuality Statement," information sheet for the news media, distributed at Texas Stadium, Irving, 28 October 1994 [cited 31 July 1998]; Web address is <www.promisekeepers.org>.

13. Ed Cole, speech by the president of the Christian Men's Network at Texas Stadium, Irving, 29 October 1994.

14. Al Janssen, James C. Dobson, Gary Smalley, and Gary Oliver, *The Seven Promises of a Promise Keeper* (Colorado Springs: Focus on the Family Publishing, 1994), 8.

15. These are the pertinent verses (all in the New International Version, a translation favored by evangelicals): Ephesians 5:22, "Wives, submit to your husbands as to the Lord"; Ephesians 5:24, "Now as the church submits to Christ, so also wives should submit to their husbands in everything"; Colossians 3:18, "Wives, submit to your husbands, as is fitting in the Lord."

16. Jerry Kirk, "God's Call to Sexual Purity," in *The Seven Promises*, 97.

17. Ibid., 96.

18. Mark Ward, "Virtual Immorality," *New Man Magazine Online*, 1998, <www.newmanmag.com>.

19. Ken Canfield, "The XXXtent of the Problem," *New Man Magazine Online*, 1998, <www.newmanmag.com>.

9. Patriarchy's Second Coming as Masculine Renewal

1. Attendance at the October 4, 1997, event was several hundred thousand; as usual, exact figures are disputed and thus unknown.

2. Figure for 1997.

3. *New Man* became an unofficial, rather than official, publication of Promise Keepers in early 1998.

10. Godly Masculinities Require Gender and Power

1. The discourses of masculinity outlined here are, of course, not exhaustive of PK's definitions of "godly masculinity." Other PK authors proffer innovative (re)constructions of issues concerning gender difference/sameness and family power. In my study, I have self-consciously opted for analytical depth over empirical breadth.

2. Edwin Louis Cole, *Maximized Manhood: A Guide to Family Survival* (Springdale, Pa.: Whitaker House, 1982).

3. For review, see John P. Bartkowski, "Gender Reinvented, Gender Reproduced: The Discourse and Negotiation of Spousal Relations within Contemporary Evangelicalism" (Ph.D. diss., University of Texas at Austin, 1997), and "Debating Patriarchy: Discursive Disputes Over Spousal Authority among Evangelical Family Commentators," *Journal for the Scientific Study of Religion* 36 (1997): 393–410.

4. Cole, *Maximized Manhood*, 72.

5. Ibid., 147.

6. Ibid., 78–79, 82.

7. Ibid., 96.

8. Ibid., 147.

9. Ibid., 77, 82, 102; also see chap. 10.

10. Ibid., 107, 111.

11. Ibid., 66, emphasis in original.

12. Ibid., 82.

13. Ibid., 34; also see 126–27.

14. Ibid., 35.

15. Ibid., 6.

16. Ibid., 62.

17. Ibid., 52, 61, 89–90, 93.

18. Ibid., 61.

19. Ibid., chap. 6.

20. Ibid., 61–62.

21. Ibid., 62.

22. Hughes, *The Manliness of Christ*; Conant, *The Manly Christ*; Case, *The Masculine in Religion*; A. T. Mahan, *The Harvest Within: Thoughts on the Life of the Christian* (Boston: Little, Brown, 1909); Fosdick, *The Manhood of the Master*; Pierce, *The Masculine Power of Christ*; Wayne, *Building the Young Man*; Fred B. Smith, *A Man's Religion*; Bouck White, *The Call of the Carpenter*; and Bruce Barton, *The Man Nobody Knows: A Discovery of the Real Jesus*.

23. Cole, *Maximized Manhood*, 62–63, emphasis in original.

24. Gary J. Oliver, *Real Men Have Feelings Too* (Chicago: Moody Press, 1993).

25. Ibid., 23–32.

26. Ibid., 19–20.

27. Ibid., 20, 61–62, 65–66, emphasis in original.

28. Ibid., 19.

29. Ibid., 37.

30. See Bartkowski, "Gender Reinvented, Gender Reproduced," and "Debating Patriarchy."

31. Oliver, *Real Men Have Feelings Too*, 230–31.

32. Ibid., 33–36.

33. Ibid., 36.

34. Ibid., 35, emphasis in original.

35. This study was underwritten by grants from the Lilly Endowment's Louisville Institute, as well as the Criss Fund and Research Initiation Program at Mississippi State University. I would like to thank Nicci Bartkowski and Sarah Haas for their comments on this chapter. I alone am responsible for the analyses and interpretations discussed here.

11. Promise Keepers Welcomed Home by Wives

1. Gilbert, "Revisiting the Psychology of Men."

2. Janssen and Weeden, eds., *Seven Promises of a Promise Keeper*.

3. "Promise Keepers Depart: Leave Mall Clean," ABC News, October 7, 1997, on-line news service, <http://www.abcnews.com/local/wjla/news/6413_1061997.html>.

4. "D.C. Covenant," Promise Keepers Web site [cited July 10, 1998].

5. Quoted in "Suburbia Seeks Salvation," *Economist*, October 11, 1997, 30.

6. Quoted in Ron Stodghill, "God of Our Fathers," *U.S. News & World Report*, October 6, 1997, 23.

7. Ibid., 25.

8. Joan Ryan, "The Promise Keepers Are an Easy Target—or Are They? What We Women Want," *San Francisco Chronicle*, October 12, 1997 [cited July 10, 1998], <http://www.examiner.com>.

9. LaRae Kemp, guest panelist on *This Week*, ABC News, October 5, 1997.

10. McDonald, "My Wife Told Me to Go."

11. Cal M. Logue and Eugene F. Miller, "Rhetorical Status: A Study of Its Origins, Functions, and Consequences," *Quarterly Journal of Speech* 81 (1995): 20–47.

12. Clella I. Jaffe, "Promise Keepers' Wives: The Rhetoric Comes Home" (paper presented to the National Communication Association, Chicago, November 1997).

13. S. J. Hekman, *Gender and Knowledge: Elements of a Postmodern Feminism* (Boston: Northeastern University Press, 1990).

14. Barbara Bate and Judith Bowker, *Communication and the Sexes*, 2d ed. (Prospect Heights, Ill.: Waveland, 1997).

15. Jennifer Coburn, letter to the editor, *Time*, November 17, 1997, 17.

16. Lee Cokorinos, letter to the editor, ibid.

17. *Book of Discipline: Doctrines, Character and Ritual of the Free Methodist Church* (Winona Lake, Ind.: Free Methodist Publishing House, 1985).

18. Holly Phillips, "In Their Own Words," *NBC Nightly News*, October 4, 1997.

19. Bill McCartney, "The Idea Behind the Promise Keepers," CNN's *Larry King Live*, October 7, 1997. Transcript available: Landover, Md.: Federal Document Clearing House.

20. Quoted in McDonald, "My Wife Told Me to Go," 30.

21. Dan Riemenschneider, "Servant-Leadership" (presentation at the Church Leaders Dessert, Free Methodist Church, Newberg, Oregon, January 17, 1996).

22. Tony Evans, *Keeping Your Promises to Your Family* (Bloomington, Minn.: Garborg's Heart and Home, 1994).

23. Jeffery L. Bineham, "Theological Hegemony and Oppositional Interpretive Codes: The Case of Evangelical Christian Feminism," *Western Journal of Communication* 57 (1993): 525.

24. Phillips, "In Their Own Words."

25. McCartney, "The Idea Behind the Promise Keepers."

26. Jaffe, "Promise Keepers' Wives: The Rhetoric Comes Home."

27. *American Heritage Dictionary*, startup software, Macintosh Performa Computer, 1996.

28. Quoted in McDonald, "My Wife Told Me to Go," 30.

29. Logue and Miller, "Rhetorical Status."

30. Cokorinos, letter to the editor, 20.

31. Logue and Miller, "Rhetorical Status."

12. Wives, Daughters, Mothers, and Sisters as Kept Women

1. The privacy of women quoted or described in this chapter is protected by the use of pseudonyms. The oral history interviews on which this chapter is based were conducted on the condition of anonymity.

2. Lyndi McCartney uses the same language. See McCartney, *Sold Out*, 235.

3. Sarah Peterson, interview with author, Raleigh, North Carolina, June 22, 1997.

4. Ron Stodghill III, "God of Our Fathers," *Time*, October 6, 1997, 34–40.

5. Richard N. Ostling, "God, Football and the Game of His Life," *Time*, October 6, 1997, 38–39.

6. In *Seven Promises of a Promise Keeper*, Evans wrote an article entitled "Reclaiming Your Manhood," where he told men, "I'm not suggesting you ask for your role back. I'm urging you to take it back. . . . There can be no compromise here. If you're going to lead, you must lead." Both scholars and reporters have picked up on Evans's advice. See, for example, Stodghill, "God of Our Fathers"; and Randall H. Balmer, "Keep the Faith and Go the Distance," in *The Promise Keepers: Essays on Masculinity and Christianity*.

7. John Yutes, "The Promise to Pray with My Wife," in *What Makes a Man? 12 Promises That Will Change Your Life*, ed. Bill McCartney (Boulder, Colo.: NavPress, 1992).

8. McCartney, *Sold Out*, 348–65.

9. Ibid., 165.

10. Janssen and Weeden, eds., *Seven Promises of a Promise Keeper.*

11. June Smith, interview with author, New York, New York, December 17, 1997.

12. Betty Friedan, *The Feminine Mystique* (New York: Dell, 1974), 147–48.

13. For information about the number of working mothers in the United States, see Elizabeth Fox-Genovese, *Feminism Is Not the Story of My Life: How Today's Feminist Elite Has Lost Touch with the Real Concerns of Women* (New York: Doubleday, 1996), 123.

14. Candyce and Rena Wentford, interview with author, Durham, North Carolina, July 1, 1997.

15. Rafe Morgan, telephone interview with author, March 21, 1998.

16. Anne Morgan, telephone interview with author, March 21, 1998.

17. Marie Johnson, interview with author, Baltimore, Maryland, December 28, 1997.

18. For a discussion of Lyndi McCartney's eating disorder, see McCartney, *Sold Out*, 207–39.

19. Sheryl Kelley, interview with author, Charleston, South Carolina, December 23, 1997.

20. Geraldine Bransen, interview with author, Newton, Massachusetts, March 3, 1997.

21. Dorthy Van Meter, letter to the editor, *Christianity Today*, January 12, 1998.

22. For a discussion of evangelical women's relationship to feminism, see R. Marie Griffith, *God's Daughters: Evangelical Women and the Power of Submission* (Berkeley: University of California Press, 1997); Brenda E. Brasher, *Godly Women: Fundamentalism and Female Power* (New Brunswick, N.J.: Rutgers University Press, 1998); and Judith Stacey and Susan Elizabeth Gerard, "'We Are Not Doormats': The Influence of Feminism on Contemporary Evangelicals in the United States," in *Uncertain Terms: Negotiating Gender in American Culture*, ed. Faye Ginsburg and Anna Lowenhaupt Tsing (Boston: Beacon Press, 1990), 98–117.

23. Laurie R. Wilson, interview with author, Trenton, New Jersey, February 8, 1997.

24. Jennifer Romano, interview with author, Providence, Rhode Island, March 18, 1997.

25. Josie Marsh, interview with author, Raleigh, North Carolina, June 27, 1997.

26. Catherine Clark Kroeger, Mary Evans, and Elaine Storkey, eds., *Study Bible for Women: The New Testament* (Grand Rapids, Mich.: Baker, 1995), 589.

27. Liz Abbot, interview with author, Charlottesville, Virginia, March 25, 1998.

28. Lisa Marcus, interview with author, Washington, D.C., March 16, 1998.

29. Rebecca Wright, interview with author, New York, New York, April 3, 1997.

30. Francis J. Beckwith, letter to the editor, *Christianity Today*, January 12, 1998, 8.

31. McCartney, *Sold Out*, 177–81.

32. Caroline Hall, interview with author, Richmond, Virginia, March 20, 1998.

33. Kimberly Nichols, telephone interview with author, October 19, 1997.

34. Lynn Stuart, interview with author, Cambridge, England, November 5, 1997.

35. Marie Johnson, interview with author.

36. For a discussion of poor women's views about marriage as a potential source of economic stability, see Fox-Genovese, *Feminism Is Not the Story of My Life.*

37. Michelle Parks, interview with author, New York City, February 3, 1997.

RELATED TITLES FROM THE PILGRIM PRESS

The Men We Long to Be: Beyond Lonely Warriors and Desperate Lovers
STEPHEN B. BOYD

Are you overburdened and hurting? Many men are. One large factor, according to Stephen Boyd, is what our culture says it means to be a "man"—to be in control and to take control. Many men become either "lonely warriors" who seek to make it without the aid of others or "desperate lovers" who have difficulty with intimate relationships. *The Men We Long to Be* offers an alternative identity for men. Using the Bible, Christian tradition, and wisdom from the men's movement, Boyd recovers a rooted view of manhood and reveals the best aspects of being a Christian father, husband, lover, brother, and son.

ISBN 0-8298-1201-6   272 pages/Paper/$17.95

Crossing the Soul's River: A Rite of Passage for Men
WILLIAM O. ROBERTS JR.

William Roberts outlines a rite of passage for men at midlife, who find themselves at the threshold of both danger and opportunity. First he addresses the importance of traversing the "soul's river" in search of personal growth and the need for guidance through this passage. Then he constructs a series of "soul tasks" to facilitate the rite of passage toward reconciliation with the self. The rite and tasks can be used individually or in a Christian men's group.

ISBN 0-8298-1259-8   160 pages/Paper/$15.95

Forgiving Our Grownup Children
DWIGHT LEE WOLTER

Do your children still blame you for the way they turned out? Have they been encouraged to trace the problems of their lives to the frustrations and trials of growing up with you? Do you feel like scapegoats who are to blame for everything? Isn't it time for all this to change? *Forgiving Our Grownup Children* helps parents come to terms with their imperfect parenting of imperfect children. Dwight Wolter's sensible, practical, very readable book is filled with encouraging examples of parents and adult children who have admitted their limitations and mistakes, recognized their problems, and found successful ways of dealing with them in order to heal old wounds and forge closer family relationships.

ISBN 0-8298-1264-4   144 pages/Paper/$12.95

To order these or any other book by The Pilgrim Press please call or write to:

The Pilgrim Press
700 Prospect Avenue East
Cleveland OH 44115-1100

Phone Orders 800-537-3394
Fax Orders 216-736-3713

Please include shipping charges of $3.50 for the first book
and $0.50 for each additional book.
Or order from our Web site at www.pilgrimpress.com.
Prices are subject to change without notice.